The Last Apocalypse

The Last Apocalypse

EUROPE
AT THE
YEAR 1000 A.D.

James Reston, Jr.

ANCHOR BOOKS

DOUBLEDAY

NEW YORK LONDON TORONTO SYDNEY AUCKLAND

AN ANCHOR BOOK
PUBLISHED BY DOUBLEDAY
a division of Random House, Inc.
1540 Broadway, New York, New York 10036

ANCHOR BOOKS, DOUBLEDAY, and the portrayal of an
anchor with a dolphin
are trademarks of Doubleday, a division of
Random House, Inc.

Book design by Marysarah Quinn

Photo insert design by Carol Malcolm-Russo

Maps designed by Martie Holmer

The Last Apocalypse was originally published in hardcover by
Doubleday in 1998.

The Library of Congress has cataloged the hardcover edition of
this book as follows:

Reston, James, 1941–
The last apocalypse: Europe at the year 1000 A.D. / James Reston, Jr.
p.   cm.
Includes bibliographical references (p. 282) and index.
1. Europe—History—476–1492.   I. Title.
D201.4.R47   1998
940.1—dc21   97-18812
CIP

FOR J.R.
in Orion

Contents

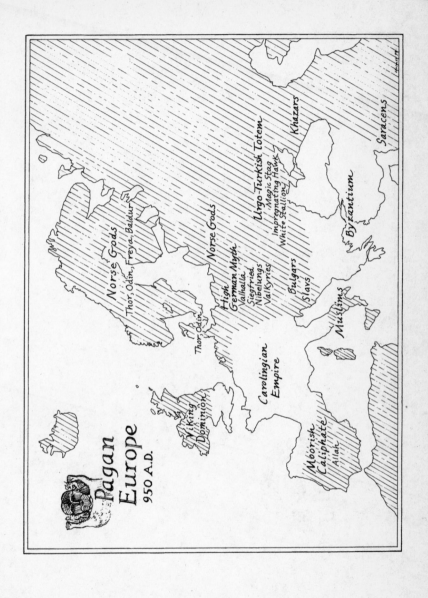

Pagan
Europe
950 A.D.

Norse Gods
Thor, Odin, Freya, Baldur

Thor, Odin

Viking
Dominion

Norse Gods

High
German Myth
Valhalla
Siegfried
Nibelungs
Valkyries

Carolingian
Empire

Urgo-Turkish Totem
Magic Stag
Impregnating Hawk
White Stallion

Khazars

Bulgars
Slavs

Byzantium

Saracens

Muslims

Moorish
Caliphate
Allah

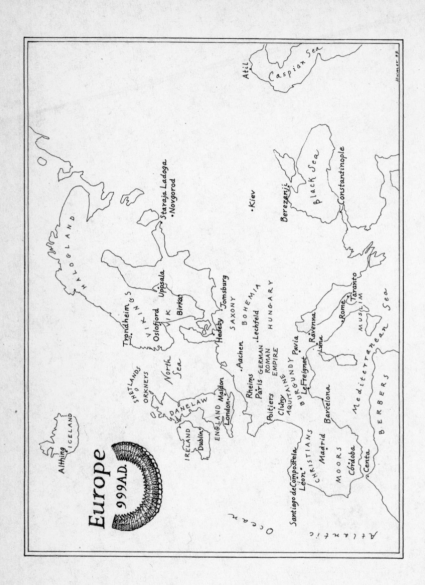

Europe
999 A.D.

The **Players**
999 A.D.

(in Greenland)
Eirik the Red
Leif Eriksson

Thorgeir
the
Lawspeaker

Olaf Trygvesson
Earl Hacon

Sigrid the Haughty
Olof the Lapking

King Brian
Boru

Svein Forkbeard
Canute the Mighty

Ethelred
the
Unready

Sigvaldi the Jarl

Boleslav the Brave

Otto I
Otto II
Otto III

Vladimir

Robert
the
Pious

St. Stephen
of Hungary

Sancho
the Great

St. Odilio

Berengar I
Empress Theophano
Otto III
Sylvester II

Nicophorus II Phocas
Empress Theophano
Basil II

Al Mansor
Little Sancho

The Last Apocalypse
circa 999 A.D.

Leif Ericksson discovers North America 1000 A.D. then converts Greenland

Iceland converts 1000 A.D.

Olaf Trygvesson converts Norway 999–1000 A.D.

Battle of Oldritari 1014 A.D. Viking Defeat

Harald Bluetooth converts Denmark 974 A.D.

Canute the Mighty becomes a King 1015 A.D.

Vladimir converts Russia 988 A.D.

Boleslav the Brave converts Poland 999 A.D.

Robert the Pious King of France 996 A.D.

King Stephen the Saint coronated 1000 A.D.

Sancho the Great King of Navarre 1000 A.D.

Otto III Holy Roman Emperor 996 A.D.

Moorish Caliphate collapses 1009 A.D.

Gerbert becomes Pope 998 A.D.

Basil II "The Bulgar-Slayer" Emperor of Byzantium 989–1025 A.D.

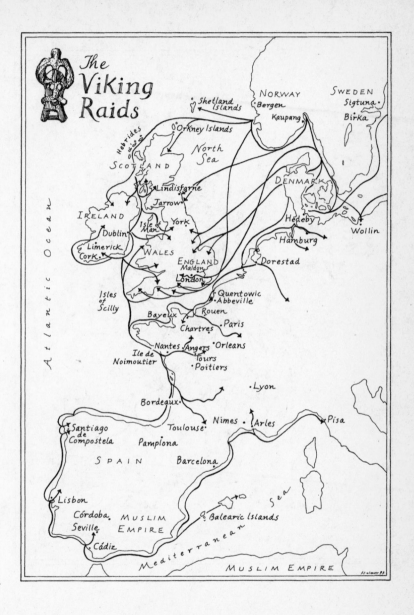

The
Viking
Raids

Shetland Islands
NORWAY
Bergen
Kaupang
SWEDEN
Sigtuna
Birka

Orkney Islands
North
Sea
Hebrides
SCOTLAND
DENMARK
Lindisfarne
Jarrow
Hedeby
Wollin
IRELAND
Isle of Man
York
Hamburg
Dublin
Limerick
Cork
WALES
ENGLAND
Maldon
London
Dorestad
Atlantic Ocean
Quentowic
Abbeville
Isles of Scilly
Bayeux
Rouen
Chartres
Paris
Nantes Angers
Orleans
Ile de Noimoutier
Tours
Poitiers
Lyon
Bordeaux
Nimes
Arles
Pisa
Santiago de Compostela
Toulouse
Pamplona
SPAIN
Barcelona
Lisbon
Córdoba
Seville
MUSLIM EMPIRE
Balearic Islands
Cádiz
Mediterranean Sea
MUSLIM EMPIRE

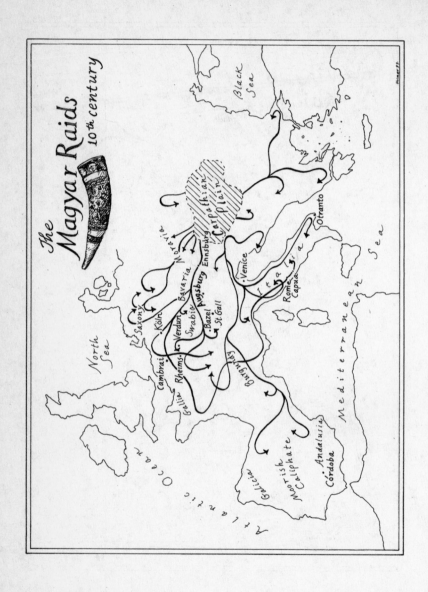

The
Magyar Raids
10th century

North Sea

Atlantic Ocean

Black Sea

Saxony

Köln

Cambrai

Gallia

Rheims

Verdun

Bavaria

Swabia

Augsburg

Bazel

St. Gall

Ennsburg

Moravia

Carpathian Plain

Venice

Italy

Rome

Capua

Otranto

Burgundy

Moorish Caliphate

Galicia

Córdoba

Andalusia

Mediterranean Sea

The
Iberian
Peninsula
999 A.D.

Spain in the time of
Al Mansor

Christians   Muslims

Bay of Biscay

Santiago
de Compostela   Oviedo
Asturias   Roncesvalles
Galicia   León   Pamplona   Pyrenees
Astorga   Burgos   Ripoll
Zamora   The   Gerona
         Meseta   Zaragoza   Barcelona
Salamanca   Calatañazor
         Madrid   Tortosa
              Toledo
Lisbon   Mérida   Valencia
      Al-Andalusia
      Córdoba   Murcia
Seville   Cartagena
         Granada
              Almería
         Málaga
         Gibraltar

Ocean

Atlantic

Mediterranean Sea

Holmer 99

The Battle of Maldon

I PARKED MY VAUXALL ROADSTER beside a hedgerow, gathered up my dog-eared copy of *The Battle of Maldon,* and set off down the straight path toward the famous causeway. The neat metal sign, white letters embossed against forest green, warned me that I needed permission from the warder to visit Northey Island. But I was not sure I could cross the causeway at this hour from the Anglo-Saxon side to the Viking side, since I had not consulted the table of tides. The gravel road led to South House farm. Past the barns and over a wood stile, marked with the medallion of the English Historical Society, I could see, far in the distance, a levee which blocked my view of the water.

With the straight path ahead of me, I opened to the epic poem, second in fame among early English poems only to *Beowulf*, and imagined the same landscape a thousand years past.

In the summer of 991 A.D., a force of ninety-three Viking ships had appeared off the English coast, menacing the Kentish village of Folkestone first, then Sandwich on the Thames, and then beaching its sea stallions and attacking Ipswich to the north. Finally, the fleet circled back and came here, to the mudflats and salt marshes of the Blackwater estuary. Their force comprised about three thousand battle-hardened men, including two future kings, Olaf Trygvesson of Norway and Svein Forkbeard of Denmark. They were allies now, bound in greed and ambition, in search of plunder and fame. But in a few years, they would turn on one another and become bitter enemies, partly because of a love triangle involving a Swedish queen called Sigrid the Haughty.

The Norsemen were bold and contemptuous, but their choice of Maldon was ill-considered. The town itself stood on high ground, and its very name, appropriately enough, meant the "cross on the hill." Appropriately, because this was to be a battle between Christians and heathens. It was also to be, in the English telling, a battle between honorable men and barbarians. Because of its strategic advantage, Maldon had long been a military encampment for Anglo-Saxon soldiers. Perhaps the Vikings thought that Northey Island, just a few yards across the causeway from the mainland, where the tides submerged the "hard" for half the day, was a safe harbor for their considerable fleet and safe ground for their pirate base. Perhaps, but we cannot know for sure. For this was still essentially an illiterate age. There is no record of what they thought. For whatever reason, they had, uncharacteristically, put themselves at a disadvantage.

The English army was commanded by a man of real consequence named Byrhtnoth. This powerful overlord of East Anglia was a tall, elderly man, sixty-five years of age, with broad shoulders and a great shock of white hair. The descendant of a long line of Essex gentlemen, he had been lord of East Anglia for thirty-five years and was outspoken in defense of the church. Byrhtnoth seemed to appreciate that he was headed for a battle of the ages. At Ely Cathedral he had met with the abbot and put his personal affairs in order. In exchange for generous grants of land to the cathedral, Byrhtnoth expressed his desire to be buried in the cathedral crypt, should he be killed.

His personal affairs settled, he marched south at the head of his army, through Cambridgeshire, in the hope that he could finally engage this insidious, elusive, fast-moving scourge of the English nation of Alfred and Ethelred. His force was nearly as large as the Viking horde, but his men were raw and untested, the peasants and servants of East Anglia who had been hastily recruited and poorly outfitted. This rabble arrived in Maldon exhausted from the long march. It was not a good formula.

MY GAZE FELL ON THE TEXT, scanning for the Vikings' first hurled challenge. Suddenly, far off in the distance, there was a frightening screeching, as if the Vikings were storming across the mudflat, and I looked up to see an enormous cloud of Brent geese swarming past the treetops of the island and disappearing beneath the levee.

On the comfortable English side, I tried to imagine Byrhtnoth's volunteers on the morning of August 11, 991 A.D. In the fields around me, the lord had "commanded each one of the soldiers to set his horse loose, to drive it far away and to proceed on foot, and turn his mind to his hands and a doughty disposition." Byrhtnoth rode along his line, his long white hair blowing in the summer breeze, arranging his ragtag soldiers on the shore, shouting out his orders, inspecting the way they held their shields, fists balled tightly, bucking them up so they would not be afraid. Perhaps a goodly number of second- and third-generation Danes were in the English line, remnants of the Viking raids that had been going on in Britain for two hundred years, and perhaps they felt a divided loyalty.

I reached the crest of the levee, and there below me stretched the causeway, its seaweed-clad rocks still dripping and slippery, but fully exposed above the mudflat. The "hard" was shorter than I had imagined from the photographs, no more than a hundred yards across, and so the Viking herald would have had no trouble being heard on this shore. I returned to the text, and even though it was low tide rather than high, and I was on the English side rather than the Viking, I held the poem high, and to the startled sheep and the wading birds, I shouted out the Viking's lines, trying to infuse them with all the derision and mocking that I could muster.

"Swift-striking seamen have sent me to you. They bid me say that you had better send them rings and bracelets in return for your protection. It will be better for you that you buy off our assault with ransom and tribute rather than engage us in cruel conflict. There is no need for us to kill each other."

This was the stiff proposition of the bully, extortion pure and simple. Pay us off rather than fight. . . . But how could one believe their word? Who had ever heard of Viking honor? Surely they would take the filthy lucre here and attack somewhere else. And then the Dane added a searing taunt, making out the proud English to be poor and leaderless, cowardly and bedraggled. "If you are wealthy enough, we offer a truce in exchange for gold! If you have a captain there, ponder this: Pay your people's ransom. Render to Vikings what they think right. Buy quiet peace at our price! With this tribute, we will turn back to our ships, sail out with the tide, and hold you as friends." Friends, indeed.

That loathsome, hateful, contemptuous taunt was too much to endure; Byrhtnoth's anger courses through the poem. He was shaken to the core of his gentleman's honor. Any reciter would be hard pressed to do justice to his rage, but for my fine-feathered audience, I tried, pale actor a millennium later. "Hear, sea-wanderer, what this nation says!" I shouted ferociously. "These men will give you spears as tribute, the poison-tipped javelin and ancient swords. Seamen's spokesman, report this back! Give your people this distasteful news: that here stands a worthy earl with his troops who are willing to defend this, his ancestral home, the country of Ethelred, my lord's nation and land." Now it was Byrhtnoth's turn to taunt his foe. "Heathens will perish in battle. It would be a pity if you were to take our riches without a fight, now that you have intruded this far into our country. Not so easily will you get our gold. First point and edge shall sort things out between us."

OR HUNDREDS OF YEARS, English schoolchildren have thrilled to Byrhtnoth's magnificent retort. There is something universal about his noble words. In the heroic actions of different leaders in other traditions, they have resonance. But what are the children being taught? History or literature or sheer patriotism? We know that a battle took place in Maldon in 991 A.D. and what leaders fought there, because it is mentioned in several independent chronicles of the time. True, we do not have archaeological confirmation in the form of arrows and spears dug up from these marshes. But medieval battlefields are rarely good places to dig, since weapons are generally collected by the victor, and the war dead are usually carted away.

Did the combatants actually say these things to one another before the battle? They could have. *The Battle of Maldon,* the poem, was written only a few years after the event, probably by a participant. The poet clearly knew the English soldiers and their leaders. He admired them as much as he hated the Danes. His epic is pure propaganda, his slant obvious. The English are here to defend their homeland and their faith against the heathen invader. With name and title, a king, a faith, a manor, Byrhtnoth is the ideal of the distinguished, noble, and ultimately poignant warrior. The Vikings, by contrast, are rootless and predatory. They are sea wanderers and wolves, without names or kings or titles or homes. They are liars, cheaters, hellhounds, barbarians. The English poem roots their reputation in our imagination.

In considering this poem, the most sober and authoritative account of a battle long ago, and arguably the greatest battle poem in the English language, we must be aware of its strengths and weaknesses. Of all the resources, poetry remains the soundest evidence we have in trying to re-create the world of 999 A.D. Beyond a poem's "historical" information, its verses usually have an enduring, internal discipline. The poem is specifically crafted to be heard and, once heard, to be repeated, from one person to the next, from one generation to the next . . . in the same form. Because of this very discipline of rhythm and meter, it is less susceptible to alternation in its repeating.

In portraying this dark and illiterate age, the oral tradition is the stuff of our history. In this work, I embrace it. There can be quibbles that this story or that myth is not written down until much later, sometimes hundreds of years later, and, therefore, we cannot rely on it. A valid criticism, but if we were to embrace it utterly, where does it leave us? We cannot discard virtually everything except the broken shards of pottery, the worm-eaten swords, the beads and horn combs of the archaeologists.

For two years, I have struggled with the problem of accuracy. The limits to the verifiable in recounting tenth-century history are severe, by modern standards. But early in the process of writing this book, I had an important interchange with a Danish professor of medieval studies in Oslo. As I badgered him about the myth of Sigrid the Haughty—Did she really exist? How do you know? Can we rely on that?—his annoyance began to rise, and it seemed that he was going to make an abrupt departure.

"You are asking the wrong questions," he snorted peevishly. "This is history, but not in the modern sense."

What follows then is not a "history" of 999 A.D. in the modern sense, because such a work, bolstered by footnote or interview or archival record, is impossible. I am not prepared to throw out oral history as worthless or "untrue" merely because I cannot prove its every word. We reconstruct as best as we are able, from the resources we have. If this provides a painting, not a photograph, we must remember that paintings transmit meaning too, sometimes an essence, stripped of unnecessary detail.

This is a *saga* of the millennium a thousand years ago. By *saga*, I mean simply, a narrative of a heroic time. Yet as I traveled through Europe on research trips, I came to see that more was at stake than mere heroism. Piecing together poetry, folklore, saga, archaeology, holy chronicle, I came to this conclusion: the turn of the millennium in 999 A.D. was a turning point in history. The change in Europe between 950 A.D. and 1010 A.D. was profound. The clash at Maldon was played out in countless venues across the continent, at Lechfeld in Germany, at Paris, at Santiago de Compostela in Spain, above Constantinople in the Black Sea. Slowly, relentlessly, despite setback, the Christian forces seemed to be winning over the three forces of heathenism that pressed in on central Europe. These were the sea dragons of the Vikings, the terrible horsemen of the Hungarian Magyars, and the proud battalions of Al Mansor and his Moors in Spain.

These victories were won not only on the battlefield. Beyond the brutal conversions of Olaf Trygvesson in Norway, these triumphs were also evident in the statesmanship of Theophano, the Byzantine empress in Rome, in the dreams of her son Otto III, in the brilliance of the first French pope, Gerbert, in the high-mindedness of Vajk, later the Hungarian king and saint Stephen I, and through the internal rot of the Moorish caliphate in Córdoba. Something great and mighty was under way throughout the continent, as if beneath the surface of the earth tectonic plates were shifting.

At the turn of the last millennium, Europe Christianized, almost all at once. The various regions of the continent—Scandinavia, Spain, Russia, and the Balkans—all came to the new religion for different reasons, but some powerful urge bound them together. No more dramatic change can be imagined, not because it was Christian per se, but because Christianity in 999 A.D. represented civilization and learning and nationhood against the darkness of heathenism, illiteracy, and tribal chaos. The forty years before the end of the first millennium is a continuous, spirited, brutal dialectic between Christianity and heathenism. For the royal players who are my main characters, the religion of Christ, the King, meant dignity and stature. The change was, in short, apocalyptic.

In portraying this sweeping transformation, ever with a critical eye and hopefully with a sense of humor, I have sifted the court poems, the Norse sagas, the myths of Cluny and Córdoba, the mysticism of Rome and Aachen, the folktales of Hungary. I have compared the meager sources and considered the prejudices of the writers. I will utilize the archaeology as confirmation or denial of the literary sources.

What seems right and true, intellectually, intuitively, emotionally in the spirit of the time, I will include. Dragons and witches, goblins, giants, and fetches are dark and fantastic imaginings that figure into the action and the psychology of the players. In the great clash of mythologies—Odinn's power versus Christ's miracles—supernatural tales were used as proof of a god's superior power. Thus, I have, on

occasion, related fantastical elements in my portraits, aware that
their propaganda value was immense.

AFTER THE LOUD EXCHANGE between the Viking messenger and Byrhtnoth, the armies faced one another warily across
the marsh. For some hours they waited, as the tide came in and then
began to recede. The Saxon line bristled impressively along the
shore, shields held fist-tight, Frankish spears at the ready. Several of
Byrhtnoth's best fighters were stationed at the causeway, and when
the water was low enough to see the rocks of the ford, several Vikings
tested the English line, only to be struck down by the defenders.

> When the hated strangers saw and understood
> what bitter bridge warders were brought against them there
> they began to plead with craft, asking permission
> to fare over the ford and lead across their footmen.

By the poet's lights, this plea to let the Vikings cross over was
cheating. It was a brazen, insolent request: to achieve by guile what
the invaders could not take by force. The cheat was all the greater
because it appealed to the English code of honor. What commander
would fall for such an absurd gambit? It was a moment of controversy which would dismay historians for a thousand years. For, aston-
ishingly, Byrhtnoth granted the request. He drew his men back, ex-
posing them to mortal danger.

"The ground is cleared for you," his lieutenant shouted out.
"Come quickly to us and to battle. God alone knows who will control
this place of slaughter."

Why had Byrhtnoth done it? In the poem, it is said that the English commander suffered from *ofermode,* but the word is subject to
different interpretation. Arrogance? Pride? Overconfidence? An over-
abundance of courage? Chivalry? Or just pure stupidity? By all accounts, the English lord was giving up his every advantage, and if he
were insistent on doing such a thing, he should at least fall upon the

enemy as they came across the causeway. But that would not be English . . . or Christian.

There is another explanation. For two hundred years the English had suffered from these maddening hit-and-run pirate raids. Rarely did the pirates ever stand for a pitched battle. When they had, as often as not, they had been defeated. With so many fat English prizes spread across the coastline, it gained the Norsemen little to tarry for a toe-to-toe battle. So long as his adversaries comprised a fast-moving naval force, Byrhtnoth could never hope to catch and engage them, since the earl had no ships of his own. So perhaps his *ofermode* was desperate cunning, a last attempt to engage and crush his country's tormenters. Byrhtnoth's mission was to search out and destroy his foes, not to prevent them from landing here and to push them elsewhere.

The "war-wolves" waded across, and the Englishmen neared the glory trial.

> The time grew on
> when fated men must fall:
> the war-cry was raised. Ravens wound higher,
> the eagle, carrion-eager; on earth—the cry.

The battle raged, bows, spears, shields clashing, their clamor mixing with the cries and howls of men, seamen against Saxons, wolves against bears. Byrhtnoth himself fought bravely, sustaining a wound as he thrust a spear through a Viking's neck. At the critical moment, a Viking thug charged Byrhtnoth, more interested, the poet tells us, in the earl's rings and bracelets than his leadership. As the English lord raised his gold-handled sword to defend himself, his arm was cut and his sword fell harmless to the ground. The end near, Byrhtnoth lifted his eyes to the sky.

"Thanks to Thee, Lord God of hosts, for the joys I have experienced in this world. Now grant my spirit safe passage to thee. Prevent these hellish assailants from harming it."

And then the "heathen churls" hacked him down. When the Saxon soldiers saw their leader dead on the ground, they panicked and fled in disarray, with the earl's retainers leading the charge to the rear. The battlefield belonged to the villain and the heathen. Only Byrhtnoth's old retainer stayed beside the body of his commander, remaining to give the English words that would last a millennium:

"Courage shall grow keener, will clearer, the heart fiercer, as our force fails. Here our lord lies leveled in the dirt. He who thinks of avoiding this war-play now shall regret it forever. Though I am white with winters I shall not away, for I mean to lie by the side of my lord, by the man so dear to me."

IN CAMBRIDGE I BREAKFASTED on eggs and kippered herring, and then, fortified with that armor, took off for Ely, fourteen miles to the north. The cathedral town lies low in a swale, on the banks of the river Ouse. As I came over the brow of a hill, I could see the Norman towers far in the distance, caught by the soft morning light. In the cathedral shop I asked the two pert ladies behind the counter of guidebooks and pendants where I might find the tomb of Byrhtnoth. They glanced at one another in confusion. Byrhtnoth? The name sounded familiar. Mr. Arthur Davies would surely know, one of them said, and just at that moment, the distinguished verger himself came striding around the postcard rack looking like Byrhtnoth himself. A slender, gray-haired man with an athletic bearing, he had an air of importance, equal to the duty of managing a great medieval cathedral. He knew the answer immediately and beckoned me to follow him through the great nave and past the ornately carved choir to a small chapel on the side of the main altar. It was the Bishop West Chapel, named for Bishop Nicholas West, who presided here in 1527.

On both sides of the chapel, empty Gothic niches imparted a forlorn, unfinished look to the sanctuary, as if this ancient church were still a work in progress. Mr. Davies sensed my confusion. Almost apologetically, he explained that during the English Reformation, with Henry VIII raging over Rome's refusal to grant him a divorce from Catherine of Aragon, "rebels and rowdies" had invaded the cathedral and smashed all the statues of the Catholic saints and heroes, following the king's orders to expunge all vestiges of Catholicism from Britain. The perches had been left empty, a stark reminder of the passions of that time.

Then he pointed to my right, to a vault with four small chambers, each too small for a man's body, yet decorated ornately with Gothic scrollwork. Beside one of the compartments was a small plaque. Byrhtnoth, d. 991, Saxon earl of Essex. The words spoke of his generosity to the abbey and his desire to be buried there, and then:

"Learning of his death, monks set out for Maldon, recovered the headless body of their benefactor and brought it back to Ely for burial."

Headless? The poem mentions nothing about the severing of Byrhtnoth's noble head.

I was startled, but imagine the shock of the English in 991 A.D. Foreign heathens had hacked to death a proud and noble English leader, mutilated his body, and then taken his head as a prize, as the English army had scattered in terror and cowardice. Maldon was only one battle with brutal Norsemen, not the first or last by any measure. The battles and raids and invasions were to grow in number and ferocity as the first millennium of Christ grew closer, until the whole nation was subdued and humiliated. Who were these raiders from the north? Where did they come from, and why were they tormenting the English so? What were their motivations?

Throughout England, from the great cathedrals to the small Saxon churches, the devout prayed for deliverance. It was the fashion of the time that the mass was said in Latin, a language understood by a precious few, except for the homily, which was spoken in the vernacular. That homily was the only part that was widely understood by the common people. It was the part to remember and to repeat. Twenty years before the Battle of Maldon, a set of popular homilies was composed and distributed widely to priests. Called the Blickling Homilies (because the manuscripts were preserved in Blickling Hall in Norfolk), they were crude but passionate, powerful and often poetic. "The redness of the rose glitters in thee, and the whiteness of the lily shines in Thee," the angel Gabriel says to the Virgin Mary.

Of the nineteen Blickling Homilies, the tenth is entitled "The End of the World Is Near." After Maldon, it took on new vigor and new relevance.

"See and know and understand this: the end of this world is very nigh. Many calamities have appeared and men's crimes and woes are greatly multiplied. From day to day we hear of monstrous plagues and strange death throughout the country, that have come upon men. Nation riseth against nation. We see wars caused by iniquitous deeds. We hear frequently of the death of men of rank whose life was dear to us, and whose life appeared fair and beautiful and pleasant. . . .

"No man need think that his body may change the sin-burden in the grave. He shall rot to dust and there await the great event, the Doom, when the Almighty will bring this world to an end, when He will draw out his fiery sword and smite all this world through and pierce the bodies, and cleave asunder this earth. The dead shall stand up, then shall the flesh garb be as transparent as glass. Nothing of its nakedness will be concealed. . . . We must believe in the forgiveness of sins and the resurrection of the body on Doomsday."

Perhaps, it began to be whispered, these horrible Norsemen were agents of God's wrath. Could they be an advance guard? Was this the prelude to Doomsday? Was the apocalypse taking shape before their eyes?

"This world is altogether transitory," the homily concludes. "When it was first formed it was full of all beauty and was blooming in itself with manifold pleasures. . . . Now there is lamentation and weeping on all sides; now is mourning everywhere and breach of peace. Now is everywhere evil and slaughter. . . . We follow it, as it flies from us and love it although it is passing away. Lo! we may perceive that this world is illusory and transitory."

And so we enter the world of 999 A.D. When the Christian calendar is about to turn three digits, the pace seems to quicken; the heart beats faster; and passions seem to grow stronger and more urgent. It can be a time of anxiety, but also of creativity, a time of extravagance but also a time to take stock, to prepare for what is unknown but felt nonetheless. For some, faith is heightened. For all, the anticipation is great. There is, about this hinge of time, an odd and unsettling mix of sobriety and celebration.

It was like this, the last time around.

CHAPTER ONE

King Olaf Trygvesson

THE BATTLE AT MALDON was but a minor way station in the already heroic life of a huge and athletic young prince of Norway known to the English as Anlaf, but to his own people as Olaf Trygvesson. The son of a petty king around Oslofjord, Olaf had fled the Vik as a babe, almost Christ-like, with his mother, after his father was murdered. They had gone east to Sweden, then south to the Orkney Islands, and eventually to Russia, while spies of the reigning queen, Gunnhild, the wicked widow of Eric Bloodaxe, followed them. But in Estonia, Vikings captured their ship, separated the queen from her son, and sold the boy into slavery, first for a good ram, then for a cloth cloak. For six years Olaf toiled in the service of his master. By chance, a cousin who was a tax collector for King Vladimir of Russia came through Estonia and noticed the handsome, towheaded boy in the market-place. Upon learning who he was, the relative bought Olaf from his master and took him to Novgorod. There, in the court of Vladimir I, Olaf flourished, becoming a special favorite of the queen. When the boy was twelve, the Russian king put twelve ships under his command, sent him into battle, and the poets began to sing his praise.

The Viking days of Olaf Trygvesson had begun. His soldiers loved him, partly because he was generous in his pay, partly because he was so superior an athlete. With each battle, each Baltic victory, his standing in the court of the Russian king rose until, inevitably, jeal-ousies were aroused, and the king's councils whispered of the mistake to make this popular, impressionable foreigner so power-ful. The youth could be exploited, they told the king, and, moreover, they did not know "of what he can have to talk so often with the queen."

With this invidious innuendo sweeping through the court, Olaf's situation became intolerable, and he asked permission to leave Rus-sia. He wanted to return at last to his homeland, he told Vladimir, after this exile of many years. With regret, the Russian king acceded to the youth's request.

Sailing south to the island of Bornholm, where he fought a battle with the natives, and then to Poland, Olaf fell in love with a Polish princess, Queen Geira, and married her. For three years of bliss, he remained in "Wendland." But then his bride fell sick and died. And Olaf's grief turned to vengeance. Now twenty-one years, he had grown into a superb Nordic specimen. His physical prowess was ex-traordinary. In climbing and swimming and leaping, he was un-matched, and it was said that he could juggle five daggers in the air, always catching them by the handle. A favorite of his warriors, he went west to Holland with a fleet of nearly ninety ships, manned by Swedish Vikings from Russia. When he had finished with the Dutch, he went to France, then back to Jutland, leaving in his wake a great harvest for the ravens and wolves, to whom the poet gives the name "witch-wife's horses."

Olaf's broad axe of shining steel

For the shy wolf left many a meal.

The ill-shaped Saxon corpses lay

Heaped up, the witch-wife's horses prey.

She rides by night: at pools of blood,

Where Friesland men in daylight stood,

Her horses slake their thirst, and fly

On to the field where Flemings lie.

The raven-friend in Odinn's dress—

Olaf, who foes can well repress,

Left Flemish flesh for many a meal

With his broad axe of shining steel.

And thence to England, the greatest prize of the northern pirates: Olaf made the most of it. At the mouth of the Thames, he beached his long ships and fought the battle at Maldon, extorting the tribute of 10,000 pounds of silver from the weak Anglo-Saxon king, Ethelred, after the victory. From there, he moved north, plundering in Northumberland and Scotland, then to the Hebrides and then to fight other Vikings on the Isle of Man. After that, he turned south to Ireland, Wales, and Cornwall before he jumped over the Channel to taste the pleasures of France. "The young king drove a bloody game," a poet wrote. "The Irish fled at Olaf's name, fled from a young king seeking fame."

With his fleet now fortified to ninety-four ships, he came back to England, joined forces with the Danish king Svein Forkbeard, and together, as if they were taunting the Christians inside the town, they stood before London on September 8, 994 A.D., on the day celebrated as the Nativity of St. Mary.

Over the past century and a half, London had been victimized four times by the Norsemen. Only twelve years before, Danish Vikings had occupied and burned the city, so the terror was fresh in English minds. Olaf and Svein kept up a furious assault, but they could not breach the stout English defense, organized by King Ethelred. "God be thanked, they [the Vikings] came off worse than they ever thought possible," boasted the English chronicler, but then, "they went away thence, doing as much harm as any host was capable of, in all kinds of ways wherever they went."

Judging from his easy ransom after the Battle of Maldon, Olaf had good reason to believe that Ethelred would crack under pressure. So the Vikings went south along the Kentish coast where they met feeble opposition. Thus emboldened, they left their ships and moved inland on horseback, into the hills of Sussex and Hampshire, "burning villages," a horrified English chronicler tells us, "laying waste the lands, putting numbers of people to death by fire and sword, without regard to sex, and sweeping off an immense booty." Seizing horses, they rode wildly through many provinces and slaughtered the whole population with savage cruelty, "sparing neither the women nor children of tender age." At last, Ethelred could not stand it any longer and sued for peace. A formal treaty was concluded between the parties to cement this pitiful deal, a treaty which had such formal provisions as these:

If an Englishman slays a Dane, he is to pay for him with 25 pounds or the actual slayer is to be surrendered; and the Dane is to do the same for an Englishman, if he slays one.

If an Englishman slays a Danish slave, he is to pay for him with one pound, and the Dane the same for an English slave, if he slays one.

If eight men are slain, then it is a breach of the truce. If a breach of the truce is committed within a borough, the citizens are to go there themselves and take the slayers, alive or dead—or their nearest kinsmen—head for head. If they will not, the ealdorman is to go there; if he will not, the king is to go there; if he will not, that ealdorman is to be excluded from the truce.

"Then the king and his councilors decided to offer them tribute," wrote the Anglo-Saxon chronicler. "This was done and they accepted it, together with provisions which were given to them from the whole of the West Saxon kingdom, the sum amounting to 22,000 pounds."

So the price of peace had inflated in three years, and it would grow much higher. A terrible precedent had been set: instead of a fight, the terrorist was to be rewarded with "danegeld," and the gold would lure the bandit back time and again, each time with a higher demand.

In the weeks it took to consummate this shabby deal and to refurbish his fleet, King Olaf lay off the Cornish coast, fatigued and fretful. To ensure that the ransom was paid on time and in full, he took several prominent hostages and soon perceived the value of this technique of extortion as well. Biding his time in the Scilly Islands, off Land's End, the Viking heard of a local fortune-teller who was said to possess the gift of prophecy. Intrigued, Olaf decided to test the seer's powers. Given his widespread reputation as a magnificent figure of a man, huge, athletic, and elegantly dressed, Olaf decked out one of his larger soldiers in royal attire and sent him to the prophet, posing as "Ole" the Dane.

"Thou art not the king," the seer declared derisively, but then, out of an abundance of caution, he added, "but I advise thee to be faithful to the king."

The story intrigued Olaf when it was reported to him, and he was determined to meet the fortune-teller personally. Rowing off in a sea buck to the hermit's rocky retreat, Olaf asked if the prophet could foresee Olaf's future. Would the prince be successful in battle? Would he regain power in the north?

"Thou wilt become a renowned king and do celebrated deeds," the hermit replied. "And that thou not doubt the truth of this answer, listen to this." And then he predicted that Olaf would soon suffer a mutiny among his men. In the ensuing fight, he would be wounded and carried to his ship on his oblong shield. After seven days, he would recover and thereafter would allow himself to be baptized a Christian.

"Many men wilt thou bring to faith and baptism," the prophet said, "and both to thy own and others' good."

Shortly afterward, the mutiny took place precisely as the hermit had predicted. After his recovery in seven days, Olaf Trygvesson hastened back to the seer and asked him how he had gained such wisdom.

"The god of the Christian has blessed me," the hermit replied, "so that I can know all that I desire."

Presently, Olaf allowed himself to be baptized. When King Ethelred heard about this, he sent his bishop and his high reeve to Olaf, proposing a glorious confirmation at Andover. There amid the chalk hills, along the bank of the Test, the solemn ceremony was held in grand style. Ethelred presented his tormenter with royal gifts and, in return, Olaf promised never again to visit war upon England. To Ethelred, Christianity was more effective than gold, and to Olaf, his new faith conferred upon him a dignity and stature among kings that he had lacked before. The benefits on both sides were evident . . . if, in the case of Ethelred, the reprieve was temporary. Svein Forkbeard also left England after this, his greed satisfied, but the Danish king would soon be back for another spree.

FOR SOME MONTHS, through the winter of 994–95 A.D., Olaf Trygvesson remained in England, pondering his new wealth, his new power, his new faith. During this period, a gathering of English nobility was held in the Wessex countryside, for the purpose of choosing a husband for the young widow of an English lord and the daughter of the petty king of Dublin (which was a Viking town). A handsome woman with a brassy demeanor, Queen Gyda was considered a prime catch. She had many suitors, but none of them had as yet pleased her, except vaguely the best fighter in the region, a broad-shouldered swain named Alfin. At the parliament, the suitors presented themselves once again in a kind of medieval cattle call, including Alfin, who was turned out beautifully in his most splendid outfit. Olaf arrived late at the occasion, in a somewhat bedraggled state. Tired from a long ride through the reeds and bogs of southern England, he had on his "bad-weather" clothes, and his coarse cloak was splattered with mud. Out of curiosity, he stood on the edge of the elegant crowd of Gyda's suitors. When she passed down the line in review and noticed this tall, grimy figure in the rear, she was startled.

"What sort of man is this?" she asked, and it is unclear whether she meant his beauty or his impertinence.

"I am called Ole," Olaf boomed, "and I am a stranger here."

"Wilt thou have me if I choose thee?" Gyda said with breathtaking forwardness.

"I will not say no to that," Olaf replied. But he did not say yes either. He was now a Christian leader, foretold to accomplish great deeds, and the king-in-waiting of Norway. Not any Irish wench would do. Who was she? he asked, and what were her attributes?

"I am called Gyda and am daughter of the king of Ireland," she replied. "I was married in this country to an earl who ruled over this territory. Since his death I have ruled over it, and many have courted me, but none would I choose as a husband."

He liked her spirit, but first Alfin had to be dispatched. As was the custom, the two suitors met in a "holm-gang," single combat usually fought on a deserted island with deadly weapons. To Alfin's expert sword, Olaf matched his Nordic axe, with which he knocked his English rival senseless, bound him, seized his property, and then banished him. Then he and Queen Gyda were betrothed.

Early in 995 A.D., a bright comet appeared in the English sky which the people called "the long-haired." Olaf Trygvesson, reborn in his luminescent new faith and flush with his new bride, must have regarded this as a good sign. While he was consorting with his new in-laws in Dublin, more good news reached him from Norway. A merchant from the north, paying a visit to him at the court of the Irish king, spoke of dissatisfaction in Norway with the current leader. He was no other than Earl Hacon, the murderer of Olaf's father, King Trygve. While the earl had done some good things in the land, such as consolidating his rule over coastal Norway and winning important battles, he had degenerated into a lecher in his middle age, seizing the comely daughters of estimable gentlemen, keeping them as his concubines for a week or two, and then discarding them, limp and used, back to their homestead. This was causing an uproar in the land, although few dared to criticize the earl to his face.

The merchant told another story that raised the ire of Olaf even further. Earl Hacon had accepted Christianity under threat from the German emperor, Otto, but then had reverted to heathenism when he was safely home. He had been busy restoring many heathen temples to their honored place in the provinces. When the earl fought a terrible battle whose outcome was in doubt, he prayed to his personal heathen goddess, offering her his best horses as a sacrifice. But she seemed angry, for she did not respond. The earl offered more valuable things without any supernatural deliverance until he offered his youngest son, a handsome and promising seven-year-old, as a sacrifice. The boy was given to a slave who broke the boy's back on the sacrifice rock in the usual manner. And afterward, the tide of the battle turned in Hacon's favor, and the court propagandist wrote his encomium, for the earl "restores Odinn's temples to Norway's shores."

"To tell the truth," the merchant told Olaf, "many brave men would rather see a king of Harald Fairhair's race come to the kingdom. But we know of no one suited for this, especially now when criticism of Earl Hacon is so pointless."

For Olaf Trygvesson to bask suddenly in the aura of Harald Fairhair had an element of irony to it, for the legacy of his ancestor was decidedly mixed. King Harald was one of the great strong men of the Viking era. He had united Norway and ruled it sternly for seventy years, from 860 to 930 A.D. His reign was the stuff of legend. It had begun on a peculiar note of Viking romance. He longed for the hand of a hot-blooded, large-minded maiden from Hordaland, but she was not interested in a union with a petty lord and told him to return when he was the self-respecting king of an entire country, not of just a tiny province. While Harald found this demand overbold, "I make this vow and God who made and rules all things shall be my witness," he announced, "that I shall never cut my hair or comb it till I possess all Norway in scot."

Harald's quest for his ladylove and all Norway took him ten years and, by the end, he must have been quite a sight and smell. His campaign culminated in the great sea battle at Hafursfjord against an alliance of lesser Norwegian earls led by the thick-necked lord called Kjoltvi the Rich. In the famous battle, the "berserks were roaring and the wolf coated warriors howling," the ships were eager for battle "with grim gaping heads and rich carved prows," and Kjoltvi's men ended up "upthrowing their buttocks, their heads in the bottom." When Harald's victorious forces headed home, "they thought of the mead horns."

The king's body finally got a bath and his hair was cut, and lo! his thatch appeared thick and beautiful. He called for the reluctant maiden, married her, and had children, the eldest of which was named Alov the Fecund. Later he took other wives, including Ragnhild the Mighty, who gave him his favorite son, Eric Bloodaxe.

Harald's rule was harsh, especially over conquered provinces where he seized the "odal rights" to all land, making himself the official owner of property, undercutting the traditional independence of the farmers, and exacting very heavy taxes. His brutal new order drove many of Norway's finest men into exile, including those who fled west over the sea and settled Iceland. Among Harald's dubious gifts to his land was Eric Bloodaxe, the worst Norse king of the Viking era, who got his name by the axes he lodged in the skulls of his brothers and who ruled Norway for ten intolerable years before he was driven out.

If now Norway wanted more of Harald Fairhair's style of governing, Olaf was willing. The time was ripe, he decided, for his triumphal return to his homeland. With the aid of his Irish father-in-law, the Norwegian prince outfitted five ships. He closed the English chapter of his life with a certain ingratitude, for he left his forward Irish wife, Gyda, on the shore as he sailed north to the Orkney Islands.

On these fertile keys, at the northern tip of Scotland, his ancestor King Harald Fairhair had put his bloody hand as well. The islands had become the lair of refugees who had fled Harald's tyranny and who had made the Orkneys a base for much pirating. This had annoyed King Harald. So he had sailed there in 875 A.D., cleaned out the nest, seized the odal rights, and left the islands a Norwegian fiefdom. He installed his puppets in power, beginning with the ugly, one-eyed Turf-Einar (who got his name as the first man to dig and burn peat for fuel). Turf-Einar might have acquired a more sinister name. His island rule had been challenged by Halfdan Long-Leg, one of Harald's sons, but Turf-Einar finally came out on top and took his revenge in the most distinctive Viking way. He carved the fearsome *rista orn,* the blood eagle, as vicious a torture as man has ever devised. He stuck his sword in the prince's back, cut all his ribs away down to the loins, and then pulled the lungs out the back.

Turf-Einar knew what a howling his act would cause when "the corbie croaks over carrion in Orkney." His deed brought King Harald Fairhair racing back across the North Sea after the villain and his son, Thorfinn Skull-splitter, and the cycle of violence continued. The bloodletting would proceed for another 120 years, with visitations by Eric Bloodaxe, wicked intrigues by scheming women, and wars with the Scots of Caithness.

In the summer of 995 A.D., Olaf's fleet of five ships put in at Osmundwall. There in the southern Orkneys he began his peculiar crusade in the service of Jesus Christ. Confronting the earl of Orkney, Sigurd, with an offer that was hard to refuse, he said:

"I want you and all your subjects to be baptized. If you refuse, I'll have you killed on the spot, and I swear that I'll ravage every island with fire and steel."

Earl Sigurd promptly saw the light of Christ and was baptized. As security for the conversion, Olaf took Sigurd's son hostage, a technique of persuasion that he was to use later in Iceland with better results. But unfortunately for Olaf and for Christ, the boy was sickly and, during the voyage to Norway, he died. After that, Earl Sigurd refused to pay any more tribute to King Olaf. (Earl Sigurd was later killed in the Battle of Clontarf in 1014 when Brian Boru, king of Dál Cais and of all Ireland, defeated a Viking force and ended, at the price of his life, the Viking occupation of his country.)

AS OLAF TRYGVESSON sailed across the North Sea toward home, he must have felt the nobility and the grandeur of his holy mission. He was a hybrid of Odysseus and Michael, avenger, exile, and zealot all in one. He was coming, in justice and in glory, as the royal scion of Harald Fairhair's race, as the king of whom great deeds were predicted in the name of Norway and in the name of Christ. He was returning to avenge the death of his father, the exile of his mother, the slavery of his youth. His passion was to convert his heathen homeland, and he was prepared for holy war. By his athletic stature, by his superior skill in the martial art, by his campaigns across the Baltic and through England, and by his zealot's faith, he was the Viking warrior *non pareil:* bold, cruel, and skilled.

As he approached Norway's shore, Olaf possessed no fine sense of what Christianity meant, especially its gentler side. But he must have had some sense of the calendar. The world was approaching the thousandth year after Christ's birth, and with it, Christ the King would come a second time. There would be a final climactic battle between the forces of good and evil. It was not hard for Olaf to view Earl Hacon as the Antichrist. The earl was the murderer of his father, the rapist of Norway's daughters, and the high priest of heathenism. Nor was it hard to imagine Hacon's soldiers as the forces of Gog and Magog.

If there was any imagery in the Christian bible to which a Viking warrior, raised in the heathen tradition, could relate, it was the magical language of Revelation. For beasts and monsters, giants and trolls were the most familiar of notions.

"And as I stood upon the sand of the sea and saw a beast rise up out of the sea, having seven heads and ten horns, and upon his horns ten crowns, and upon his heads the name of blasphemy," reads Revelation 13 about the first beast. "And the beast which I saw was like unto a leopard, and his feet were as the feet of a bear, and his mouth as the mouth of a lion; and the dragon gave him his power, and his meat, and his great authority."

How different was that from the apocalypse of the heathens? For in the villages and temples of Olaf's upbringing, in Norway and in Russia, there had been talk of Ragnarok, that terrible end-time when the world sinks into moral chaos, into anxiety and greed, into an intoxication with gold, when brothers kill brothers and incest is rampant. In this wolf's age, Odinn becomes an agent of violent death and is himself killed violently, when war breaks out between the Vanir and the Aesir, and the gods mete out punishment to oath breakers, murderers, rapists.

In the day of Ragnarok, the wolf will swallow the sun. Another wolf will seize the moon. The earth and the mountains will tremble so violently that trees will be uprooted, mountains will crash down. The sun will go black. The earth will sink into the sea. And the heavens will lose their stars.

In this final battle between the good and the evil gods, all will die. There are no winners, only losers. Into this chaos and conflagration,

Inn riki, the Mighty One, will ride triumphantly. And with him the world will be renewed and purified, and afterward, only innocent gods will rule.

When Olaf Trygvesson finally approached the nose of Norway, he touched land offshore on Moster Island, pitched a tent, and held a great mass. Afterward, he considered his situation. Should he make a big noise in the land or try to take Earl Hacon by surprise? He decided on the latter course and moved quietly up the coast to the mouth of the Trondheim fjord. On its southern point, he sent a few spies inland, and they came back with excellent news. Earl Hacon was indeed in the area, and he was up to his old escapades. He had just tried to seize the wife of a respectable farmer and had been turned back by a rabble of the farmer's friends. Now the earl was feasting at a place called Medalhus and could not leave well enough alone. He had sent his slaves to seize the beautiful wife of another freeholder named Orm. But Orm was no more compliant. He delayed the earl's messengers with food and drink while he sent a call to arms, and the farmers were gathering in great anger, ready to kill Earl Hacon. Olaf could scarcely have wished for better intelligence.

Moving stealthily into the fjord with his five ships, he spotted the earl's three ships, lying at anchor near Vigg. The earl's handsome son was watching over the royal fleet, and when he saw Olaf's sea stallions bearing down on him, he weighed anchor and tried to get away. But Olaf caught up and hurled a tiller at the young man, striking him on the head and killing him instantly. Soon after, Olaf made contact with the rebellious peasants, who by this time had blocked off the roads and were ready to pounce on the lecherous earl.

But Earl Hacon was already on the fly. His own troops having deserted him, he took refuge in the area with his mistress, an estimable woman of great power named Thora. Her cozy relationship with the earl was well known and it could be expected that Olaf and his farmers would come to look for the fugitive there first. So Thora had her slave dig a hole beneath her pigsty. Logs were placed over the hole, and manure on top of the logs. With his slave named Kark, the earl crawled into the poke, hoping to wait out the trouble, if he could stand the smell.

As expected, Olaf soon turned up. His rebels searched the house inside and out, and when they could not find the earl, Olaf climbed up onto a large rock next to the pigsty and gave a speech to his troops, promising great reward and honor to anyone who could find the earl and kill him. Earl Hacon and his slave Kark heard the speech through the seeping timbers, and the earl turned on his slave suspiciously.

"Why are you so pale?" he whispered. "Do you have a mind to betray me?"

"By no means, master," Kark replied.

"Remember this," the earl said. "We were born on the same night. The time between our deaths will be short."

After Olaf went away and the night came, the earl and his slave tried to sleep. But Kark had a bad dream, and at his moans, Earl Hacon woke him up. "What on earth is the matter with you?"

"I had a bad dream," the slave replied. "I was at Lade, and Olaf Trygvesson was laying a gold ring around my neck."

"It will be a red ring Olaf lays around your neck if he catches you," the earl snapped. "Take care. From me you will enjoy good things, so do not betray me."

They tried to go back to sleep, but each was now so suspicious of the other, they tried to keep an eye open. Eventually, the earl dropped off, and he too slept so fitfully that he cried out in his sleep. Horror-struck, Kark woke up with such a fright that he pulled a knife from his belt and plunged it into Earl Hacon's throat, killing him. Then thinking of the reward and honor that Olaf Trygvesson had promised from the rock, Kark cut off the earl's head, took it to Lade, and presented it proudly to Olaf.

Olaf thanked him, gave him a gold ring, and then had him beheaded.

In 996 A.D., a national assembly was held, and Olaf Trygvesson was proclaimed the king of all Norway. One by one, the petty earls and chiefs of the country paid him homage, even the leaders of the Uplands and the Vik, who before had been in league with Svein Forkbeard, the king of Denmark. In his first winter and summer as king, Olaf traveled along his rocky coast to consolidate his realm, as the heirs of Earl Hacon, full of vengeance, fled to Sweden.

S INCE THE DAYS OF KING HARALD FAIRHAIR, the propaganda of the royal court had been its poetry. Iceland had
provided elegant bards—their talent coming, no doubt, from the long
winters, the long nights, the isolation of their native land. They were
called *scalds,* and they received stature and gold for their words.
When the greatest of them, Egil Skallagrimsson, neared death, he
wondered who would

> Fill high hawkfell of my hand
> With scald's reward for skilled word?

And he spoke of the poet's craft unabashedly:

> I am pat of speech for praising of princes,
> But slow-spoke of the stingy-minded
> Open-mouthed of war-lord's deeds,
> But tongue-tied 'mid tittle-tattle.

Because the rhyme and meter was such an exacting art, their
poems endured.

Of all the scalds to write poems about the great deeds of Olaf,
Hallfred was the most noteworthy. Olaf called him the "troublesome
scald" because he was so obstinate and independent and even
bloody-minded, but also because for him conversion to Christianity
was such agony. He was also something of a romantic, even though
his face was swarthy and his nose ugly. In his youth he gained a
reputation for being sarcastic and fickle. He hailed from the north of
Iceland where the polar icecap was no more than a day's sail and
where the sun in the summer was perpetual. When he came first to
Norway, he persuaded Earl Hacon to let him be the poet laureate,
and the old heathen showered him gratefully with fancy clothes and
a silver axe.

When the change of leadership came, the bard was on a journey, and he knew his royal status in the court was in jeopardy. He had heard the stories of Olaf's insistence on the new faith and of the king's stern measures for those who did not go along. In truth, Hallfred loved the pagan pantheon, for literary reasons. Poetry was "Odinn's mead"; to lose Thor and Odinn, or Freya, the goddess of love, or the glorious Baldur, the god of beauty, was a literary disaster. It would rob him of his imagination, kill his muse, and deprive him of his art. He would flee rather than lose his gift. He would put Norway and its stern king with his bloodless faith behind him, he decided. With his friends he made a promise: if they could reach Iceland, he would pay tribute to Thor, but if they reached Sweden, he would bow down to Freya.

But on the day Hallfred expected to leave, a stiff wind blew him back into Trondheim harbor. The wind became a gale, the gale a storm, and suddenly even his anchor would not hold under the force. But then from nowhere appeared a very large man, wrapped in a green cloak and commanding a force of thirty men, and he came to Hallfred's rescue. Hallfred asked the man his name. "Anchor-shank" was the reply.

Just then the walrus-hide cable snapped completely, and Hallfred's *snaekke* began to drift. But Anchor-shank dove into the turbulent water, retrieved the rope's end, and reattached it in the roiling water. Such was the poet's introduction to the heroic life of Olaf Trygvesson. After the storm, the king summoned the bedraggled and crestfallen Icelander and announced the price of his rescue: salvation in Christ. Give up your old pagan beliefs, the king demanded, and take up the new faith.

"Only at a price," Hallfred replied stubbornly. "That you will never turn me away, whatever misfortune befalls me."

"Receive baptism," the king demanded. "And your wish will be granted."

"I have another request."

"You ask much, Hallfred."

"That you be my godfather."

At the king's side, his bishop leaned down and whispered into Olaf's ear. "The more you do for God's true faith, the more he will do for you." After it was done, Hallfred exulted in his godfather, the greatest man of all who "dwelt under the dome of dwarves' northern sky-burden."

But once he was in the king's service, Hallfred had trouble getting the king's ear. Matters worsened and finally came to a head when Olaf put his bard off one last time after Hallfred had composed a very special poem.

"That is for you to decide," Hallfred snapped. "But if you will not listen to my poems, I shall forget your teachings, for those teachings are not a whit more poetic than the *drapa* I made for you." Impertinent though this was, the king reacted benignly. "In truth, you are a troublesome scald," the king answered indulgently. "Proceed with your poem." But the king was ill-pleased with what followed:

> Time was I worshiped him
>
> Who, well-skilled, governs Valhalla.
>
> Lo there is a shocking shift!
>
> Men's ways are other these days.

"That is not a good verse," snapped the king. "Make amends." The poet's next, begrudging effort was this:

> To praise thy power, Odinn
>
> Poets have ever made sacred songs:
>
> For me it is pleasant to remember.
>
> Reluctant I was
>
> To despise the spouse of Frigg
>
> Since Christ alone must I now serve.

"You think too much about the gods," the king said. "It does you no credit." Hallfred tried again, but to reject the old and embrace the new was hard.

> I am finished with the raven-god
>
> Who was honored by all
>
> Whose guile was acclaimed by all nations.

"Stop," cried the king. "That is not much better. Speak again."
Hallfred spoke:

> Let fiends find Hoodman's favor
> Though Freya be angry
> . . . and Freya and Thor the Mighty.
> I recant the errors of the witches outright.
> To Christ with all faith henceforth.
> Fearful of his anger
> Who under the World-Father wields wide sway
> and to God, will I pray.

With this, the king was satisfied. "This is well done," he said. "But
make another." Hallfred complied:

> Rites of blood are banned.
> In Olaf's house all must shun
> The witches rite
> All forsake the rood-cross
> I, sprung from the witches' issue,
> Now worship only Christ.

The stormy relationship between the king and his bard continued
for some time. Hallfred stood always in danger of imbibing the mead
of Odinn, like some unrecovered alcoholic. But his verses were not
all somber and tortured. There were lighthearted moments as well.
Once, as a kind of poetic calisthenic, the warrior-king asked his poet
if he could compose a verse with the word *sword* in every line. Hallfred went to the mat . . . and almost succeeded.

> This sword of swords is my reward.
> For him who knows to wield a sword,
> And with his sword to serve his lord,

Yet wants a sword, his lot is hard.

I would I had my good lord's leave

For this good sword a sheath to choose:

I'm worth three swords where men swords use,

But for the sword-sheath now I grieve.

If his poet was worth three swords, that was fine with Olaf, for the king would need all he could get.

TOWARD THE END of the first millennium, Norway was a sparsely peopled kingdom. It was ruled by a motley group of petty lords and cultivated by self-reliant freeholders who farmed and fished along the coast and the riverbanks and took orders from no man. The total population of the country did not exceed fifty thousand people, and it was spread along the rocky, crenellated coastline. The trading towns like Kaupang on the western point of the Oslofjord or Trondheim and Lade in the north had no more than about five hundred people, even in high season. Few ventured inland, into the dense forests toward the keel of mountains that separated Norway from Sweden. The greatest concentration of people was in the Vik, that region encompassing Oslo's fjord which was the domain of Olaf's martyred father, King Trygve. It was there that Olaf began his crusade to Christianize his land.

In the Vik, during the summer and fall of 996 A.D., he had easy sailing. Many of his relatives were still powerful, and the supporters of his father were legion. In the preceding decades when the Christian king of Denmark Harald Bluetooth held sway over the area, many had converted to Christianity. But when the Thor-loving Earl Hacon took over, the converted reverted, and once again, the gods of Aesir were transcendent. King Olaf burned with messianic fire, however, and the days of choice were over. Olaf gathered his relatives together and deputized them as Christ's captains.

"I shall make you great and mighty men for doing this work," he told them. "All Norway will be Christian or die."

The east and west shores of the Oslofjord acceded immediately to the king's demand, but in the northern part of the Vik the resistance was greater. He treated the holdouts without mercy, killing some, mutilating others, and banishing the rest. By the end of the year, between his sword and his axe, he had claimed all of the Vik for Christ and dared anyone to claim otherwise.

In the early spring of 997 A.D., he moved west into Hordaland with a great force, to the Agder along the tip of Norway's nose, and into Rogaland. The farther west he moved, the stiffer and more organized became the opposition. Local chiefs conspired to plan a defense of the old traditions, conferring the dubious honor upon three of the region's most eloquent talkers to speak out against the king and his new religion when a general assembly was held. Legend holds that the three had sudden attacks of discombobulation. The first and most eloquent was seized with a cough and shortness of breath and could not utter a word; the second became so confused that the audience laughed him down; and the third developed a sore throat. Some supernatural force was clearly at work. Thereafter, the region voted for Christianity and the people were baptized.

The king moved on, north to the fjord country, the south and north More and Raumsdal. He was a model of consistency. Sometimes he began whimsically, challenging a heathen to a swimming race or a shooting contest, and to the winner's faith goes the loser. Once he is said to have shot a chess piece off the head of a boy to impress the child's agnostic uncle. Generally, however, the challenge was more direct: Christianize or fight. Few were ready for the latter.

And so they did what he asked. They pretended to convert and wept battle tears at their loss. The heathen gods were proclaimed to be evil spirits: anyone who trafficked in such evil was to be banished, especially the sorcerers. Once, at a place on the river Göta, he gathered all the wizards and the troll-wise high priests of the region in a longhouse for a great feast, then closed the doors and burnt the building to the ground. But their leader escaped through the smoke hole, and when he was caught, King Olaf marooned him and his fellow incorrigibles on a rock far offshore at low tide. Afterward, the rock was called the Skerry of the Warlocks.

When he came to Trondheim, the lair of the late Earl Hacon, he took more extreme measures, burning heathen temples and desecrating heathen idols. At one temple, he found a gold ring of Earl Hacon, hung it on the door of the pagan temple, and when the crowd gathered, he torched the place. This caused anger in the fjord, and again, the local chiefs rose against him, sending out the war arrow through the region as a message to prepare for battle. Faced with this unrest, King Olaf went away to the Vik for the winter, but returned the following summer with a larger army and thirty ships, weighing anchor in the river Nid. Inviting the local chiefs to a fine feast, as an apparent gesture of peace, he indicated his willingness to attend a heathen sacrifice.

At the feast the guests got quite drunk on Viking ale. The following morning, King Olaf attended a mass and then gathered the hungover chiefs together. "It has been agreed between us that we would meet and make a great sacrifice," the king said. "If I am to return to making heathen sacrifices, then I will make the greatest sacrifice of all. I will sacrifice men, not slaves. I propose to take the greatest men only and offer them to the gods." And he named the eleven most prominent leaders of the opposition. When the horrified farmers howled in protest, he took the eleven hostage instead, until everyone was baptized. Finally, he set the eminent men free only when their sons and brothers were swapped for their prominent fathers.

In nearby Trondheim, King Olaf employed another method. Again at the assembly of the local farmers, he appeared open to attending a heathen ritual. "We want, king, that you should offer sacrifice, as other kings before you have done," said the leader, whose name was Iron Beard. The king agreed readily and the crowd went to the local temple. Once the door was closed, Olaf raised his golden axe, struck the image of Thor and ransacked the niches of the other gods, and then killed old Iron Beard. After the survivors agreed to be baptized, King Olaf took Iron Beard's comely daughter as his wife.

As the king moved still farther north, even as far as the Lofoton Islands, the population of potential converts grew sparser and more obstreperous. None was more obstinate than a rich farmer and devout heathen named Raud the Strong, who was the chief of the region, had a large company of Laplanders at his disposal, and commanded a formidable long ship, larger than the king's flagship, with a gilded dragon head on its prow and an upturned serpent's tail in its stern. When Raud heard that the king was coming with his bitter message, Raud mobilized his force, and a fierce sea battle was fought . . . with predictable results.

Raud, however, escaped and took refuge in his island hideout in the Saltenfjord. The entrance to the fjord was protected by a narrow throat through which the tidal water gushed in torrents, and only the most skilled sailor could navigate it. For more than a week, King Olaf lay offshore, waiting for the wind to calm and the high seas to slacken, trying to figure out when to make a run for it. The problem was greater, we are told, because Raud was expert in witchcraft and had placed a hex on the king. Countermeasures were called for, and so King Olaf summoned his bishop, who laid his holy robes on the stem of the king's ship, sprinkled holy water over the ship, read the gospels, and then gave his blessing to proceed. By some miracle, it is said, the Christian ships passed through the narrow passageway, the water curling gently around the keels, while a few paces away the waves raged so furiously that the nearby mountains were obscured.

Once in the fjord, the royal men quickly apprehended Raud and brought him to the king, who ordered the chief to accept baptism.

"I will not take your property from you, but instead will be your friend," said Olaf sweetly, "if you make yourself worthy to be so."

Raud declined and even made fun of Christ and the Christian God. This enraged Olaf, and he declared that Raud would die "the worst of deaths." The blasphemer was bound to a wooden beam, his mouth was forced open with a wooden pin, and the king's henchmen tried to force an adder down his throat. But Raud's breath came from the pits of hell, and the adder recoiled at the first whiff. So the king took a horn, placed it in Raud's mouth, stuffed the reluctant adder in again, and put a hot iron to the snake's tail. The treatment of Raud was a powerful lesson, and the region, feeling the heat of Olaf's poker, quickly came over to Christ.

By 999 A.D. Olaf Trygvesson, as Christ's supreme hatchet man, had conquered all of Norway for Christianity. The time had come for him to settle down, to rule and to turn his attention beyond his shores to other distant lands. On the Trondheim fjord, he built his royal house along the bank of the river Nid and put his mind to developing the village there into a trading center, looking especially to Iceland. That country, still in the grip of pagans, loomed as the king's next target.

Meanwhile, his domestic affairs preoccupied him. After he paid just compensation to the relatives of old Iron Beard for slaying the heathen in his temple, he took Iron Beard's daughter, Gudrun, home as his bride. On their wedding night, they went to bed, and when Gudrun thought the king was spent and asleep, she took a knife and prepared to plunge it into his neck. But Olaf woke just in time and took the knife away. Gudrun gathered up her clothes and left.

Pity King Olaf: he was happy in holy war, cruel in his rule, devout in his faith, and unlucky in love.

Thorgeir the Lawspeaker

IN MIDSUMMER OF THE YEAR 1000 A.D., the long ship of two Icelandic chieftains hugged the inhospitable southern coast of Iceland, moving slowly west. After a seven-day voyage the sailors reached their safe harbor in the Westman Islands. Their journey from the west coast of Norway had been uneventful, but the chieftains found themselves now in a high state of excitement about the possibilities that lay before them. They passed by the vaulting, troll-like rock sentinels outside, then slipped between the sheer, cackling, puffin-filled cliffs of Ystiklettur on one side and the fire mountain of Eldfell on the other. The earth itself seemed to taunt them.

They were not superstitious men. Gizur the White was the battle-hardened chief at Mossfell, a high talus plain west of the hooded, heathen volcano of Hekla and on the road to the Parliament place. He had been a central figure in the politics and the lawmaking and the blood feuds of the previous few decades. Just two years before, Gizur the White had stood at the Law Rock and declared the greatest fighter in Iceland, the awesome Gunnar Hamundarson, to be an outlaw in the land. The following summer Gizur led the death struggle against the great warrior. Gizur's band of forty men surrounded Gunnar's hut, pulled the roof off his house with ropes, and finally overcame the great fighter—when Gunnar's grudge-filled wife refused to lend locks of her hair to restring his bow. Afterward, as Gunnar lay bleeding on the ground before them, Gizur the White had said in admiration:

"We have felled a great champion, and we have not found it easy. His last defense will be remembered for as long as people live in this land."

Two years before his battle with Gunnar, Gizur the White had converted to Christianity. This had been a bold and unpopular act, especially for one of Iceland's thirty-nine chieftains, for the pagan way was strong and popular in Iceland and attempts at conversion, largely promoted by King Olaf Trygvesson of Norway, had failed miserably. The king's first missionary, a baleful bishop named Stefni, had resorted to the radical measures of destroying sanctuaries and altars and sacred images of the gods. For this, he was driven away and narrowly escaped with his life. As if by divine intervention, his ship was blown out to sea, and the pagans gloated.

"The gods must still be in the land," one said.

Despite the storm, Stefni made it back to Norway and reported to King Olaf that he had been received by the Icelanders in "a most inhospitable way." (He should not have taken his rejection personally. Ten years earlier, the very first attempts to Christianize Iceland had ended in failure, when the first missionaries killed a few men at the Parliament place, after the heathens lampooned the missionaries. Lampooning was a dangerous sport in Iceland.)

Afterward a law was passed at the Parliament, and Gizur the White, an important chief of the Rang River valley, had offered no opposition. Henceforth, any man who dishonored the gods of Aesir or their temples would be outlawed, meaning he would be ostracized and could be killed on sight. The relatives of the accused, second and third cousins and all degrees in between, were obligated to administer the punishment, because "the devout call Christianity [was] a shame to one's kinsmen."

Then King Olaf dispatched the infamous Bishop Thangbrand to Iceland. To pick this Saxon priest for so important a ministry was an odd move for the king, since Thangbrand was passionate but uncontrollable, a good scholar but also a murderer. In him, learning and brutality and impulsiveness were joined in equal measure. The king's motivation seemed to be as much to lose a nuisance as to gain a missionary. To Thangbrand, King Olaf gave a simple order: convert Iceland in two years.

Thangbrand met with no less opposition than his predecessor. The pagan witches took a special dislike to him, turning on him with fury. Things went especially badly for Thangbrand after the Christian bishop killed two poets when they made fun of his religion. Once, in the north country, it was learned that Thangbrand was passing through, and the heathens prepared a great and sinister sacrifice to the gods. Shortly afterward, not far from the bogs of Lake Myvatn, the earth opened up, and the bishop and his horse fell headlong into a soggy pit. The swamp swallowed the horse, but the bishop climbed out of the ooze (a soft depression first made by a melted iceberg) and escaped.

In this event the pagans saw further evidence of Thor's fury against the outside agitator and wished only that their god had used his hammer. But Thangbrand gave thanks to his God. His escape was a miracle. The place became known as Thangbrand's pool.

It would not be the only body of water named after Thangbrand. There was also Thangbrand's brook in Oxarfjord, Thangbrand's ship shelter in the river Hitara, and Thangbrand's harbor in Alftrafjord. They were all bad, forbidding places, and Thangbrand himself was now branded in Iceland as "a pervert god-outcast." The last of these places was the bay in eastern Iceland called Berufjord place. That was where the bishop's ship, called the *Bison*, was blown out to sea and wrecked.

"Did you ever hear how Thor challenged Christ to a duel," a pagan sorceress would ask Thangbrand later, "and Christ did not dare to accept the challenge?"

"I have heard that Thor would be nothing but dust and ashes if God did not permit him to live," he replied.

"Do you know who wrecked your ship then?" she asked.

"Who do you think?" Thangbrand asked.

She answered with a verse:

> It was Thor's giant-killing hammer
> That smashed the ocean-striding Bison;
> It was our gods who drove
> The bell-ringer's boat ashore.
> Your Christ could not save
> This buffalo of the sea from destruction;
> I do not think your God
> Kept guard over him at all.
> Thor seized the great ship,
> Shook its frame
> And beat its timbers
> And hurled it on the rocks;
> That ship will never sail the seas again,
> For Thor's relentless thrashing
> Smashed it into fragments.

But Thangbrand would not be deterred. His method of conversion was rough, but occasionally it worked. When he killed his attackers, he used a cross for a shield, and this made an impression. Sometimes, it was said, he used magic along with violence to make his case. Once at a festival of a wise heathen, he was confronted with two hundred angry heathens and one wild-eyed, hair-shirted berserk, and the bishop proposed a test of gods.

"We shall kindle three fires," he told the assemblage. "You heathens hallow one of the fires. I will hallow another, and we will leave the third unhallowed. If the berserk is afraid of the fire I hallow, but walks unharmed through your fire, then you must accept the new faith."

The wise pagan accepted. Not long after, the berserk approached the fires, sword in hand, and walked right through the heathen fire, but stopped and cowarded before Thangbrand's. Then he saw the heathens hiding behind a bench and went for them, but Thangbrand leapt from his place and knocked the berserk's sword out of his hand with a crucifix before he ran the crazy man through with his sword. Thereafter, the heathens honored their promise and were baptized. When Thangbrand asked his new convert, the wise heathen, about the possibilities for the whole land turning Christian, the wise man replied:

"A tree does not fall at the first stroke."

On another occasion, Bishop Thangbrand said mass for a chieftain, and the chief asked in whose honor the ceremony was being performed.

"The angel Michael," Thangbrand replied.

"What power does this angel have?" the chief asked.

"Great power," replied the bishop. "He weighs everything you do, both good and evil, and he is so merciful that the good weighs more heavily with him than the evil."

"I would like to have him as my friend," the chief replied.

"You can do that easily," Thangbrand said. "Give yourself to him in God's name this very day."

"I will, if he can become my guardian angel!"

And so it must have been with Gizur the White as well. Through Thangbrand's crude ministrations, Christ was presented as a friend. He was a friend you could trust. But he was also a warrior-king. Jesus Christ was conquering all of Europe, and this was compelling for Icelanders who in these last days of the first millennium felt themselves to be very much part of the wider world. The king Christ had befriended and strengthened and protected the mighty King Olaf Trygvesson, and that was enough for Gizur the White. Besides, in a real pinch, one did not really have to give up the thunder of Thor or the muse of Odinn or the beauty of Baldur to accept Christ. In the dangerous life of an Icelandic chieftain, Thor came in handy if one got into a real fight.

IN HIS LONG SHIP, for this voyage home, Gizur the White had a companion. He was Hjalti Skeggjasson, the outlawed chieftain of Thjorsriverdale, the long, broad valley of the bull river just west of the slumbering Mount Hekla. Theirs was the comradeship of accommodation, since Gizur and Hjalti had not always agreed with each other. Hjalti Skeggjasson had refused to join in the legendary attack on Gunnar Hamundarson a few years before, for example, because of an old promise of neutrality which he had given to Gunnar himself. Yet he had married Gizur the White's daughter, and he was family.

Two years previously, at the annual parliament of chieftains, not long after Bishop Thangbrand had also converted Hjalti Skeggjasson to Christianity, the heathen chieftains gathered around Thangbrand to kill him. A fierce argument broke out between the Christian and the heathen chiefs, and this was lucky for Thangbrand, for he escaped with his life.

But in the course of the fight, Hjalti did the unthinkable. Turning on the heathens, he slurred their gods publicly . . . not just any gods, but the All-father, Odinn, the universal ruler over all, the spirit manifold in all nature, the god who had given one eye in exchange for wisdom and whose other eye was the sun, the lord of Valhalla where all brave warriors go to drink and fight and frolic. That is not all. Hjalti blasphemed Freya as well, Freya, the beautiful goddess of passion and fertility whose plumage is falcon feathers and whose carriage is drawn by two cats, the goddess to whose care half the fallen warriors on the battlefield are entrusted.

"I don't mind mocking the gods," Hjalti had said to the chieftains, "because I think that Freya's a bitch! Either that, or Odinn is a dog!"

For his sacrilege Hjalti Skeggjasson was banished from the community. And shortly afterward, he and Gizur the White sailed into exile to Norway. In Trondheim, in the estuary of the river Nid, they paid homage to King Olaf Trygvesson. The king welcomed them warmly and treated them well. There they found themselves in the company of many Icelanders, because there was still a robust trade between the two countries. Many of these were still heathen, and this angered the king. So in late September 999 A.D., Olaf ordered that a splendid mass and great feast be given for St. Michael, the archangel, the slayer of Satan, the avenging angel with his sword in his hand. And he invited the Icelanders. In public they seemed to enjoy the music and the bells, but when they got home, they made fun of the ceremony. This reached the ears of King Olaf and made him angry.

At about the same time, Bishop Thangbrand returned from Iceland quite downcast. To the king, he reported that the Icelanders were incorrigible, that they made fun of him and his faith with verses and even tried to kill him. So strongly in the grip of superstition were they, the bishop said, there was little chance of Iceland becoming Christian. They had even used their witchcraft to open the ground in front of him, and their marsh had gobbled up his horse.

Forthwith, King Olaf ordered the Icelanders to be brought before him. In a fuming rage, he proclaimed that he would kill (or at least maim) all the Icelanders in Trondheim. While he did not say it overtly, he left the impression that he was prepared to invade Iceland, to conquer the heathen land for Christ. In the vigorous commerce between Norway and Iceland, the king had even more leverage. For over a hundred years Iceland had exported wool, sheepskin, hides, tallow, falcons, and sulfur to Europe in exchange for desperately needed timber, flour, malt, beer, and linen. The king could interrupt this flow in a minute. To show that he meant what he said, Olaf took a few leading Icelanders hostage.

But Gizur the White stepped forward and beseeched the king to reconsider. "However much any man may irritate thee, sire, thou wilt forgive him, if he turns from heathenism and becomes Christian," he said. "All the Icelanders here are willing to be baptized. Through them we can find a means to bring Christianity into Iceland. For among Icelanders here, there are sons of considerable people in Iceland, whose friends can advance the cause. But your priest, Thangbrand, proceeded there, as he did here in your court, with violence and manslaughter. Such conduct offended my people, and they would not submit to him."

Instead of the mayhem, Gizur the White offered himself as the king's emissary to Iceland, to take with him a gentler preacher than Thangbrand and to try a different approach. He was confident that he could succeed. For Gizur the White, the question was political as well as religious, and in the political realm he had influence.

King Olaf was pleased with this offer and granted the chieftain's request. He lifted his death penalty on the Icelanders in Norway, but just for insurance, he took into custody the sons of four chieftains from the four corners of Iceland, promising to release them when he heard the blessed news of Christ's victory. To increase the chances of success, the king gave the chieftains a considerable cache of silver, should it be needed to sway beliefs in Iceland.

This charge brought Gizur the White and Hjalti Skeggjasson to the cliffs of the Westman Island in late August, in the year 1000 A.D.

SINCE THE TRADITION had been established seventy years previously, the entire country gathered once a year, in the twelfth week of every summer, at a dramatic field known as the Thingvellir in western Iceland. From the far corners of the island they came, by boat and by horse: from Svinafell in the east, the glacial home of Flosi the Burner, from the hofs along the Rang River, the home of the Njal family, to the sacred fjords around Snaefellsness and Helgafell where one of the first Norwegian settlers, Thorolf Mostur-Beard, had tarried over a hundred years before and thrown overboard the high-seat pillars from his temple, graven with the image of Thor, and declared that he would settle wherever the sacred pillars came ashore. When the islanders arrived at the revered gorge, they set up their stone-and-sod "booths" along the banks of the Axe River and readied themselves for the debates and socializing and the lawsuits.

Gizur the White and Hjalti Skeggjasson had arrived in good time for this Parliament. They took a small boat across the channel to the mainland and landed near Bergthorshvoll, the flat plain where Njal had his place and also not far from the gravel delta of the lovely Markarflot River where the farm of the mighty Gunnar Hamundarson now stood empty. The fields looked just as Gunnar had seen them that last time, golden pastures and new-mown hay against the red-scree slopes with their cascading, wispy waterfalls, that last time before Gizur the White and his band of forty had arrived to kill him.

The two chiefs set off walking west along the rich, flat coastal plain, across the forested, glacial valley called Porsmork. After crossing the Rang River, they pressed on to Hafur on the bank of the Thjorsa River, where they borrowed some horses and turned north into the steaming valley. At Gizur's place on the high mound at Skalholt, they stopped briefly and then rode north sixty miles past the geysers and the paintpots to the smoky shoreline of Laugarvatn.

Upon this long ride, it could not escape them that the traditions of their young country were in jeopardy. A rough, tender democracy had incubated in this barren, volcanic soil. The isolation of the land, free from foreign threat, had nurtured a sense of safety, and the modesty of the place nourished its equality. The thirty-nine chiefs across the land were more or less equal in their power. Some had inherited their positions, but there was nothing sacrosanct about that, because they could be removed by popular vote. Some had been elected outright, in the semblance of a democratic vote. Until now, no king or central authority had been needed, because there had never before been an outside threat. Refugees from the tyranny of the Norwegian king called Harald Fairhair had settled Iceland, and that was well remembered. There was no economic basis to have an aristocracy of knights and princes—the land was not wealthy enough to support such a luxury—but, more than that, the intrepid natives recoiled from the idea of royalty for philosophical reasons. Though he was Christian and that was good, King Olaf was alien to Icelandic soil and alien to the Icelandic spirit. Gizur the White and Hjalti Skeggjasson were coming, therefore, as agents of a foreign power, charged with the mission of delivering an ultimatum.

Now the island was in jeopardy from abroad and from within. The chieftains who doubled as the high priests were divided. The new faith of Europe had split the land, pitting leader against leader, family against family. If the long ships of King Olaf did not appear offshore, the long knives of the warring chieftains might be unsheathed in civil war.

Aware of these perils and of the historical moment, the two chiefs tarried at Laugarvatn, thirty miles east of the Parliament place, partly to send word to other Christians of Gizur the White's return and partly to spread the story of King Olaf's threats against the nation.

Hjalti Skeggjasson should remain behind, they decided, so that this outlaw's very presence would not be a provocation. Gizur the White rode ahead, to the northeast side of the large lake bordering the Parliament plain. At a place called Vellankatla—the "boiling cauldron," where the bubbles rise beneath the shallow water and the steam rises in great plumes over the shoreline—he stopped again and sent word to the moot field, only two miles away, for his Christian friends to join him.

As the force gathered, Hjalti Skeggjasson rode up. How could he miss the action, no matter what the consequences were for him personally or for their cause? He had heard that the heathen forces were gathering and that they intended to block the entry of the Christians to the Assembly. They rode on, thirty Christian soldiers now, to the moot field.

Out of the hot lake, like the back fin of a great prehistoric fish, the rift rises, brown, craggy, towering thirty feet above the surrounding plain, extending far up the slope of the far mountain. Over its edge, just above the moot field, the Axe River drops in a thundering waterfall and then winds past an eddy below the cliff, known as the drowning pool. That is where girls who abandon their unwanted female babies to the cold and death are themselves drowned in a cruel justice. The gorge had more significance than the chiefs could know: it separates the European tectonic plate from the unknown regions far across the sea to the west, regions which during that very summer Leif Eriksson was exploring.

When the column of Christians arrived at the moot field, the place was in an uproar. Armed and angry, the pagan forces milled about, primed for a fight, and they far outnumbered the small band of Christians. One man approached the outlaw Hjalti and, pointing to steam coming out of the ground across the lake, he said:

"It is no wonder that the gods are angry with your talk."

But a Christian named Snorri stepped between them. "Over what are the gods angry as this lava field burns under our feet?" he asked. There were hotheads among the heathens, men who wished to exclude the Christians altogether, who wanted to kill the intruders, especially the outlaw Hjalti, and to reimpose the traditional faith upon the nation by law.

But something in the bearing of the Christians made the pagan extremists hesitate. Moderates in the heathen faction spoke of the generous, welcoming nature of the gods of Aesir. Christ could join the pantheon. There was no need to choose one or another. More compelling was the worry, especially among their powerful families, about what King Olaf would do to his Icelandic hostages in Norway if his emissaries were harmed. This moderate element stepped between the opposing forces now and kept the situation from disintegrating into bloodshed on the first day. In the booths along the Axe River, however, the situation remained tense.

The following day, Gizur the White and Hjalti Skeggjasson strode up the sloping pathway to the Law Rock to state their case. With the high brown cliff towering behind him—it was a jagged stage set worthy of the moment—Hjalti spoke first. He was eloquent and persuasive. "The heathen sacrifice the worst men and kill them with stones," he said. "We want to appeal to your good side. This is the victory sacrifice, dedicated to our God, Jesus Christ. We want to live a better life. We who sin will be watched over more than before." Gizur the White then took the platform. His message swung between the carrot and the stick. On the one hand, there were the king's stern threats to independence, but on the other were the positive qualities of his mighty king, Christ, the king who had conquered Europe. To become Christian, he argued, dignified their nation in the eyes of all of Europe. Moreover, the commonwealth could not survive half Christian and half heathen.

Yet the rule of Icelandic law was based in the values and standards of the heathen religion. It had been so since the constitution of the land had been written seventy years before. To espouse Christianity was to read oneself out of society, to disqualify oneself for leadership, to spread shame among one's kin, to renounce the community of laws which yearly the lawspeaker spoke from the Law Rock and which had been agreed upon by the people. Gizur the White was, therefore, assaulting the very foundations of the society. Below him on the moot field, there was a great commotion. A succession of speakers followed him, both Christian and heathen. They too argued their principles and trumpeted their readiness to fight for them.

In the chaos, Gizur the White proposed that one Hall of Sida, the powerful chieftain from Thvattriver in the east, promulgate the new laws under Christianity. It was a clever suggestion, since Hall of Sida had considerable standing. He possessed noble lineage: he was the grandson of Eystein the Noisy, the brother of Thorstein Broad Paunch, and one of his sons was said to have been killed by elf women. Bishop Thangbrand had converted him to Christianity several years before, and therefore his pronouncements were sure to be advantageous to the Christian side . . . advantageous and likely to lead to bloodshed.

Hall of Sida was not the lawspeaker himself. Proclaim he might, but he did not have the authority to impose new laws upon the entire people, at least not without a fight. The lawspeaker was the most distinguished man in the land, and also the wisest. His calling was to know the entire law code by heart and to be prepared to repeat the laws, chapter and verse, from the Law Rock each summer. He was the final arbiter of all major disputes, and for his troubles he received a fee, as well as half the fees imposed in cases that were adjudicated at the moot field.

In 1000 A.D. the lawspeaker was Thorgeir, the son of Thorkel the Long. Thorgeir the Lawspeaker hailed from a deep river valley in northeast Iceland called Lightwater, and his relatives included Grim Hairy-Cheek and Hallbjorn Half-Troll. He had three wives, one of whom was Finnish, and eleven sons, one of whom was called Finni the Dream-wise because he could interpret dreams. Thorgeir was popular. For fifteen summers, ever since he first sanctified his office by killing a ram and smearing its blood on the walls of his house, he had been elected and reelected. He was devoutly heathen.

Hall of Sida now declined the invitation of his Christian comrades to promulgate new laws and went instead to Thorgeir. For openers, he pressed three pieces of the king's silver upon the old pagan chief to discharge this important and unpleasant task of resolving the dispute. Whether the silver was a fee or a bribe did not matter. Either way, the final decision of the lawspeaker would have to be acceptable to the heathen as well as to the Christian chieftains. Peace was the issue. Hall of Sida made things more difficult for Thorgeir now. He had one nonnegotiable demand: whatever the lawspeaker's decision might be, the Christians, under no circumstances, would give up their faith. Was it possible to proclaim separate laws for Christians and for heathens?

Thorgeir withdrew to his booth alone, lay down on his bed, spread a woolen cloak over his head, and listened to the water cascading over the rocks a few feet away. This was a common practice for poets and madmen, sorcerers and prophets alike, and to those who peered into the lawspeaker's tent, thinking the priest was either asleep or dead, it was not clear from which of these conditions Thorgeir would emerge. For a full day and night he remained in meditation, still and silent except for the occasional mumble into his cloth, listening to the waterfall and to the voice of his own conscience, appealing for strength and for wisdom to his own gods. It was the act of a mystic and a shaman. The consequences were profound.

The next morning, he sent word for all to gather.

"And now this seems the best to me," he shouted from his high perch, "that we do not let those prevail who are most strongly opposed to one another. Let us reach a compromise between them so that each side may win part of its case. Let us all have one law and one faith! If we sunder the law, so we will sunder the peace and we lay waste the country."

Murmurs and grumbles of discontent rose from the river. Thorgeir asked for silence. "The situation is impossible if we do not all have one and the same law. If the laws are divided, the peace will be divided, and we cannot tolerate that. Now, therefore, I want to ask both heathens and Christians. Will you accept the law which I am going to proclaim?"

Again the dissension was noisy, but eventually the din quieted, and a kind of consensus was reached. For Thorgeir the voice vote was not enough. He insisted upon their pledges, and these were given.

"Then this is my decision," he said finally. "The first principle of our laws is that all men in this land shall be Christian. They shall believe in one God—Father, Son, and Holy Ghost. You shall renounce all worship of idols. You shall not abandon children to die at birth, nor shall you eat horse flesh. The penalty for carrying on these practices openly shall be banishment. But they shall not be punished if you do them in private."

After that, he explained about the Sabbath and fast days, Christmas and Easter. And about baptism. But the people were not keen on being baptized in the icy Axe River, and so they marched off to Laugarvatn, as fair-weather and warm-water Christians.

At the shoreline of the thermal lake of Laugarvatn, the Christians knelt to be baptized. Among them was a chief named Runolf, who had been vocal in the banishment of Hjalti for blaspheming the pagan gods several years before. Over him the priest invoked a rough version of Matthew 5:13:

"Ye are the salt of the earth: but if the salt have lost his savor, wherewith shall it be salted? It is thenceforth good for nothing, but to be cast out, and to be trodden under foot of men," or words to that effect.

As Runolf reached for the salt, Hjalti shouted out good-naturedly from the fringe:

"And now we teach the old fart to eat salt!"

ICELAND BECAME CHRISTIAN, all at once. Conversion had been a political act, the consequence of arbitration rather than enlightenment. The Trinity remained a mystery. The Father, the Son, and the Holy Ghost melded into the image of the mighty king, the conqueror of Europe, sword in hand, gold crown upon his head, the king you could trust as a friend. This benign deity was useful in times of peace, for questions of right and wrong (though not in any moral sense, but rather as a balance sheet between good and bad). His ceremonies for birth and marriage were pleasing. He was the god of happy times.

But when war came and men faced death, the Northmen needed stronger drink, and they imbibed the old thinking greedily. The Christian concepts of sin and guilt found few takers in the north land. When a man killed another man, the penalty was vengeance, if it could be exacted, and, if not, cool, hard cash as fair compensation. "I call upon God and all good men," said one angry warrior brandishing the bloody shirt of a dead friend and urging on his followers, "that I charge you in the name of all the powers of your Christ and the name of your courage and your manhood, to avenge every one of the wounds that marked his body . . . or be an object of contempt to all men." On another occasion a man had a private mass sung before he went out to burn down the house of his enemy.

To mix one's faith was the fashion. Men could believe in Christ, but call upon Thor for voyages and other large undertakings. In adversity when the sword and the hammer and the shield were needed, they turned to Thor, and not so secretly either. When they died in a blood feud, the limp Christian heaven was no match for Valhalla, that boisterous mead hall where the fighting and the drinking and the bantering could continue eternally. Angels remained Valkyries, those lusty maidens of Odinn, who blessed the brave and left the cowardly to the ravens. When the Valkyries descended through the lightning, with bloody bodices and flashing swords, when their horses shook their manes and spread dew through the valleys and mountains, they spirited away the brave in a manner that suited the heroic deeds of the true champion.

Where in Christianity could one find the goddess of fertility? or the god of beauty? or anything like the heathen concept of the divine spirit residing in every blade of grass, every rock, every drop of water? To the heathens, the blood of the earth lay immediately below the surface, the way the blood of a man lay just beneath the skin. How else could one explain the steam and the lava and the ice of Iceland?

On that historic day at the moot field, Thorgeir the Lawspeaker had commanded the heathens to give up a rich and textured divinity. They went away, unswayed, feeling a bit betrayed and yet at the same time confident that their traditions could continue. Thorgeir had given each side half a loaf. He had forbidden certain pagan practices, but only if they were performed in public. There would be no more eating of horse flesh, a practice tied directly to pagan sacrifice, where horse flesh and horse blood were part of the sacrificial mead. This disgusting ritual was easy to give up. Women were forbidden to abandon their children to death, but slave mothers were the chief culprits of this despicable practice, and the authorities were still trying to stamp out infanticide six hundred years later.

It is true that after the decision at the Parliament, some newborn Christians performed a public repudiation of their heathen ways. One group of the converted climbed the peak of Bulandstindur in eastern Iceland, looked down on the bay where three years before they had cheered the wreck of Bishop Thangbrand's bison ship. Now they proclaimed this to be "God's Rock" and threw their pagan idols over the cliff. In the north country Thorgeir himself passed by the sacred waterfall now known as Godafoss on his way home and threw his heathen engravings into the roil. On the other side of the country, in the Westfjords where the high-seat pillars of the first Norwegian settler had floated ashore at the first days of settlement, priests began to build churches on the old pagan shrines such as Helgafell (near the home of Thorstein the Cod-Biter, who had once reported seeing the mountain open up into a fiery Valhalla where he witnessed dead warriors carousing). They promised the farmers as many places in heaven as there was standing room in the church. This encouraged the building of more churches, and a little disappointment as well.

In the Westfjords, the new saver of souls was Snorri the Priest. In the past he had been better known for his sword play than his evangelism, for in a celebrated killing he had slain one Vigfus Bjarnarson of Drapuhlid and left his corpse "as carrion for crows to gorge their greed on gobbets of his flesh." But now Snorri was a priest. He was in great demand to say the mass. One farmer in the area named Thorodd the Tribute-Trader (who a few years before had paid a woman named Thorgrima Witch-face to cause a blizzard) built a church on his farm in Frodriver, but then could not get Snorri or any other priest to say mass in it.

FROM THESE PRIMITIVE EFFORTS at law and parliament, Thorgeir's peacemaking produced an event to be remembered and celebrated for a thousand years. It was not, however, the only long-ranging event to grow out of the Icelandic assemblies around this time. Some time before, in the summer of 985 A.D. (the year that Thorgeir first assumed his lawspeakership), another historic happening was taking shape far to the west of Iceland. It began with fugitives from justice, and the moral of the story seemed to be that, if the punishment is harsh enough, outlaws can sometimes serve history well.

A few years before, a cutthroat named Eirik the Red, the son of a Norwegian murderer, had himself been involved in a series of vicious killings in the Hawk's Valley and around Thor's Ness. His taste for blood revenge was great, and in this case it had been provoked by nothing more than an argument over the borrowing of some decorative bench boards. The Thor's Ness Assembly had banished Eirik from Iceland. To serve his three-year banishment, the scoundrel decided to sail off into uncharted waters. With a handful of men, he sailed west, chasing the rumor of legendary lands called the Gunnbjarnar Skerries that the wind-blown Gunnbjorn Ulfsson was supposed to have seen some eighty years before. In 981 A.D., after the perilous four-day sail, he saw land: the mysterious Blue Shirt, Blaserk, the glacial mountain towering six thousand feet above the horizon, came into view. From this landmark, Eirik turned south along the uncharted coast and ended up on the tip of Greenland on an island that became known as Eirik's Island. He gave his harsh new land the inviting name of Greenland.

Yet it must be remembered that the world's climate in 1000 A.D. was more moderate than it is today, especially in the North Atlantic. In both Greenland and Iceland, the temperature was one full degree centigrade warmer, and that is a considerable difference, since the global temperature of the Ice Age was only three degrees cooler than it is today. Greenland was a more hospitable place then.

Eirik the Red stayed three winters in that hostile land, serving out his official sentence of exile. Upon his return to Iceland, he wintered over, and in the following summer of 985 A.D. he mounted an expedition to colonize the new land. His flotilla comprised twenty-five boats upon departure, but only fourteen arrived safely at their destination. In succeeding years, the Greenland colony, between its eastern and its western settlements, grew to three thousand inhabitants, and it provided a sturdy trade in walrus and narwhal teeth, walrus and seal skins, caribou and polar bear hides, which were often transported directly to the trading port of Bergen in Norway, bypassing Iceland. Eirik the Red, once so ferocious and bloodthirsty, now became the colony's most distinguished citizen, with a large farmstead surrounded by 190 smaller ones.

The voyage to Greenland was dangerous, far more dangerous even than the longer voyage from Norway to Iceland. By 1000 A.D. the latter, through the warmer aquamarine water of the Gulf Stream, was a well-traveled route. Between Iceland and Greenland, the north winds took over, the frigid polar currents were unpredictable, there were occasional submarine earthquakes, and the fog, that foul breath of Odinn's hag, that infernal brew of the bog woman, could defeat the best of mariners. The dangers of the passage were enough to make any man pray to his god, and many did.

"May He whose hand protects so well the simple monk in the lonely cell," went one prayer, "and o'er the world upholds the sky, his own blue hall, still stand me by!"

Navigation was a crude business. There were no charts, only oft-told stories. Eirik the Red was drawn west by the rumor of a single voyage, many years before, a story which had been embellished by several generations at the hearthside. Where they could, the mariners hugged the familiar coastline. To determine latitude, they depended on the sun and its shadow. Portable Canterbury sundials had just come into use, but it is unlikely that the Norse mariners had them. When there was no sun, they toyed with a sunstone, a piece of opaque Icelandic feldspar that was supposed to pick up the dim rays. This was more magic than science. The flight of birds was important and was carefully monitored. Occasionally, the mariners released their own birds in the belief that the birds would guide them to land. But they might as well have rolled the dice.

In the passage to Iceland from Norway, the route was due west, a dead reckoning, since to the medieval sailor Iceland was "opposite" Norway, just as the Shetlands and Scotland were a straight shot from distinct landmarks on the Norwegian coast. By gauging his speed at a steady ten knots an hour on an average day, the mariner knew what to expect in a day or two.

"He bade a seaworthy wave-cutter be fitted out for him," reads the passage about Beowulf's voyage. "They whetted his quest-thirst, watched omens. Time running on, she rode the waves now, hard in by the headland. Away she went over a wavy ocean, boat like a bird, breaking seas, wind-whetted, white-throated till the curved prow had ploughed so far—the sun standing right on the second day—that they might see land loom on the skyline, then the shimmer of cliffs, sheer fells behind, reaching capes."

Until Eirik the Red first sighted the Blue Shirt hovering high and mysterious above the distant horizon, there was no prominent guide-post to give comfort to the sea captain. Even the contemplation of Greenland could bring bad dreams and terrible imaginings.

"I can see death in a dread place, yours and mine," said one way-farer before he left Iceland. "North-west over the waves, with ice and cold and countless wonders."

Once it was established, Greenland became the westernmost out-post to the European world. Without it, the further exploration of America would have been impossible. It drew the land-hungry and the quest-thirsty from Denmark and Norway, and they somehow found their way there via the Shetlands and the Faroes, bypassing Iceland altogether. In the important summer of 985 A.D., a wealthy merchant named Bjarni Herjolfsson, a descendant of the first Ice-landic settler who had sea adventure in his veins, set off from Iceland to join his father at Eirik the Red's settlement at Brattahlid, Green-land. After three days, the old hag and the north wind blew him off course, and for a number of days he did not know where he was. Soon after the weather broke, his crew sighted land. But at a safe distance offshore, they could see no glaciers, only forests and low hills. The sylvan scene was not what they expected, and they were afraid to land.

"I think we should sail in close," Bjarni told his crew.

So they put out to sea once again. After two days on a northeast tack, they again sighted land but still no glaciers. So they caught a southwest wind and after three more days, they at last spied the high snow mountains, a sight only a Viking could love. "Now this tallies more closely with what I have been told about Greenland," Bjarni told his crew. In a few more days, they found Brattahlid. After his scare, Bjarni gave up sea trading and became a farmer.

Star-crossed and lucky though he may have been, Bjarni Herjolfs-son became a famous man. His adventure became legend in his own time, and it captured the imagination of many, including kings and chieftains. Among the most fascinated was the eldest son of Eirik the Red, whose name was Leif. Leif Eriksson had grown to be tall and impressive, and he had already been to Norway where he had visited with King Olaf Trygvesson. With his eye for talent, the king knew a leader when he saw one, and in leaders he saw his soldiers for Christ.

"Are you intending to sail to Greenland this summer?" King Olaf asked of Leif Eriksson.

"Yes, if you approve, sire," Leif replied.

"It would be good for you to go there with a mission from me, then, to preach Christianity in Greenland."

"The mission would be difficult," Leif replied, no doubt thinking of his own father.

"Your good luck will see you through," the king responded benignly.

"That will only be if I have the benefit of yours, too," Leif said.

Once in Greenland, Leif Eriksson visited Bjarni Herjolfsson and listened, excited and envious, to the old man's tale of misadventure. But Leif Eriksson was not put off. The young adventurer promptly bought the transoceanic cargo ship from the retired mariner, outfitted it with dried fish and smoked meat, butter, cheese, and water, axes, tongs, and sledgehammers, and recruited thirty-five men for an expedition to Bjarni's far-flung lands. Leif begged his father to come on the voyage, and Eirik the Red agreed. But on the way to the long ship, on the day of departure, Eirik's horse stumbled. The rider fell off and broke his leg. This was a bad omen, and Eirik decided to stay home.

Like Beowulf, quest-thirsty and wind-whetted, the explorers traveled due west, retracing Bjarni's route in reverse. After only two days at sea, a far easier journey than between Iceland and Greenland, and having traveled only about two hundred nautical miles, they came upon a barren, rocky land. The colony at Greenland had brought the American continent close at hand.

"Now we have done better than Bjarni," Leif Eriksson told his crew buoyantly. "At least we set foot on it." But this land was worthless, and Eriksson dubbed it Helluland, "Slab-land." Six hundred years later, the large island would be renamed for its British explorer, William Baffin.

Pressing southward along the coast, surfing downwind at nearly sixteen knots an hour, they crossed a wide channel and next came upon a flat, wooded land with sandy beaches and gently sloping shorelines. This Leif named Markland or "Forest-land." But they hoped for more than mere forests.

Still farther south, bathed now in the warmth of summer, they crossed another broad strait and came upon a lovely high headland. Their long ship beached, they ran through the high meadows overlooking the sea, high-spirited and boisterous, scooping up the dew from the tall grass and finding it the sweetest nectar they had ever tasted. In their newfound land the salmon were large and bountiful in the nearby lakes and streams, and the meadows were rich in wild wheat. The warmth drew them still farther south, below the fiftieth parallel. Somewhere in a place where wild grapes were plentiful and the forests were full of large maple trees, they settled in for the winter, building lodges and boathouses, excavating cooking pits, looking for bog iron, even building a sauna. Vinland was the name Leif Eriksson gave to his new paradise, the land of wine and honey. They built large maple houses.

"Now I want to divide our company into two parties and have the country explored," Leif announced. "Half of the company are to remain here at the houses while the other half go exploring. But they must not go so far that they cannot return the same evening, and they are not to become separated."

(These precautions were sound, but apparently not needed during this first Viking winter in America. Leif's successors in the new millennium would not be so lucky. Several years later Leif would give his brother Thorvald his long ship and in Vinland the younger brother would be killed when strange, short, coarse-haired, marrow-eating, evil-looking natives came across the water in moose-skin boats and attacked the Viking settlement. They shot Thorvald in the armpit with an arrow.)

The following spring, Leif's men loaded down their long ship with the exotic woods and grapes of Vinland and headed back to Greenland. Blessed as he appeared to be with bravery and good fortune, Leif Eriksson turned to his promise to King Olaf Trygvesson. He was determined to use his new fame to preach the Christian faith to Greenland. As he expected, his father was obstinate in the old ways but his mother, Thjodhild, accepted the faith immediately and promptly moved out of the heathen household, much to the annoyance of Eirik the Red. Nearby, she built a tiny church of sod and American timber. More than nine hundred years later, this tiny church was found behind a fold in the hill above Eirik's fjord.

Thus, in the year 1000 A.D., through threat and intimidation, through good missionaries and strong leaders, King Olaf Trygvesson

had added both Iceland and Greenland to the Shetlands, the Orkneys, and the Faroes as conquered lands for the Mighty King Christ.
And the new world had been discovered.

This news of the North Atlantic was slow to reach Norway that
fall. By the time it did, King Olaf was dead.

CHAPTER THREE

Queen Sigrid the Strong-Minded

KING OLAF TRYGVESSON was happy in holy war and cruel in his subjugation, but he was unlucky in love. His first and most memorable passion had been the Polish princess Geira, and her premature death, after three years of youthful bliss, had turned Olaf into a brutal sea warrior. After tasting France and battling at Maldon and extorting blood lucre from Ethelred the Unready, he had come upon the feisty Irish widow Gyda, or, more exactly, she had discovered him in her lineup. Her father, lesser Irish potentate though he was, had launched Olaf's triumphal return to Norway and the Norse king was surely grateful for that. But somehow this Irish damsel disappeared from the scene.

Then there was his trophy wife, Gudrun, Iron Beard's daughter, who had returned his embraces with vengeance and a dagger to his throat on their wedding night. Now that Olaf was the mighty king of all Norway, thirty years of age, loved, dreaded, and obeyed, it was time to put aside young girls and cloying widows to search for a true Viking queen.

To the east, in Sweden, there was such a woman of stature. She was Sigrid, the widow of the Swedish king Eric the Victorious, and she was a lusty older matron with several grown children, who enjoyed the company of bawdy drinking men. She was, however, still in search of an equal. A rash of lesser lords pursued her, and she had had a recent fling with a petty chief called Harald the Greenlander. His lesser status was an annoyance—not to mention the fact that he was already married. Still, the Greenlander doted on Sigrid, and after a drunken assignation in her bedchamber, in which she had been the initiator, he offered to leave his wife. His wife was a good woman and all that, he told Sigrid, but "she is not as well-born as I am." This put Sigrid off, since the Greenlander's lineage was nothing to brag about, and she replied, "Your kin may be more eminent than hers, but she is a good wife for you. Besides, I hear she is pregnant."

The Greenlander went away, heavy-hearted, but could not stay away, and after a few months he returned, to the displeasure of Sigrid, just at the inopportune time when she was also being hounded by a Russian wolf named Vsevolod, the boorish prince of Volhynia. So Queen Sigrid put the oafs in the beer hall and let them get drunk. Then she torched the place and had her soldiers finish off any who might crawl out. That should teach "small kings" to come courting her, she proclaimed, and afterward she was called Sigrid the Strong-Minded.

But Olaf Trygvesson was not a small king. And he needed a great queen. In the winter of 998 A.D., when he was in the Oslofjord, he sent word to Sigrid that he wished to court her. She, of course, had heard of his reputation and his manliness, and she was intrigued. To show that he was earnest, King Olaf sent Sigrid a gold ring from the temple at Lade. The gift pleased her, but her goldsmiths exchanged furtive glances when they weighed the prize in their hands. Sigrid, ever eagle-eyed, noticed this and asked why they were smiling. Finally, she pried out of them that they thought the ring was fake. Forthwith, the ornament was smashed and found to be copper inside. This did not mark an auspicious beginning for the royal courtship, nor was Sigrid the right lady with whom to trifle. The Norwegian king would deceive her in more ways than one, she told her courtiers.

Still, a meeting between them was arranged the following spring at the mouth of the Göta River. The magnificent specimen of a man who presented himself did not fail to impress the well-traveled Sigrid, and she quickly got over her pique. The negotiation proceeded cordially (since a marriage uniting Norway and Sweden was a powerful inducement beyond any physical attraction), until it came to a sticking point. Olaf insisted that Sigrid convert to the true faith. She demurred.

"I cannot part with the faith I have had before, and my ancestors have had before me," Sigrid said sweetly. "But I will not speak out against you if you believe in a god that pleases you."

Olaf flew into a rage. "Why should I marry you, you heathen bitch," he shouted, "you faded old woman!" And he struck her across the face with a glove.

She recoiled coldly. "This may well be the death of you," she whispered. She left hurriedly and made her way back to Uppsala.

To spurn a strong Viking woman was a dangerous game. To strike her in the face could be suicide. Far to the west in Iceland, the legendary fighter Gunnar Hamundarson had found that out. He had once slapped his wife, Hallgerd Long-Legs (for considerable provocation since she had stolen cheese from a neighbor and then burned down his storehouse), and she had promised to remember it. She did so at an unfortunate time, when a blood feud raged and her husband was set upon by his enemies, their house surrounded, and spears and arrows flying all around. One of the arrows had severed Gunnar's bowstring.

"Let me have two locks of your hair and help my mother plait them into a bowstring," he demanded.

"Does anything depend on it?" his wife asked.

"My life depends on it," said Gunnar, "for they will never overcome me as long as I can use my bow."

"In that case," said Hallgerd Long-Legs, "I shall remind you of the slap you once gave me. I do not care in the least whether you hold out a long time or not."

"To each his own way of earning fame," said Gunnar, and he was soon dead.

If Hallgerd Long-Legs harbored such a profound resentment against her husband for the insult years before, it is a quandary why she had not dissolved the marriage. For in Viking Scandinavia around the time of the millennium, women had equality with men far in advance of other European countries. They could obtain a divorce simply by a public declaration, and the grounds could be mere incompatibility, lack of consummation, or homosexuality. Moreover, the honor of a single woman was also protected. In millennial Iceland, composing love songs to a spinster was against the law, for such trifling compromised the woman's prospects for marriage.

When Sigrid spoke of holding on to her ancestral faith, her attachment was partly because of the stature women had in her tradition. In the heathen way, the woman did not cower a step behind her husband. There was no such thing as obedience to the "stronger half." Women were equals, powerful and often daunting. Consider the style of one high priestess, known as Thorbjord, the "Little Sybil." She sat on her high seat stuffed with hens' feathers, decked out in a blue cloak adorned with stones down to the hem, gathered with a belt of decayed wood from which hung a pouch, full of her magic charms. She carried a staff with a brass knob studded with stones. On her feet she wore calfskin shoes with tin buttons, and on her hands were white, furry cat-skin gloves. When she sat down to eat, she began with a gruel of goat's milk and followed that with a main course of various animal hearts. When she sang her warlock songs— how beautifully she could sing!—the spirits were drawn in and better weather followed, just as she predicted. Who would dare cross a woman like that?

For the love of a Viking woman, King Harald Fairhair had conquered all Norway and left his thick hair uncut for twelve years. His son Eric Bloodaxe had found his wife, Gunnhild, deep in a Finnish forest, practicing witchcraft and imprisoned by two hunters with whom she slept before she slew them. Later, she would kill an enemy by putting snake venom in his mead. Cruel and promiscuous, she inspired passionate hate, especially in the most famous of the Norse poets, Egil Skallagrimsson.

For the evil, Gunnhild had exiled him, and the poet, in turn, vowed revenge. From his exile on a distant shore, Egil climbed up on a rock, planted a hazelwood pole, put a horse head on it, and turned it toward Gunnhild's land. "Here I erect a spite-pole, and turn this spite against King Eric and Queen Gunnhild," Egil said. "I turn this spite against the spirits that inhabit this land, so that they may all lose their way, and not reach nor find their homes until they drive King Eric and Queen Gunnhild out of the land."

And it was this same sinister queen, Gunnhild, later called Mother of Kings, who had sent her bloodhounds to pursue the baby Olaf Trygvesson and his mother with the intent to kill them.

In the heathen pantheon, the goddesses were all powerful. The Fates were three maidens who established the laws and decided how the lives of men were to be led. The Valkyries decided who would live and who would die on the battlefield and then decided who would enter Valhalla. These bloody maidens served the manly heroes their Viking ale. And with her bridal veil, her golden necklace, and her belt with the keys that symbolized wealth and authority, Freya, the goddess of fertility, was everyone's favorite deity.

To Viking women, men were strong but gullible. Deep in Viking lore are the stories of women appealing to their men's baser instincts, egging them on to seek revenge, exact retribution, betray their friends, usually for some wicked scheme. An example:

> Gudrun went into the store-room
> From the chests she found the helmets
> For her sons, and full length chain mail
> Roused, they flung themselves on horseback.

And thus, when Queen Sigrid arrived back in Uppsala, she doubt-less repaired to the gleaming, golden Hall of Goddesses, there in the company of Valkyries and Norns, to ponder her revenge on this Norwegian paragon of manliness and Christian virtue.

UPPSALA WAS SACRED, royal land, the seat of old kings, the home of Frey, God of the World, Sovereign of the Swedes. Frey made the earth fruitful, nourished it with sunshine and rain, and ruled over the light and the dark elves. In Uppsala a grand temple had been built in a theatrical setting, surrounded by mountains, gilded on the outside, with a golden chain spread around its gables and with a monumental phallic statue of Frey upon the high throne within. After Frey's death in the heathen apocalypse, his sister, Freya, became the preeminent deity. At last, a woman ruled heaven and earth.

Uppsala had also been the site of a legendary sacrifice in ancient times when, under a bad king named Domaldi, Sweden had presided over a succession of poor seasons. To change their fortune and to restore the fruitfulness of their earth, the Swedes had sacrificed first oxen and then slaves to no avail, so finally they sacrificed Domaldi, and, at last, as the bad king's blood was smeared on the stalls of horses and cows, Freya was pleased.

From this ancient lore a Swedish custom arose where every year during "good month," from mid-February to mid-March, a festive blood offering for peace and victory and prosperity was held for nine days in Uppsala. For this "midwinterblot" people would gather from all over the country. The ceremonies were described by a Christian missionary:

"Of every living thing that is male, they offer nine heads, the blood of which placates the gods. They hang the bodies in a sacred grove adjoining the temple. Now this grove is so sacred to the heathen that each and every tree in it is believed to be divine because of the death or putrefaction of the victims. Even dogs and horses hang there with men. A Christian man told me that he had seen their bodies suspended promiscuously. Furthermore, the incantations customarily chanted in the ritual of sacrifice are manifold and unseemly. Therefore, it is better to keep silence about them."

The sacrificial blood was called hlaut, and it was put in vessels called hlaut bowls and in a sprinkler called a hlaut tein. "With all the hlaut should the stalls of the Gods be reddened," it was proclaimed, "and the walls of the temple inside and out, and the men-folk should also be sprinkled."

The Swedish royal line began in Uppsala about 500 A.D., and it produced not only Swedish nobility but also Norwegian kings including the forebears of King Harald Fairhair. On Lake Malar, south of the royal lands, was the trading town of Birka. It was the Swedish jewel in the necklace of Baltic and Scandinavian towns including Kaupang in Norway, Ribe and Hedeby in Denmark, Wollin in Poland, and Hamburg in Germany. For all the terror that the Vikings occasioned throughout Europe, the sea warriors had no real population center. In its heyday, Birka was a mere village of about nine hundred people. But the land was fertile, replete with streams and lakes, good for crops and cattle, especially in the country's midsection of East and West Gautland, and it supported a population of about a half million, six times the population of Norway.

During Queen Sigrid's time, around 995 A.D., the Swedes minted their first coins in a new village on royal land north of Birka called Sigtuna. But the metal was not local.

For Sweden looked east, toward the vast hinterland of Russia and on to Byzantium. For nearly two hundred years, Swedish Vikings had ventured across the eastern expanse. The colonists and merchants went first to their Baltic trading post called Staraja Ladoga and then divided along two trading routes. Some went due south to Novgorod, then down the Dnieper River to Kiev, which they conquered after subjugating the Slavish peoples. From there they floated far south, gathering furs, hemp, and salt, to a village on the Black Sea called Berezanji. This became a Viking base for gathering slaves before the Viking merchants sailed across the Black Sea to Constantinople to exchange their slaves for spices and glass and the silver Islamic coins called the *dirham*.

With such wealth in Constantinople, the Viking warriors inevitably followed the Viking traders. On June 18, 860 A.D., a force of two hundred warships descended on the Black Sea coast, entered the Bosporus, and disgorged the Nordic soldiers into the suburbs. The city was surrounded, and the mayhem began. It was the bad luck of "New Rome" that the Byzantine emperor Michael was with his army far in the east on an expedition against the Arabs, and, therefore, his capital lay open and ripe for plunder. The pillage was awful, the slaughter appalling. Houses were burned indiscriminately; people were slashed and thrown into the sea to drown; those who resisted had their hands tied behind their backs and iron spikes driven into their skulls; palaces were gutted.

Even as the devastation continued, on the first Sunday after the attack began, June 23, the archbishop of Constantinople, Photius, ascended the podium at San Sofia to cast this pestilence in apocalyptic terms. These pirates, unorganized and unchecked and indiscriminate, from some obscure nation of no account to the north, were the forces of the Lord, he said, sent to punish the wanton people of Constantinople for their sins. They had come like wild boars, devouring the citizens of Constantinople like grass or straw.

"Why has this thick, sudden hail-storm of barbarians burst forth, not one that hews down the stalks of wheat or beats down ears of corn, or lashes the vine-twigs or dashes to pieces unripe fruit or strikes the stems of plants or tears the branches apart? Rather, he miserably grinds up man's very bodies and bitterly destroys our whole nation. Is it not for our sins that all these things have come upon us? O Queenly City, what a throng of evils has poured around thee, as the depths of the sea and the mouth of fire and sword have cast lots according to barbarian custom for the children of thy belly. What a calamitous threat, what a mass of horrors have inundated thee all round and have humbled thy celebrated glory! O city reigning over nearly the whole universe, what an uncaptained army, equipped so crudely, is sneering at thee as at a slave!"

As the story would later be told—and it would be told often and luridly for decades to come—the Viking marauders had left only when Photius took the holy shroud of the Virgin Mary and dipped it into the Bosporus, whereupon a terrible storm brewed up suddenly and drove the Viking ships away.

But the New Rome was not free of Nordic terrors. Eighty-one years later, in 941 A.D., the Viking sea dragons again emerged to threaten Constantinople, and, again, the Byzantine army was far away on a foreign expedition. This time the invading fleet was even more awesome, more than twice as large as it had been in 860 A.D., more than a thousand ships. What veil, what miracle might save the queenly city now from its God-sent punishment? But it was saved, not by divine intervention but by human science. At least, this time, there had been a little advance warning, and the Byzantine commander mobilized nearly every boat and raft that could float. These scraps and hulks were outfitted with a strange new contraption, a hose that was connected to an ovenlike cannister which was heated underneath until it was boiling hot. These boats then were dispatched to the mouth of the Bosporus to await the approach of the Viking ships that were then on the horizon.

When the sleek boats came upon the motley Byzantine line, its Greek fire was uncorked. The hoses turned into a crude flame thrower, spewing fire for a considerable distance and terrorizing the Vikings. The flame was a kind of medieval napalm, a soup of kerosene, crude oil, paraffin, and sulfur, heated in its airtight tin container, pumped through a tube by pressure, and then lit at the nozzle. The Vikings leapt overboard in terror, and their ships were consumed like matchboxes. When the few survivors straggled back home, they spoke of this Greek fire as "lightning from heaven" that had set their ships on fire and rendered their attack useless. It was said that this doomsday weapon could burn underwater and incinerate stone. No armor could defend against it. With this defeat, and perhaps more importantly with the legends it spawned, the Viking threat to Constantinople evaporated.

The roar of these Byzantine torches and the crackle of the Nordic ships was the distant sound signaling the end of an era. The weapon of the Viking ship, which had terrorized Europe for 150 years, had met its remedy.

After this profound turning point, a few Vikings stayed on in Constantinople, leaving their runic graffiti in the mosques and serving as bodyguards to the occidental emperors. They became the medieval counterparts of the modern Swiss guards of the pope and were called the Varangian Guard.

The Black Sea and Constantinople were not the only southern destinations of the eastern Vikings. A more easterly route took the Swedes along the Volga to a place called Bulgar, then downriver with their timber and wool to a village called Itil on the Caspian Sea. From there they ventured overland to Baghdad. That fantastic metropolis of two million people was the jewel of the world, the most cultivated city on earth. To the Vikings it was the wealthy capital of Sarkland (the land of the silk) and the royal seat of the Arabian caliphate.

On the southern shore of the Caspian Sea some of these Swedes bypassed Baghdad and turned farther east toward Afghanistan, for that was the site of fabulous silver mines. Beginning in 850 A.D. they mined the silver greedily, melting it into ingots and transporting it north, where it was made into jewelry and fine cups or cut into shards as primitive barter. Eight ounces of refined silver (or one "mark") could buy four milk cows or one concubine. So important was the metal that this became known as the Silver Age, supplanting the gold and iron of previous eras. By 950 A.D., however, the Swedes had exhausted the mines. Just as significant, the Arabian and Moorish caliphates had grown stronger militarily. The Mediterranean was abruptly shut off to the Norse pirates, and the Vikings became more crude, desperate, and brutal than before.

"The Vikings are like donkeys running wild," a sophisticated Arabian diplomat named Ibn Fahlan would write when he found himself marooned in the Volga town of Bulgar. "They bring their slave girls with them, and they never bathe after eating or sexual intercourse. And on the riverbank they put up a wooden pile with an image of a face, bow down before it, and say, 'Oh my God, bring me a customer, and let me do a good business without bargaining.'"

And yet this same Arabian found the Vikings beautiful to behold, even if they were a bit dull-witted and humorless as well as weak in faith because of their cold climate. "Never have I seen people of more perfect physique. They are tall as date palms, blond and ruddy," Ibn Fahlan wrote. "They wear neither coat nor mantle, but each man carries a cape which covers one half of his body, leaving one hand free. Their swords are Frankish in pattern, broad, flat, and fluted." And it was to this sword that the Vikings often resorted in plundering the Slavs and selling their spoils to the Khazars and the Bulgars.

When these exiled Vikings died, the burial rite was elaborate and even mystical. The wake lasted nearly two weeks, as the dead man was fitted for his elaborate burial gown and his mourners became drunk on fermented Viking ale. The text for the funeral was taken from the legend of Baldur, the Apollo of the Scandinavian pantheon. The most beautiful and eloquent of the gods, the second son of Odinn, Baldur was killed by a mistletoe dart, guided by the evil god Loki, and thereafter the grieving was widespread. At Baldur's death, his wife, Nanna, was overcome with grief and died of heartbreak. She is, therefore, placed beside him on the long ship before it is set afire during the funeral rite and pushed out to sea. (Afterward, Baldur is revived, and mistletoe is taken into the care of Freya and sealed with a kiss; it becomes the everlasting symbol of love, so long as it is suspended overhead and never allowed to touch the ground.)

In the burial on the Volga, the chieftain's wife relied on a surrogate. The chieftain's slave girls were gathered, and the question was asked:

"Who will die with him?"

There were no lack of takers. To die with a chieftain was to raise the slave and her descendants out of bondage. It meant to die in dignity, if not as the chieftain's wife, then at least as his consort. On the appointed day, the ship was readied on the shore, and the corpse was brought on a tablet, covered with oriental carpets, dressed in a brocaded mantle, festooned with gold buttons, a sable cap on his head. The body was placed in a tent on shipboard. The attendants brought Viking ale, a stringed instrument, fruit, and sweet-smelling herbs, bread, meat, and onions, and placed them beside the tent. Two horses, lathered with sweat from galloping, were butchered, and their flesh thrown into the ship. Two cows were brought and also slaughtered, and their flesh was added.

Then a grim, heavyset old woman called the Angel of Death brought the slave girl to the side of the boat. (It is significant that in Scandinavian lore the messenger of death and the executioner is a woman. The woman personifies death.) The tent lord said to the slave girl: "When you see your master, say this: I have done this out of love for you." Then other men gather around her and lift her skyward three times, so she can see over the gunnels into the land of the dead. As the Arabian diplomat Ibn Fahlan watched this ritual, somewhat aghast, his guide whispered to him: "The first time they lifted her she said: 'Look there! I see my father and my mother.' The second time, 'Look! all my dead relatives are sitting there.' And the

last time, 'I see my master sitting in Paradise, and Paradise is beautiful and green, and with him are men and boy-servants. He calls me
. . . so lead me to him.'" They handed her a hen. She lopped off its
head and placed it reverently with the other provisions for the journey. Handing her golden arm rings to the angel and her anklets to
death's daughters, she took a cup of ale, and after she sang over it,
she drank it as a gesture of farewell to her girlfriends. Appearing
confused and hesitant, she was offered another cup, and after she
drank it as well, she entered the tent. Outside the men began to beat
sticks against their shields.

Then six men entered the tent and ravaged her. For the girl this
was the last promiscuous act of slave status, before she swore her
fidelity to her surrogate husband. She was the substitute wife, and
they were the substitute husbands. Why there had to be six of them
is left to the imagination. The six professed to perform the act out of
sheer love for the master, not lust for the girl. They were breaking
her in for her new role. Afterward, she lay down next to her master,
and the Angel of Death put a noose around her neck. At the signal,
the men pulled on the noose as the Angel of Death plunged a dagger
into her heart.

At that point, the chief's closest relative came upon the scene. He
stood stark naked and held a torch in one hand, his other hand over
his anus. His nakedness symbolized his inheritance of eminent status
in the clan. The hand over his anus was to protect him from a suspicion of unmanly man love, for there was nothing more degrading in
the Viking code than for a man to be taken sexually from behind by
another man. He put the first fire to the wood, and others followed
his lead. As in *Beowulf,* "the roaring of flames mingle[d] with weeping." Then the burning ship was launched, as a strong wind caught
the sail.

"Out of love for him, his Lord has sent the wind, so that it will
take him quickly," Fahlan's interpreter whispered. "We burn him in a
moment, and he enters Paradise at once."

Where the ship had been on the shore, a round hill was con-
structed, and in its middle, a large piece of birch wood was erected.
Upon it was written the name of the chief and of the king of the Rus.
And if the late chief had been the king himself, his poet would have

been at the pyre, as was the scald of Hacon the Good, the king of Norway, thirty years before Olaf Trygvesson, imagining the fighting Valkyries Skogul and Gondul waiting to welcome the hero:

Said the rich Skogul,
"Gondul and I shall ride
To the gods' green home
To tell Odinn
That quickly the prince
Comes to see him."

Now it is known
That the king has guarded
Well the temples
So Hacon the Good
Was welcomed with gladness
By the kind gods.

Wealth dies,
Kinsmen die,
The land is laid waste.
Since Hacon fared
To heathen gods
Many are thralls and slaves.

BUT WHAT OF A GREAT HEATHEN QUEEN? What did Queen Sigrid the Strong-Minded have a right to expect when Skogul and Gondul came for her?

For starters, she had a choice. She could decide to be cremated or to be buried, and this could have a bearing on whether she would ascend to the throne of Odinn or to the chamber of Frey, god of fertility with his enormous phallus, and his surviving sister, the goddess of carnal pleasure and fruitfulness, Freya. According to the pagan scriptures, Odinn had been burned after his death. And the fire was very glorious. And the higher the smoke went aloft, the higher the place in heaven he would achieve. The more goods that were burned with him, the richer he became. That would appeal to a man.

When Frey died in the apocalypse, he was put in the earth and afterward there were always good growing seasons. "When all the Swedes marked that Frey was dead, but that good seasons and peace continued, they believed it would be so, so long as Frey was in Sweden. Therefore, they would not burn him, but called him god of the earth and ever after sacrificed to him, most of all for good seasons and peace." Only the goddess Freya lived after the apocalypse, and she continued her sacrifices. "She then became so very renowned that they called all their noble women by her name." That would appeal to a woman.

As a proud, powerful woman, with her sense of being equal to any man, in her desire for immortality and in her fruitfulness, Queen Sigrid identified with Freya. She would choose to be buried and thereby to make the earth more fertile. How she was buried followed the example of another Viking queen who had lived before Sigrid. She had been buried in her finest gown, upon a lovely feather bed, covered with splendid blankets, her head on an eiderdown pillow, in a magnificent, decorative ship. Unlike the raunchy, macho burial on the Volga River, where the mourners expected the wispy spirit of the dead chief to enter paradise at once, there was no telling how long the queen's passage might take. Perhaps it would take all winter, and, therefore, aboard ship, butter and cheese were provided, along with unkneaded dough, berries, apples, and walnuts. There were pots and ladles, knives and spoons, shovels and pitchforks. For the queen's grooming table, there were reindeer-antler combs, glass beads made from Italian mosaic pieces, and peacock feathers, as well as needles and thread and fine cloth.

On her extended journey to the otherworld, she too was accompanied by a slave girl. In the royal ship, not one but twelve stallions had been sacrificed, along with four dogs and a few goats. Should they encounter snow, the long ship contained four decorative sleds, carved with the most fantastic animal shapes and laced with intricate serpentine designs. In case the journey lasted into the following summer, there was also a decorative wagon, with Freya's beloved cats as the central motif, their eyes as silver beads.

And just in case there were a few boring nights on this long, starlit, queenly journey to paradise, a few pounds of hashish were on board.

SIGRID THE HAUGHTY was not ready for this celestial journey in 999 A.D. She still had pressing business in the here-and-now. Her fury over her humiliation at the hand of Olaf Trygvesson was unbridled, and it lapsed into a lusty contempt for his religion. But she had a problem. Ever since a German bishop named Ansgar, later called the Apostle of the North and sainted by Rome, came to Sweden in 830 A.D. and founded the first church of Scandinavia at Bjorko, missionaries from Germany and England had been fanning out across the country. This was an organized campaign which was supported by a succession of popes including the strong current pope, Sylvester II. The conversion crusade was executed by German, Danish, and British bishops. In West Gautland, the crusade had been the most successful, partly now because that region fell under Olaf Trygvesson's zone of influence. If Olaf could not have the Swedish queen, his agents at least could nibble away at her domain.

Christianity was infiltrating Sweden from the east, as well as from the south and west. The Swedish Vikings were bringing back from Byzantium more than tales of giants and trolls, strange diseases and bizarre sorceries. They also brought back an exotic brand of Christianity. This was the eastern orthodoxy of Constantinople, and to the Christian missionaries who came from Rome-centered Germany and England, it was unrecognizable. Nevertheless, around the turn of the millennium, more and more graves in Sweden were Christian, with Christ's cross rather than Thor's hammer inside, and the body laid out east and west to see the rising sun rather than the heathen way of north and south. In the assemblies around the country, the leadership of these orthodox Christians was beginning to be felt.

Even within Sigrid's own house, Christianity was making inroads.

The new faith intrigued Sigrid's son Olof, who had been made king of Sweden in 995 A.D. and was first given the unflattering label Olof the Lap-King because he became king while still in his nurse's lap. (Later he was known by an even unhappier moniker, Olof the Tax King.) At first quietly and unobtrusively, Olof had converted. Just how and where and even when that happened is a matter of dispute, and while his conversion appears less than heroic, he has the honor of becoming the first Christian king of Sweden.

The Lap-King was caught between two powerful forces. While the spread of the new faith was a noble goal, he did not want to offend his illustrious and intimidating mother. Nor did he want to offend the heathen ways of the Uplanders. Further, he wished to convert his people by quiet example rather than by the cruel method of Olaf Trygvesson. But few followed his example, at least in his part of the country. In the eastern part of Sweden, where royal lands encircled the heathen mecca at Uppsala (which his Christian bishops wanted burned), his conversion was an unpopular act.

Olof the Lap-cum-Tax King was vain and conceited. At one point he had not one but two scalds in his court to praise his actions. This competition of dueling poets did not turn out well. One poet was Hrafn, but he was joined in court one spring by another scald named Gunnlaug the Worm-Tongue. The king turned to Hrafn to ask what sort of man was the newcomer. "He is of the best family and himself the most valiant man," Hrafn replied precipitously.

"Then go and sit by him," the king said.

Then Gunnlaug spoke up. "I have a poem to recite to you," he said to the king.

"Go first and sit," said the king. "There is not time just now to hear poems." The two poets sat together and shared their experiences in life and art. But Gunnlaug was persistent. The next day, he said to the king in court, "Now, lord, I want you to hear that poem."

"Perhaps that is possible now," the king answered.

"But I want to recite my poem," Hrafn objected.

"Perhaps that is also possible."

"I will recite my poem first," Gunnlaug insisted.

"No, I should go first," Hrafn said. "I came to you first."

"Since when did it happen that my father would be a towed-boat for your father?" Gunnlaug lashed out. "Never. And so it shall be with us."

"Let us not dispute this. The king should decide."

"Gunnlaug will recite first," King Olof said indulgently, as if he were adjudicating a dispute between children, "because it displeases him if he does not have his way." So Gunnlaug recited a heroic *drapa*.

After the poem, the king turned to Hrafn. "Hrafn," he said, "what do you think of the poem?"

"It is a big-worded poem, lord, unbeautiful and somewhat stiff-spoken as Gunnlaug is himself."

"Now you shall recite your poem," the king said to Hrafn. And when it was over, the king asked Gunnlaug how Hrafn's poem was crafted.

"This is a poem as Hrafn is himself, of poor appearance. Why did you compose so short a poem about the king?" he said, turning to Hrafn. "Did he not seem worthy of a *drapa* to you?"

The poets parted badly. Soon after, Hrafn prepared to leave the court on a journey. Before he left, he said to his competitor: "Our friendship is ended because you defamed me here in front of aristocrats. Sometime later, I shall dishonor you no less than you dishonored me here." Eventually, the two poets had a *holmgang,* that uniquely Icelandic form of single combat, a kind of Nordic samurai fight to the death, always held on a holm, or island.

King Olof had not handled the jealousies of his poets well, and he was worse with more weighty matters. He grew increasingly unpopular for reasons of character. His subjects considered him weak, lazy, and arrogant, a leader who squandered his forces on pointless hostilities with Norway while he let other precious Swedish lands to the east slip away without a fight. In due course, this popular dissension burst into the open when a wise man named Thorgny the Law-speaker confronted the king in public at a regional assembly.

"Swedish kings are different now from what they used to be," the old man said brazenly. "I remember your father, Eric the Victorious, and was on many a war expedition with him. He enlarged the Swedish dominion and defended it manfully. And it was also easy and agreeable to communicate our opinions to him. But you allow no man to presume to talk to you, unless it be what you desire to hear.

On this alone you apply all your power, while you allow your tax lands in other countries to disappear through laziness and weakness. You want to have the Norway kingdom under you, which no Swedish king before you ever desired, and this brings war and distress on many a man. If you will reconquer the kingdoms in the east which thy relations and forefathers had there, we will all follow thee to the war. But if you will not do that, we will attack you and put you to death."

Far more than spiritual enlightenment, foreign policy considerations drove the Tax King's emotions. With its pagan ways, his country was becoming the butt of jokes around Europe. Swedish customs were considered dumb, lascivious, clumsy, naive, and crude, Sweden itself a land of giants and barbarians and idiots. The Baltic Sea was dubbed the Barbarian Sea. The country was increasingly isolated from the rest of the "civilized" world and overtly threatened by the new Christian states: hostile Norway to the west, the Holy Roman Empire to the south, even the sister kingdom in Russia.

Given his weakness, Olof could scarcely take too much credit for the Christian inroads in Sweden. Other social forces were at work, especially the wind from the east. In Kiev, the Christian king of Scandinavian Russia was Vladimir I, who was called the Fair Sun, and Olof the Tax King's relations with Vladimir were cordial but rather intense since Queen Sigrid the Haughty had incinerated Vladimir's son Vsevolod, the prince of Volhynia, when he had the brass to come courting. (Later, Olof would marry his daughter into the Russian court.) It had been Vladimir who sequestered Olaf Trygvesson as a youth and groomed the young man for greatness. (And later, he would sequester another Christian king of Norway, St. Olaf, when he was exiled.)

In 988 A.D. Vladimir had converted to Christianity, but only after a very interesting flirtation with other faiths. To the king of the Rus, religion was a powerful unifying force for his diverse realm, and it was natural that he would look to eastern traditions, since Kiev ("the moon") and Constantinople ("the sun") had been engaging in active trade for over a century, and since the eastern Slavs, Chuds, and Krivichians whom Vladimir had subjugated were Muslim. Indeed, Vladimir had originally accepted Islam, but his was not a spiritual conversion. When he was installed as the king of the Rus in Kiev, he set up idols in the hills, the most remarkable of which had a silver head with a gold mustache mounted on a wooden post. By the fetid riverside, the sacrificing to his gods was causing mayhem.

Vladimir decided to invite the representatives of various prophetic religions to Kiev. There he questioned them sharply about their attitudes toward women and drink. This was a matter of some concern to Vladimir since he was a man consumed with carnal lust. He had two wives and eight hundred concubines spread through the realm, and his omnivorous sexual appetite had led him to impregnate the wife of his brother and to ravage married women and young girls continually. A German chronicler of the time called him *fornicator immensus et crudelis*. He was obviously not intimidated by the sordid fate of his fellow royal-in-lechery, Earl Hacon of Norway.

The Bulgar Muhammadans played heavily to the king's corruption, assuring him that in their heaven, all carnal desires were fulfilled to the utmost since each man could choose his heavenly companion from seventy beautiful women. This pleased the king, but when the mullahs told him that Islam required circumcision, forbade the eating of pork, and prohibited drink, Vladimir discharged them.

"Drink is the delight of the Rus, and we cannot live without it," he roared. "Go away."

Then the papal emissaries from Germany came. "Thus says the pope," they said to Vladimir. "Your country is like our country, but your faith is not as ours. We worship God, who made heaven and earth, the stars, the moon, and every creature, while your gods are only wood." When Vladimir asked about Catholic teaching, they replied: "Fasting according to one's strength. But whatever one eats or drinks is all to the glory of God, as our teacher Paul has said."

"Our fathers accepted no such principle," the Russian king snapped. "Go away."

Then the Jews came from Khazar. "The Christians believe in him whom we crucified, but we believe in the one God of Abraham, Isaac, and Jacob." Vladimir asked where their country was. "God was angry at our forefathers and scattered us among the gentiles on account of our sins," the Khazarian Jews replied. "Our land was then given to the Christians."

"How can you hope to teach others when you yourselves are cast out and scattered abroad by the hand of God?" the king replied. "If God loved you and your faith, He would not have dispersed you in foreign lands. Do you expect us to accept that fate also?"

At last, an emissary from the patriarch of Greek orthodoxy came. For his turn, he did his best to sour the Russian king on the other faiths. "We have heard that the Bulgarians came and urged you to adopt their faith, which pollutes heaven and earth," the Greek diplomat said. "They are accursed above all men, like Sodom and Gomorrah. The day of destruction awaits these men, on which the Lord will come to judge the earth and to destroy all those who do evil and abomination. For they moisten their excrement and pour the water into their mouths and anoint their beards with it. In this manner, they worship Muhammad. The women also perform this same abomination, and even worse ones."

Vladimir was shocked. "This is a vile thing," he said.

Eventually, he received instruction in the Greek faith which included Proverbs 5.3–6: "Honey flows from the lips of a licentious woman, and for a time it delights thy palate. But in the end it will become bitterer than wormwood." The Russian king accepted the faith of the Greeks and underwent a remarkable transformation. He became high-minded and gave up his wanton ways. After he helped the Byzantine emperor Basil II save his throne against the coup attempt of a usurper, he married the sister of the Greek emperor and reluctantly sent his other wives away. Such a scoundrel as Vladimir scarcely deserved his new wife. She was Anna, one of the precious and much-sought-after "purple-born" princesses of the Great Palace of Constantinople. She had already been denied to Otto II, the German emperor; and she was sought by the new king of France, Hugh Capet, for his son. But the Byzantines felt a particular debt of gratitude to the Russian king, since Vladimir had come to the aid of the Byzantine emperor when he was beset by rebels. The debt was so deeply felt that the court of Constantinople was prepared, for the first time, to give away the daughter of an emperor, a princess purple-born, to a foreigner. But to acquire so valuable a prize, Vladimir's conversion was an absolute requirement for the Byzantine emperor, for the sovereigns of Constantinople considered themselves to be the successor of the ancient Roman emperors and of Constantine the Great.

"Never shall an emperor of the Romans ally himself in marriage with a nation of customs differing from and alien to those of the Roman order, especially with one that is infidel and unbaptized," read the imperial rules of the Byzantine court.

Vladimir accepted this solemn condition. Thereafter, he became a model citizen. In Kiev, he built the Byzantine cathedral known as the Church of the Tithes, and he encouraged the cultural and religious influence of the east on his kingdom. After his death, he was made a saint.

Olof's relations with Vladimir I smoothed the way of eastern orthodoxy in Sweden. Eventually, King Olof's daughter married into the Russian court.

WHAT SIGRID THE STRONG-MINDED thought about all this is hard to divine. In middle age, she finally found an equal. He was a strong man of her own pagan persuasion, and she left Sweden for him. Widowed by Eric the Victorious, abused by Olaf Trygvesson, hounded by lesser nobles, consumed with a desire for revenge, she might have considered the touching words of another much-traveled Viking woman named Gudrun. Gudrun had had four husbands, all fiery, vibrant relationships, and, after the death of the last husband and after she became the first nun in Iceland, her son asked her which of the four she had loved the most. One was the wealthiest chieftain, she replied, another the most accomplished, the third the wisest lawyer, and of the last she would say nothing. But the son pressed her on which of the four she loved the most.

"I was worst to the one I loved the most," she finally replied.

Sigrid's new man was King Svein Forkbeard, the king of Denmark. When she went to Denmark, she did not leave her old resentments behind. For Sigrid the Haughty, the question was the reverse of Gudrun's: which of your husbands and lovers did you resent the most?

CHAPTER FOUR

Svein Forkbeard versus Ethelred the Unready

IN THE MEDIEVAL DOMINION of the northern light, the kingdom of Denmark was the most populous, the richest, the best organized, and the most powerful of realms. The peninsula and its adjacent islands had about a million people in the late tenth century, twice the population of Sweden, ten times that of Norway, even though in landmass the country was onetenth the size of Sweden and one-seventh that of Norway. Denmark was bustling with vitality. Moreover, it had tightened its own belt several hundred years before when it built the daunting Danevirk in the late eighth century, a kind of Chinese Wall against Charlemagne and his Saxon lords to the south. This rampart of peat and logs, twenty feet high, served to keep the Danes in, as much as it kept the Saxons out. It had been a gargantuan undertaking, a true wonder in a supposedly illiterate world, showing the Vikings to be brilliant engineers. Yet the Danes could not be contained within their own borders. They were also greedy.

As Sweden looked to Russia and Byzantium and Norway looked to Iceland, the Shetlands, and the Orkneys, so Denmark looked to the greatest prize of all, England. 793 A.D. was to be a terrible year. The English chroniclers told of dire portents: of tornados and dragons appearing in the sky, amid thunder and lightning. The deacon of York named Alcuin saw bloody rain fall from the sky north of his church's roof. "Can it not be expected that from the north there will come upon our nation a retribution of blood?" he asked. Then the terrible raids commenced. The isolated coastline monasteries were the first easy targets. At Lindisfarne, the holy island off Northumberland, the Norsemen descended like starlings upon the Christian retreat, splattering blood on the shrine of St. Cuthbert. They carried off its silver treasure and enslaved its brothers. "For 350 years we and our forebears have lived in this beautiful country and never previously in Britain has anything so fearful happened as what we've been subjected to," wrote one brother called Alcuin. "They came from the sea. Heathens! They plundered, and they murdered. Blood flew in the altar. Christians were trampled underfoot like filth in the streets. Some of the Brothers were carried off. We did not believe that such sea voyages were possible."

Alcuin saw this heathen sacrilege in starkly apocalyptic terms. Now the human race was in the sixth and final age of Christ, as the historian the Venerable Bede had predicted a hundred years earlier. This was the scourge of God at the end-time. That Lindisfarne was the holy shrine of St. Cuthbert—whose body had remained uncorrupted by the ground even a hundred years after his death—made the situation all the clearer to Alcuin. Even St. Cuthbert had not been able to prevent the disaster.

In succeeding years, other monasteries made easy pickings, on the Isle of Man, in the Hebrides, and along the Irish coast at Limerick, Cork, Waterford, and Skellig Michael. Dublin became a Viking town. London was attacked in 839 A.D. and again in 851 A.D. In the latter assault, 350 Viking ships appeared at the mouth of the Thames and plundered Canterbury. Twenty years after that, the heathen host harried from Reading to London and wintered over.

In the mid-ninth century, the depredations spread to France where the royal line of Frankish kings had declined after Charlemagne with Charles the Bald, Charles the Fat, and Charles the Simple. In 845 A.D. a fleet of 120 ships attacked Paris on Easter Day. (The Vikings seemed to have a preference for holy holidays. The year before they had burned Hamburg on St. John's Day, June 24.). "The winter was very harsh," one Christian chronicler wrote about the Paris raid. "In March Northmen forced their way as far as Paris. They raided, laid waste and met no resistance. Christians were struck down without mercy outside the monastery at St. Denis. The Church of St. Germain was plundered. King Charles took arms, but when he realized he had no chance against the Northmen, he paid them 7,000 pounds of silver to go away. When they went, they took many Christians as prisoners. God save us from the wild Norsemen who ravage our kingdom." The attack on the monastery at St. Denis was a particular sacrilege, for it was the burial ground of French kings, and its abbot was the guardian of the royal sword and crown.

If that raid was horror to the French, it was legend to the Scandinavians, for it was led by the mythical king of the Danes, Ragnar Hairy Breeks. To display the seriousness of his purpose, old Hairy Breeks had taken 111 Frankish prisoners and pinioned them to trees on an island in the Seine. This outrage seemed to soften up Charles the Bald. After Paris, according to legend, Hairy Breeks returned to England where he was shipwrecked and fought and lost a battle with King Ella. The English king threw his prisoner in a "worm-close" (a snake pit) where Hairy Breeks died singing and announcing his revenge with the line "The piglings would be grunting if they knew the plight of the boar." His pigling sons, including one known as Ironside, soon fell on the English king, and when they defeated him, they carved the blood eagle in his back.

In the pirate lairs of Scandinavia the ripeness of France became well known. "The number of ships is growing," a monk called Ermentarius wrote in 860 A.D. as he gazed at the Loire delta on the Ile de Noirmoutier. "Endless flocks of Vikings keep pouring in. Every-

Thor's hammer.
(Statens Historiska Museum, Stockholm)

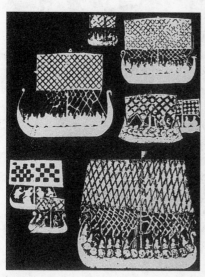

Viking ships, represented on rune stones.
(Statens Historiska Museum, Stockholm)

Norse gargoyle.
(Viking Ship Museum, Oslo)

Odinn mask.
(Den Antikvariske Samling I Ribe)

The fertility god, Frey, with his mighty phallus.
(Statens Historiska Museum, Stockholm)

Viking helmet.
(Statens Historiska Museum, Stockholm)

Trelleborg, one of the five Viking bases in Denmark.
(National Museum, Copenhagen)

Human sacrifice at the heathen temple of Uppsala.
(Midwinterblot, *Carl Larsson, National Art Museum, Stockholm*)

The Althing, where in 1000 A.D. Iceland converted as a nation to Christianity.
(*British Museum*)

Egil Skallagrimsson, the most famous of all the Viking poets.
(Stofnun Arna Magnussonar)

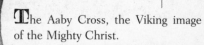

The Aaby Cross, the Viking image of the Mighty Christ.
(National Museum, Copenhagen)

The cliffs of Rugen. Nearby King Olaf Trygvesson was killed in a great sea battle in 1000 A.D.
(German Information Center)

Leif Eriksson's settlement at L'Anse aux Meadows in Newfoundland, carbon-dated to 1000 A.D.
(Canadian Heritage)

The entrance to the Mosque of Córdoba.
(*City of Córdoba*)

Al Mansor's addition to the Mosque of Córdoba.
(*City of Córdoba*)

Gormaz, the fortress from which Al Mansor launched his
attacks on Christian Spain.
(*Dr. Juan Zozaya*)

The Whore of Babylon, portrayed in Christian Spain as a
woman from Córdoba.
(*Silos Beatus, British Library*)

where the Christians are massacred, burned and pillaged. The Danes take everything that comes their way. Nobody is able to resist them. They have captured Bordeaux, Perigeux, Limoges, Angouleme and Toulouse. Angers, Tours, and Orleans have been annihilated. A huge fleet moves up the Seine, and all over the country viciousness is growing. Rouen has been devastated, plundered and sacked. Paris, Beauvais and Meaux are captured, the strong fortress of Melun has been razed to the ground. Chartres is occupied, Evreux and Bayeux plundered."

Sixteen years after the monk wrote this, on November 17, 876 A.D. to be exact, an unusual Viking turned up in France. He was Rolf the Walker, a Norwegian so big no horse could bear him, and he would conquer Normandy, a name which itself is a perversion of the word *Norway*. The English would call him Rollo, and his descendant called William the Conqueror always manifested a great pride in his Norse forebear.

Farther south the scourge spread. The pilgrimage city of Santiago de Compostela in Spain was taken. In Lisbon, in 844 A.D., looking out on the flotilla of red sails, an Arabic observer wrote, "They filled the sea with red birds, just as they filled the hearts of men with fear and horror." Passing through the Straits of Gilbraltar, they attacked Luna in Italy, thinking it was Rome. By trickery they got through the town gates by pretending that their leader was dead and in need of a decent burial. Once inside the city walls, the Viking leader rose from the dead and lopped off the head of the presiding bishop, exulting at the death of the "pope."

At the beginning of the Viking era, the first lightning strikes in England had been pure piracy. A few Viking ships, filled with cruel and greedy thieves, looked for plunder and rapine. But the early raiders were also canny advance scouts, gathering intelligence for the Danish kings on the sources of foreign wealth and spreading the news to their friends. This was the age of silver, and the chief supply of minted silver, until the Viking raids on England and France, had come along the precarious routes from the far-flung mines and kasbahs of the Muslim world. After Ragnar Hairy Breeks extorted 7,000 pounds of silver from Charles the Bald, a new method of procurement had been discovered.

There was more to these raids than the thirst for silver. The Danes needed more living space. By the mid-ninth century the attacking parties were organized naval expeditions, led by professional soldiers, in the service of the king. They came with the intent to defeat opposing armies, to conquer land and colonize it. The sons of Ragnar Hairy Breeks settled in York to the north, and Northumberland became a Danish state. By the late 870s eastern England from the Tees to the Thames was Danish. In 886 A.D. the occupation was formalized when the powerful English king Alfred the Great negotiated a treaty with the Danes. This split England in two, creating a new Danish realm which encompassed the Kingdom of York and East Anglia. Lincoln, York, Nottingham, Berby, and Cambridge became Danish towns. The new Danish state became known as Danelaw, since the Dane's law was administered there and even the Danish language was spoken.

After a ten-year period of unrest, peace finally took hold, ending at last the first era of Viking depredations in England. The pillaging had lasted one hundred years, and it had ended only because Alfred had united the English people against the invaders and had constructed a network of defensive fortresses across the land. Like the monk Alcuin a hundred years before him and the archbishop Wulfstan a hundred years later, King Alfred had seen the Viking visitations as a manifestation of God's displeasure with the English people. The king, at least, was determined to do something about it.

For about ninety years, there would be a hiatus. Only the brief and unhappy appearance of Eric Bloodaxe in Northumbria punctuated the peace. Eric and his sorcerer wife, Queen Gunnhild, had been expelled from Norway and took their vengeance out on Britain, plundering through Scotland and Wales. Instead of fighting, the northern English king compromised by giving Eric dominion over the vale of York, and the barbarian king took up residence on the banks of the river Ouse, in a limestone castle built upon Roman ruins.

This prince from hell would survive only a year before the English threw him out, but in that time Bloodaxe had a memorable interchange with the great Norse poet Egil Skallagrimsson. Queen Gunnhild had placed a curse on the bard, and he was dragged into the king's castle at York one night under the most dire circumstances.

"Why not kill him straightaway?" Queen Gunnhild said bitterly to the king. "Or do you not remember, my king, what Egil has done to us, killed your friends and kinsmen and your own son and defamed you personally? Has anyone ever done that to a king and gotten away with it?"

A friend of Egil's then stepped forward and pleaded that Egil be able to compose a poem in Eric Bloodaxe's honor to atone for his past deeds.

"We do not care to hear his praise," Gunnhild said. "Have Egil led out, my king, and beheaded. I will not listen to him, nor do I care to see him."

"The king will not let himself be egged on," Egil's friend protested. "He will not have Egil killed tonight, because slaying at night is as good as murder."

The appeal worked. "As you wish," Bloodaxe said with a wave of his hand. "Take him home with you and bring him back to me in the morning."

That night, writing for his life, Egil composed his poem. It was a *drapa* of twenty verses called "Head Ransom," and it may be the finest poem in the entire Norse canon. At York castle he presented it full-throated and bold-voiced to the scurrilous king. He spoke of sailing west on Odinn's breast, and at the king's behest, he came as guest, bearing Odinn's lore to England's shore . . . and of the sea king's great feats. After each noble deed, the poet sang his refrain:

"Great honor him gat Eric by that."

At this poetic flattery, Eric Bloodaxe sat bolt upright and was most impressed. "Most excellently has this poem been recited," the king said, and Egil was permitted to leave England with his life.

Eric Bloodaxe would not be so fortunate. Within a year he was deposed and then killed at a lonely place in Westmoreland known as Steinmore.

I N THE SECOND HALF OF THE TENTH CENTURY, Denmark began to feel an old pressure. Once again German emperors were strong, and they possessed all of Charlemagne's passion for a Europe united in Christ and hostile to the infidel. In 961 A.D. Otto the Great had conquered Italy and in the following year, on February 2, 962 A.D., he had been crowned in Rome by the pope as the Holy Roman Emperor. The coronation revived the lost glory of the first Roman Empire when the vicar of Christ and Constantine the Great were partners in a common cause. "Receive this sword with which you will drive out all the enemies of Christ, barbarians and bad Christians, and by which God gives you power over the entire Empire of the Franks."

In 974 A.D., one year after he succeeded his father, Otto II, a more impetuous, vain, and unpredictable monarch, threatened the north land. This was not to be taken lightly, for Otto II would soon become known as Rufus the Bloody. Sending word to the Danish king Harald Bluetooth that the king must convert, the German emperor demanded that Denmark become Christian or he would invade. Denmark mobilized, and Bluetooth sent word to his heathen brother Earl Hacon in Norway that he needed help. Earl Hacon responded with a large army and deployed it along the Danevirk.

At the rampart, the two armies met, and the Saxons were repulsed, falling back in the face of the stout heathen defense. The poet was there to record the event, reporting that "the sea steed's steerer drove the Saxers in flight." But the Saxon emperor retreated to the east into Schleswig where he reinforced his army with Polish forces (which included a young Norwegian prince called Olaf Trygvesson). Renewing his attack on the Danevirk and concentrating on a gap in the fortifications called Wieglesdor, Otto finally broke through, and in the open country of south Jutland the two armies met. This time, Otto prevailed over Bluetooth. Bluetooth fled north to a large island in the Limsfjord called Morso. From there he sued for peace. At the summit meeting Otto had his bishop, a man named Poppo, preach the faith. Under these adverse circumstances, the Danes and even Earl Hacon were in no position to resist any imperial demands. They were open to Christ, they declared, but they insisted that their Norse gods were stronger because they revealed themselves to men with signs and miracles. Bishop Poppo replied that this was superstition and nonsense and declared his readiness to prove the superiority of his God in an ordeal of the flesh. Taking an iron glove, he thrust it into the coals, and when it was red hot, he put the glove on his hand. When he removed his hand, he held it up to reveal to his doubters that the hand was unburned. Harald Bluetooth and Earl Hacon promptly became believers and were baptized.

These conversions satisfied the German emperor, who withdrew his army from Denmark, declaring that from this point forward the Danish people need pay taxes only to the Christian bishops. Bluetooth kept his word about Christianity (while the recalcitrant Earl Hacon reverted to heathenism immediately after Otto was safely south). At the Morso meeting, Bluetooth's own infant son Svein was baptized, and Otto was made the boy's godfather.

But if Bluetooth kept his word on the faith, he was determined never to be humbled again. His humiliation hardened the Danish king in his military preparations. He set about to strengthen the Danevirk further, and near Jelling his engineers built an immense seven-hundred-meter-long oaken bridge at Ravning Enge. His trading towns of Ribe, Arhus, and Hedeby were fortified. In Trelleborg, Fyrakt, Aggersborg, Nonnebakken, and Trelleborg II in southern Sweden, impressive fortresses were constructed. Their usefulness was threefold: they provided a chain of defensive installations; they could be used to suppress domestic unrest and consolidate internal administration; and they could be staging areas for offensive operations.

Harald Bluetooth was a brilliant military thinker. His fort at Trelleborg was laid out in a perfect circle, one hundred yards across, surrounded by a daunting forty-foot earthen work and appointed with four thatch-roofed barracks. These halls housed about five hundred marines and their families. The fort was situated on a small stream not far from the ocean, so that the warships could be beached inland and launched at the first sign of danger. At the northern tip of Jutland, facing Sweden and Norway, Aggersborg was the largest of the five forts, with about fifteen hundred warriors, and these succeeded in recapturing and stabilizing northern Jutland, which had been subject to foreign encroachments for decades. More significantly, Aggersborg was the prime staging area for foreign invasions.

Besides his extraordinary forts and his impressive bridge at Ravning Enge, Bluetooth also counted another remarkable military achievement. As an outpost against the Poles and the Saxons, he established a unique fortress at the mouth of the Oder River near the village of Wollin, in the shoals of Peenemunde, and called it Jomsborg. Here he trained his most severe and single-minded fighters, swore them into a blood brotherhood under the strictest rules and discipline, and called them Jomsvikings. No women were allowed in this austere base, nor any man over the age of fifty. Leave from the camp could not last more than three days, and no leatherneck could have any personal treasure from summertime forays. It is said that 360 ships could be anchored in its port, which could be closed and defended behind huge iron doors.

If the geometric precision of these fortifications was impressive, Bluetooth's administrative organization was no less sophisticated. The so-called Leidang system was instituted whereby the king taxed each community to raise a local militia, train it, and supply a battle-ready warship. As many as fifty assembly points existed around Denmark, so that on short notice the king could muster a fighting fleet of a thousand ships, each carrying up to forty men. That meant that for this country of about one million people, there was an army of more than forty thousand men at the ready. The soldiers were armed with a shield, spear, and iron helmet. The officers also carried a battle axe and a sword, and their bodies were protected with a coat of mail. This force was not a large standing army, but rather a highly proficient, well-trained militia, led by professional farmer-soldiers and poised to strike quickly. The training was rigorous, especially for the archers who were nurtured from the age of six and developed extremely powerful shoulders.

Their ships were a marvel of craftsmanship. The sea stallions of kings could be thirty meters long, with sixty oar posts, and a crew of one hundred warriors. At top speed they could reach twenty knots, and they were limber, able to bend stem to stern in the roughest storm. They rode high in the water so they could slip through shoals and beach and just as quickly be launched again at the first sign of danger. With the fleet came the cargo ships carrying the cavalry and its horses as well as the supplies for the entire naval force. The logistical support for a Viking fleet of several hundred ships was a complicated enterprise, and no rabid band of thick-headed barbarians could accomplish it.

In their order of battle, they were disciplined. Small raids were hit-and-run affairs. They burned, looted, and took slaves—their instinct sheer greed—but these commando raids were also probes, designed to see how stoutly an area might be defended and also to weaken that defense for a larger invasion to follow. Once the marines hit the shore, they took up positions on high ground in a stationary line, the troops armed with spears and axes and shields. If the opposing line broke, a wedge of axe men would charge through the defensive position. (What more horrible sight can one imagine than a phalanx of Bluetooth's hoary fellows running toward you!) Moreover, the Viking forces were well versed in the tactic of the false retreat, where the line would seem to buckle, encouraging the enemy to charge, whereupon the cavalry would outflank it. This linear order of battle went back to the third century, but it would be used quite effectively some decades later, when the troops of William the Conqueror, proud man he was in his Norse lineage, outflanked the English at the Battle of Hastings.

In 978 A.D. a new epoch was about to begin. The new era was announced in the heavens when over the English countryside a mysterious red cloud suddenly appeared. The harbinger, "red as blood," looking like fire, its rays changing color, suddenly rose around midnight and disappeared at dawn. Worse things soon began to happen. In that year the benevolent English king Edmund was murdered, and he was succeeded by his thirteen-year-old brother Ethelred. With this unrest, mayhem, and infant leadership, England was weak and ripe for the taking. Bluetooth smelled his chance.

In 980 A.D. the Dane's military machine swung into action. Southampton and Chester were attacked. The following year, the coasts of Devon and Cornwall were picked clean. In 982 A.D. the Danes landed at Dorset, ravaged Portland, and set London ablaze. In that same year, Bluetooth bathed in sweet revenge. When he heard that Otto II had overstepped and had been disastrously defeated by Saracens in the south of Italy, Bluetooth's Danes scrambled over the Danevirk and attacked towns in northern Germany.

The second wave of Viking raids had begun. But now the intention was far more than theft.

For all his might King Harald Bluetooth was becoming a bit disoriented in his old age. By 985 A.D. he had ruled Denmark for thirty years, and since his conversion he had pushed his Christian faith too far for some. He had his detractors, and they were particularly vocal in Iceland. The basis of the scorn was an incident in which an Icelandic ship had been stranded in Denmark, looted, and wrecked, and it was the king's own bailiff, a man called Birger, who was thought to be responsible. Part in disgust, part in jest, an Icelandic national assembly passed a law that every citizen should make a lampoon about Bluetooth. Soon enough, a popular libel called a scurvy rhyme swept the country. In it, Bluetooth was transformed into a horse.

> The gallant Harald in the field
> Between his legs dropped his shield;
> Into a pony he was changed,
> And kicked his shield, and safely ranged.
> And Birger, he who dwells in halls
> For safety built with four stone walls,
> That these might be a worthy pair
> Was changed into a pony mare.

When he heard this impertinent scurvy rhyme, Bluetooth flew into a rage. He called out the fleet and announced his intention to invade Iceland. Fortunately, he calmed down and thought better of the idea, sending instead a wizard to Iceland in place of the fleet. But the sorry sorcerer brought back word of being attacked by serpents and toads and gigantic birds in the far-off island, and Bluetooth decided to let the matter slide. But his bizarre behavior won him no credit with his people.

As restlessness grew in the land, Bluetooth had problems within his own house as well. His son Svein was now fifteen, full of questions and manly ambitions. The boy's questions had to do with his parentage, for he was, according to legend, a love child, the offspring of Bluetooth and a poor but accomplished servant girl who had attended the king during a royal banquet and had given birth the following summer . . . to the considerable dismay of the king. Apart from Svein's baptism under the watchful eye of the German emperor Otto, Bluetooth had played no part in his son's upbringing, preferring instead to park the child with foster parents. Now as he reached manhood, Svein Forkbeard was a bundle of resentments, and he demanded to be made the rightful and legitimate heir to the Danish throne. In this ambition, he did not shrink from speaking his mind to his father. The presence of this unwanted and impertinent child in his court displeased the king greatly, and he showed it.

"I can see from your speech that the stories they tell about your mother are not lies," Bluetooth said to him one day. "You must be a fool and a simpleton."

"I would have preferred a mother of nobler birth if you had provided me with one," Svein replied tartly. "But you are my father. Now let me have three ships. If you don't I shall play some evil tricks on you that will cost you more than ships."

"I think you can be bought off in this way," the king said. "Never come back here again."

Young Svein took charge of three ships and a hundred men, and went off plundering in his father's land, behavior which occasioned loud grumbling among the farmers who were the victims of the bastard prince. The following spring, Svein confronted his father again, demanding an additional three ships and another hundred men, which he was given, and he plundered more widely through the island of Zealand and in Sweden. Bluetooth ignored the rising outcry, until after another rampaging season, Svein returned, doubling his demand a second time to twelve ships.

"I have never seen the likes of you for impudence," Bluetooth roared. "You dare to come to me, a thief and a robber, and ask for more! I will never acknowledge you as my kin."

"Most certainly I am your son, and there's no denying our relationship," Svein replied. "But I shall not spare you for all that. We shall fight it out right here if you don't give me what I want. And you'll have no chance to slip away."

"You are a difficult man, and your manner shows me that you must be of noble birth," Bluetooth said. "You shall have what you demand. Go then and never come back again into my sight."

With the ships he had extorted from his father, together with others that came from his foster father, Svein now had a formidable fleet of thirty ships, and he created havoc throughout Denmark, robbing day and night and causing great anger in the populace. Finally, Bluetooth could bear the protests of his people no longer and he took out after his son with a fleet of fifty ships. On Novemeber 1, 987 A.D., off the Helgenaes headland on the east coast of central Jutland, not far from the village of Arhus, the two fleets met. In the customary fashion of sea battle, the ships were lashed together as fighting platforms, and ferocious combat ensued. With the local people rising to the king's defense, Bluetooth got the better of it. He lost ten ships to Svein's twelve, and the engagement broke off at dusk.

At nightfall, Harald Bluetooth made for the shore with eleven men. They hacked their way inland to a clearing and made camp. The king undressed and was warming himself quite naked by the campfire when one of Svein's cohorts saw the blaze from a distance and crept through the woods to the camp's edge. Seeing the king naked, the warrior grabbed an arrow, took aim, and shot the king in his royal behind. In this undignified fashion, King Harald Bluetooth bled to death that night.

In the chaos of the following day, Svein was taken prisoner and spirited away to Jomsborg where he was presented with a choice. The fierce Jomsvikings would support him as king of Denmark if he would make peace with the Polish king. If he would not, Svein would be handed over to the Poles, who would surely torture him to death. Either to sweeten or sour the deal, an additional stipulation was that Svein must marry the uncomely daughter of the Polish king. In this manner, Svein Forkbeard became the king of Denmark.

Once he was ensconced on the throne, Svein Forkbeard threw a great party. The murderer of Harald Bluetooth now turned into his celebrant, and many cups of ale were raised in honor of the dead king, the monarch who had "united the Danes and made Denmark Christian." But Svein's feast was more a celebration of himself. It was called an heirship ale, a time of boasting and posturing. When the time came for Svein Forkbeard to speak, with most of the Vikings dead drunk, he raised his cup, vowed to conquer England, and kill its king, Ethelred, before three winters were gone. Not to be outdone, the head of the Jomsvikings raised his cup and promised to do the same to the heathen Earl Hacon in Norway within three winters.

When the Vikings awoke the following morning, they were ashamed of their boasts, but a vow was a vow and they could not welch on their promises. The preparations for war began.

"I hear," whispered the poet excitedly, "that in this Danish land long-ships slide down the strand, and floating with the rising tide, the ocean-coursers soon will ride."

S VEIN FORKBEARD CAME TO POWER in Denmark in 987 A.D., and it would not be three years . . . nor thirteen . . . before he succeeded in conquering England. The delay was not, however, for want of trying. Four years after he became king, Forkbeard was with Olaf Trygvesson for the victory of Maldon that netted the victors 10,000 pounds of silver. In 994 A.D. the Viking warriors were together again at the burning of London and the rape of Kent, which brought them 16,000 pounds of silver. After that tidy extortion, it seemed that they had reached the limit, and they went their separate ways. Olaf set off for Ireland and Norway, while Svein went to Wales and on to the Isle of Man before he returned home, weighed down with English spoils and spoiling to come back as soon as he could dispense with a few domestic annoyances like throwing Swedes out of his trading center at Hedeby.

In 997 A.D. Svein's forces were in Wales and Cornwall. They destroyed the magnificent abbey of St. Mary and St. Rumon at Tavistock in Devon, before they gutted Lydford and Watchet. The next year the rolling countryside of Dorset was the target, and Forkbeard's men established a base in the Isle of Wight, just off Portsmouth.

For the woebegone English under the woeful king Ethelred, things went from bad to worse. In 999 A.D. the Danes sailed up the Thames again, meeting Ethelred's men outside Rochester. The English king was not known as Ethelred the Unready for nothing. Besides his laziness, he was incompetent. "These Danes are also advantaged by the Unactiveness of King Ethelred, surnamed the Unready," a contemporary scribe wrote about the English monarch. "The Clock of his Consultations and Executions is always set some Hours too late, vainly striving with much Industry to redresse, what a little Providence might seasonably have prevented. Now when this Unready King meets with the Danes, his over-ready Enemies, no wonder, if lamentable is the Event thereof."

In this instance, the king's men "all too quickly gave way and fled, because they did not have the support that they should have had," the Anglo-Saxon chronicle tells us. "The Danes held the field; and then took horses and rode withersoever they would and ruined almost all West Kent. The King decreed that the Danes should be met both by a navy and a land-force. But when the ships were ready there was delay from one day to the next day. The wretched crews in the ships were harassed, and ever, as things ought to have moved forward, they were from one hour to another more behind. Ever they let the host of their foe increase. Ever the English withdrew from the sea, and the Danes followed them up. In the end, the English resistance came to nothing, save toil of the people, and waste of money, and encouragement of the enemy."

In the year 1000 A.D., as if to mark the apocalypse by the lack of it, Svein Forkbeard gave England a respite by taking his armageddon to Normandy instead (as well as attempting to defend his wife Sigrid's honor by exacting revenge on Olaf Trygvesson, as will be seen later). But in 1001 A.D. he was back in Hampshire and Devon, burning the town of Teignton and destroying the large but disorganized English armies of Devon and Somerset.

With each skirmish, each battle, Svein Forkbeard grew stronger and bolder. His purpose was shifting from piracy to conquest to colonization, and each payment of danegeld made him salivate for more. No longer a Viking adventurer bent merely on wealth and glory, he was becoming the Viking Caesar, bent on empire and land. Still his drunken promise fifteen years before remained only half-fulfilled.

In 1002 A.D., seeing that further resistance was pointless, Ethelred threw up his hands and went to his exchequer once again, handing over 24,000 pounds of silver in exchange for a temporary truce. The wolf went away, sated for the moment, but then the lamb grew paranoid and listened to rumors that certain Danes were plotting on his life. At this report, Ethelred the Unready became Ethelred the Unstable. Disastrously and insanely, he ordered the massacre of all Danes in southern England, where the Scandinavians now made up half the population. The Danes were to be rooted out "like cockle amongst the wheat."

Of all the irrational acts of all the irrational rulers of the Middle Ages, this horrendous order ranks among the most stupid. The massacre was carried out on November 13, 1002 A.D., St. Brice's Day, with uncharacteristic efficiency, and the dead included Svein Forkbeard's sister. Did the Unready One think Forkbeard would ignore the atrocity? He did not. The Nordic Caesar came back to England with a vengeance, with more men and more passion than ever. For once there was a legitimacy, even a certain nobility, to Svein Forkbeard's enterprise, and he had no trouble rallying his greatest force of all.

It would be said of Ethelred's kingdom that it was split into three groups: those who fought, those who labored, and those who prayed. With the appearance of Svein Forkbeard's fleet offshore, the third group of Englishmen predominated. Ethelred's own commander went pale at the sight of the Viking host, and as the Anglo-Saxon chronicle put it, "When the General grows faint-hearted, the whole Army suffers a severe check." In this case, more than a check. Seeing his foes wilt, Forkbeard marched into Wiltshire, burning its episcopal seat of Wilton, and thereby avenged the insult that Alfred the Great had given the Danes there 120 years before. In the next three years, Forkbeard crisscrossed southern England at will from Salisbury to Exeter, Norwich to Reading. He chose to pass up the English famine in 1005–6, returning to Denmark, but was back in 1007 when the crops were better to accept 36,000 pounds of silver that Ethelred forked over for a little relief.

The English were entirely demoralized, their king in hiding or on the run, their dispirited and mismanaged forces reduced to guerrilla tactics. The Danish romp attracted the Jomsvikings and the Norwegians to the gorge, and, soon enough, there were so many predators at the trough that they began to trip over one another.

For his part, the baleful King Ethelred retreated into apocalyptic thinking. In 1009 A.D. he issued a royal edict identifying the "Great Army" of heathens with the forces of the Antichrist and calling upon his people to fast for three days before Michaelmas (September 26–28), when every man was to go barefoot to church and to pay alms to the church; when the votive mass "Against the Heathen" was to be said at matins; and when, at each of the canonical hours, the whole community, prostrate before the altar, was to sing the psalm "Why, O Lord, Are They Multiplied?" Even slaves got three days off from work so they could fast and confess, and if they did not, they were flogged. The nation was to do all this "until things become better," but there was no optimism that things were going to get better anytime soon. In the same year Ethelred minted a penny called the Agnus Dei coin, with the alpha and the omega printed on the back, to beseech divine deliverance from the enemies. But God did not show the English mercy.

In this period, the celebrated battle at London took place. The challenge for the invaders was to capture London Bridge, which had proved to be a formidable obstacle, even to a combined force of Danes and Norwegians. Under the command of the Norwegian prince Olaf the Stout, the invaders had been unable to break past the bridge, which was well fortified with towers and ably defended by soldiers armed with heavy stones and spears. But eventually, the Vikings covered their boats with staves and wicker mesh and shields, rowed under the bridge where they tied ropes to the pilings, and then rowed with all their might back downstream, as they shouted;

"Odinn makes our Olaf win!"

If Odinn was behind all this, no wonder he was worshiped. After the Danes burned Oxford and Cambridge and martyred the archbishop of Canterbury by clubbing him to death with cow bones, there would be one last tribute to Caesar. This time, the sum was so large that the English king needed a few months to extort the money from his own people. In 1011 A.D. 48,000 pounds of silver was paid to Forkbeard. "All these calamities fell upon us through evil counsel," the Anglo-Saxon chronicle reported about the ransom, "because tribute was not offered to the Danes at the right time, nor yet were they resisted. But when they had done the most evil, then was peace made with them. And notwithstanding this peace and tribute, they went everywhere in companies, harried our wretched people, robbed and slew them."

For show, Svein Forkbeard left England. But he left a sizable force in place, knowing that any pretext, real or imagined, would bring him back to the ripe English table. The interval was two years, not exactly decent, but long enough to give the impression of starting afresh.

In 1013 A.D. Svein Forkbeard declared his right to the English throne. His Viking fleet of more than three hundred wave stallions appeared off Sandwich, and it was an awesome, terrible, and profoundly beautiful sight:

"When the warriors gathered, they went on board the towered ships, having chosen their own leaders on the braxen prows. On one side lions, molded in gold were seen on the ships, and on the other side, birds on the mast tops indicated the direction of the wind, or dragons of various kinds poured fire from their nostrils. Here there were glittering men of solid gold or silver, nearly comparable to live ones, there bulls with necks raised high and legs outstretched, were fashioned, leaping or roaring like live ones. One might see dolphins molded in silver and gold, and centaurs in the same metal, recalling ancient fable. Sides of the ships were not only painted with ornate colors, but were covered with gold and silver figures. The royal vessel excelled all others in beauty as much as the king preceded the soldiers in honor and in dignity.

"When the signal was given, they set out gladly, and as they had been ordered, placed themselves round about the royal vessel, some in front and some behind. The blue water, smitten by many oars, might be seen foaming far and wide, and the sunlight cast back in the gleam of metal, spread a double radiance in the air."

His forces marched wherever they wanted across the south of England. Now whole boroughs and shires and whole peoples submitted to him, offering him tribute and hostages, and before long all of England north along the ancient Roman way called Watling Street was his. London was the one exception. The last resistance centered there, but now, instead of a costly siege of the town, Forkbeard outmaneuvered its defenders, and their situation was hopeless.

When London submitted, Ethelred slipped down the Thames on a stolid English boat, tarried briefly in the Isle of Wight, and then crossed over to Normandy. Svein Forkbeard became the Viking king of all England.

"At this time," wrote the Anglo-Saxon chronicler, "nothing went right for this nation, neither in the south nor in the north."

The noble and passionate archbishop of York, Wulfstan, saw the situation more profoundly. The darkness descending in England was the apocalypse. The Gospel of St. Matthew had predicted it: nation would rise against nation; the sun and the moon would be darkened by the appearance of the cross. Upon his high pulpit in the York minster, he saw damnation at hand. "Beloved men, realize what is true," he proclaimed. "This world is in haste and the end approaches." The sins of the people had brought the Antichrist into their midst, and the people now were getting what they deserved. "The English have been for a long time now completely defeated and too greatly disheartened through God's anger," Wulfstan preached, "and the pirates so strong with God's consent that often in battle one puts to flight ten." The misery and the shame were the consequences of God's anger. "We pay them continually, and they humiliate us daily. They ravage and they burn, plunder and rob and carry on board. And lo, what else is there in all these events except God's anger clear and visible over his people?"

RAIL AS ARCHBISHOP WULFSTAN might about pirates and heathens and the Antichrist in Danish battle armor, Svein Forkbeard was no holy warrior. The German emperor Otto had forced baptism on him and his blue-toothed father, but there was nothing in Christianity, until the very end of his life, that suited Forkbeard's passions or his goals. In adolescence, when he rebelled against his father and formed his grand designs for conquest, he had reverted to paganism. His very rebellion against his father comported with Denmark's rebellion against his father's religion. Then Sigrid, the haughty heathen from Uppsala, had raced into his arms—Svein had long since divorced his homely Polish queen and sent her back to Poland. The union between Svein and Sigrid brought peace between Denmark and Sweden and enabled Svein Forkbeard to make war on England.

Sigrid had never forgotten, much less forgiven, Olaf Trygvesson for his violent insult, and she remained full of hate for the Norwegian king. Now she urged Svein Forkbeard on and, no doubt, invoked the gods of Aesir as his inspiration. Most of all, in his campaigns in England and France, and in his battles with Olaf Trygvesson, it was not Christ, but the power of Thor, the ravens of Odinn, the succor of the Valkyries, and the promise of Valhalla that suited Forkbeard's heroic ambitions.

In the fall of 1013 A.D., he was the triumphant conqueror of England, but he had only a few months to live. For twenty-five years, he had been at war in England, almost continuously. At last, he had accomplished the quest of his youth. He could not have understood that in those twenty-five years a quiet process had been taking place behind his battle lines. The Danish Vikings were settling into their conquered land and becoming part of its life and its traditions and even its language. With each successive Viking victory, the Viking Age drew nearer to a close. The colonizers had found the land and the life and the wealth that Denmark alone could not give them. They were becoming happy and contented. England was transformed, and the outlines of its modern nationhood became apparent.

Glory still lay ahead for Svein's son Canute. Unlike his father, he would become the most exemplary and most beloved of kings, accepted and much admired by his adoptive English and much feared by the rest of Scandinavia. Canute the Mighty, as he would come to be known, would consolidate the Viking empire that Svein Forkbeard had established and would extend its boundaries beyond England and Ireland, to Norway and Sweden. From the beginning, Canute escaped the nefarious influence of his father and Swedish stepmother on religious matters. He was a devout Christian.

In January 1014 A.D., Svein Forkbeard grew ill, and the approach of death gave him a change of heart. He summoned Canute to his bedside, counseling him on the governing of the kingdom and, no doubt to the surprise of Canute, exhorting his son in the zealous practice of Christianity. Should Canute ever return to Denmark, he should take the body of his father back with him, and not, as a contemporaneous account put it, "let him be buried a stranger in a foreign land, for he knew that he was hateful to the English people. Soon after, he paid his last dues to nature, returning his soul to the heavens, and giving back his body to the earth."

CHAPTER FIVE

ARMAGEDDON AT SEA

IN 999 A.D. the Viking domain was a region in flux and in doubt. Yet it was on the precipice of a new millennium in the widest sense. Huge animosities between the countries still existed, and these were bound up with marriage and faith and geopolitics. On the human level, the tensions between the kings and queens of Scandinavia had the feel of interfamily strife, where kings competed for the same women and queens transformed their resentments into national goals. Having reverted to paganism, the Dane Svein Forkbeard was in the grip of his Swedish wife, Sigrid the Strong-Minded, who was the mother of the Swedish king, Olof the Lap-King. Sigrid, in turn, was filled with hate for

the Norwegian king, Olaf Trygvesson. Olof the Lap-King had not yet converted to Christianity and was petrified of the traditionalists all around him in the heathen mecca of Uppsala. To make things even more complicated, Olaf Trygvesson's sister had married the earl of Vastergotland, the area of western Sweden that lay between Christian Norway and the heathen regions around Uppsala. Meanwhile, Svein Forkbeard had married off his daughter to the exiled son of the heathen Earl Hacon, whom Olaf Trygvesson had supplanted in Norway. It was as if the sides had been chosen in what should have been a friendly match. It would be anything but that.

Both Olaf Trygvesson and Svein Forkbeard had had Polish dalliances in their youth, and this widened the playing field. Olaf's first and only love had been a Polish princess, and her pubescent death, when Olaf Trygvesson was only twenty-one years of age, had turned him into a harsh Viking warrior. Svein Forkbeard's tie to the Polish court was less romantic. As the price of the Danish throne, after he had spearheaded the rebellion against his father, Harald Bluetooth, he had been forced to take a homely Polish wife whom he later left for Sigid the Haughty.

On the Polish side, with equal ferocity, religion had complicated royal matchmaking. Since 992 A.D. the leader of Poland had been Boleslav the Brave. He was a strong, ruthless, and powerful ruler who had inherited a struggling principality and had transformed it into a thriving nation, first by conquering Pomerania and thereby acquiring a coastline and then by marching south into Bohemia and making Cracow his. Eventually, he would rule a kingdom that extended from the Baltic to the Carpathians, from the Elbe to the Bug. In pursuit of his ambitions, his tactics were both brutal and clever. Blinding was a common punishment, and he did not hesitate to order it when he felt it was needed.

Until quite late in both life and rule, he had been also vigorously heathen. After failed marriages to German and Hungarian princesses, Boleslav was attracted to a Danish beauty called Tyri, who was Harald Bluetooth's daughter and Svein Forkbeard's sister. His marriage to Tyri was to be the fulfillment of a long-standing promise which had been made years before as part of the Forkbeard deal (whereby Svein Forkbeard was forced by the Jomsvikings to marry a

Polish princess, and the Polish king was promised a Danish queen).
Boleslav dispatched the leader of the Jomsvikings, Earl Sigvald, to
Denmark to execute this long-delayed arrangement. The Polish king
would wait no longer.

But there was a problem. Tyri was the stubborn and very Christian widow of the first founder of Jomsborg, and she now declined to
marry Boleslav, even if he was a king. He was older and, more importantly, still quite heathen. Boleslav the Brave would have none of this
foolishness, and when Earl Sigvald arrived in Denmark, Svein
Forkbeard also brushed aside the sobs of his sister, delivering her up
promptly to the Poles. In an effort to assuage her anguish, however,
Tyri was promised large and valuable holdings in Pomerania. They
would not suffice. Upon boarding a vessel for Poland, Tyri wept pro-
fusely.

In grand and opulent style, the royal wedding was held, with the
bride's reluctance well hidden from view. On her wedding night,
however, Tyri took the notion to refuse food and drink from the
pagan banquet table and persisted in her fast for a week. She then
fled into the woods, making her way first to Denmark and eventually,
fearing the wrath of her bearded brother, on to Norway. There she
threw herself on the mercy of King Olaf Trygvesson. King Olaf liked
what he saw in this handsome, well-spoken, and vulnerable princess.
Impulsive as ever, the king promptly proposed marriage. Under the
circumstances, Tyri was in no position to refuse so attractive an offer,
nor so attractive and celebrated a man, and she was prepared to
overlook Olaf's unlucky past with women. After the wedding the
royal couple wintered in Trondheim.

This complex intermingling of blood ties, marriage, faith, and geopolitics came to a climax in the shallow waters off the flats of
Peenemunde and near the island of Rugen in the late summer of
1000 A.D. In legend this would become known as the Battle of Svold.

In the spring of 1000 A.D., Queen Tyri had developed a severe
case of homesickness. She had quickly tired of the cold rocks of
Norway, and her mind rested on the rich Pomeranian lands that she
had forgone for her faith. The news from Poland encouraged her
longings further. In the intervening time, Boleslav had converted to
Christianity, partly, the queen must have hoped, because of his hu-

miliating loss of her, but just as powerfully for reasons of statecraft. Geopolitics had compelled his conversion. In the conquest of the Slavic tribes between the Oder and the Elbe Rivers, Christianity was useful to his policy of subjugation. In 996 A.D. Adalbert, the former bishop of Prague and later a martyr and saint, arrived in Poland and took over Boleslav's missionary effort. In fact, he was now so passionately Christian that the punishment for breaking fast on a holy day was to have your teeth extracted.

This startling change of spirit had immediate, tangible benefits. With Boleslav's rebirth in Christ, the new French pope, Sylvester II, made the central Polish town of Gniezno the episcopal see of Catholicism. Fulfilling a desire long felt by lesser Pomeranian dukes before Boleslav, this emancipated the Polish church from German control and accorded independence to the indigenous church and state. To dignify the new arrangement, Otto III, the mystical Holy Roman Emperor, made a state visit. Encamping in Gniezno, he was entertained magnificently by Boleslav, so splendidly, in fact, that he decided to crown Boleslav as the first Christian king of Poland. Thus, with one swoop, Boleslav became the first Polish ruler to bear the royal and papal imprimatur. The king and his nation were elevated into the community of European states. This moment, in 1000 A.D., marks the birth of the Polish nation.

During the spring of 1000 A.D. Queen Tyri was relentless in her pleading to King Olaf about an expedition to the "new Poland" to recover her promised lands. The king was noncommittal. His councilors sought to dissuade him from the adventure. They were not sure that a newly acquired faith was as strong an inducement to friendship as being cuckolded was an inducement to revenge. One day, while Olaf was strolling in the Trondheim marketplace, he came upon a stall that was selling unusually large angelica roots. Thinking this aromatic plant, so fine for perfume, flavored liqueur, and sweetmeats, would make a fine present for the queen, he took a few home.

"See here, queen, a great angelica stalk for you."

But Tyri threw the tuber down. "My father, Harald, gave my mother a greater present than a root. He was not afraid to go out of Denmark and take what he wanted. He came here to Norway and seized all the scatt he needed. You don't dare to venture across Danish dominions for fear of this brother of mine, King Svein!"

The king leapt from his chair and loudly protested:

"Never have I been afraid of your brother, never! If we meet, he shall give way before me!"

FOR A FEW YEARS the sea king had been reinforcing his considerable fleet with several titanic ships of war. In the fall of 996 A.D., a long ship with thirty benches was constructed on the banks of the Nid. Thin and nimble, with a keel fashioned from a single tree and a hull flattened amidships to increase its open-sea speed, this was the *Crane,* which King Olaf thought was the largest and fastest warship in the world. But then he had come up against Raud the Strong in the north and had been astounded by Raud's still larger warship. It also had thirty benches but it was longer and more magnificent, with a gilded snake's head upturned at the bow and a wooden tail coiling off its stern. This was called the *Serpent,* and King Olaf seized it with joy as his prize after he put Raud to his horrible serpent's death.

In the winter of 1000 A.D., as Queen Tyri badgered him about an expedition to Poland, King Olaf requisitioned a still larger battleship, and it went under construction near Lade. Its keel measured 150 feet, and it was designed to be broader abeam than the *Serpent,* with four more rowers' benches. Upon its completion, the king regarded his ship with satisfaction. In its size, its speed, and sheer beauty, it was unmatched in the world. This magnificent warship would be his *Long Serpent,* he declared, while Raud's ship was downgraded to the *Short Serpent.*

In the spring, he levied an army to be raised and then sailed south to the river Göta to show off his new ship to his sister and her new Swedish husband. The excursion was an opportunity for Queen Tyri to persist in her entreaties, and she was in a position to influence the king more than ever. The year before, the royal couple had had a son, named Harald, who had died before he was a year old. The tragedy had made the queen more emotional than ever. By the end of the sail south, King Olaf had acceded to his queen's desires.

In midsummer, sixty ships had been mustered, and the Norwegian fleet sailed south, passing by Denmark without incident and arriving expeditiously in Poland. Boleslav put on a brave face, greeted Olaf cordially, entertained him lavishly, negotiated peaceably about the Pomeranian lands, and gave no hint of pique.

That is how it was on the surface. But in the background more sinister plans were afoot. News of Olaf's presence quickly reached Denmark, and Queen Sigrid prodded Svein Forkbeard to seize the moment. All her old resentments poured out of her, and she added another grievance for Svein's benefit: King Olaf had married Svein's sister, Tyri, without his permission, and "your predecessors never would have agreed to that!"

Svein Forkbeard did not need much persuading. He sent word to Sigrid's son Olof the Lap-King and to Earl Hacon's son Eric, both of whom were in Sweden, that they should mobilize their fleet, fill its ships with stout-hearted men, and hasten to the attack. Olof the Lap-King was coming out of loyalty to his mother, Sigrid, and awe of his stepfather, Svein. Earl Eric was coming with a stronger emotion. He had revenge in his heart for the death of his heathen father, and he carried the torch of the old pagan religion. Now married to the daughter of Svein Forkbeard, Eric had named the first son of this union Hacon after the martyred patriarch. Earl Eric had a lot to fight for.

When the armies massed, the force was immense. It was the last great heathen army of Europe, and it was coming to holy war. Ragnarok and Armageddon were conjoined: the battle was between men, but it was also a battle between gods and between good and evil. As usual, the princes were accompanied by their battle-poets as well. Earl Eric's scald was Haldor the Unchristian, and he wrote expectantly that "the ravens of the sea waited for food, and every warrior then longed to follow Eric into battle."

On the heathen side, a shadowy third player would be pivotal in the unfolding drama. That was the ever-present Earl Sigvald, leader of the Jomsvikings, who seemed to be eager for all missions of love and war. Sigvald's loyalties were divided between the parties, and he seemed to operate as an independent agent. Technically under the command of Svein Forkbeard, he had married Boleslav's daughter, who in turn was the sister of King Olaf's first wife. Now Forkbeard dispatched Earl Sigvald to Poland with instructions to renew his friendship with King Olaf and, by any pretext he could find, to delay Olaf's departure until the Swedish armies had arrived from the north. In the Polish court the treacherous Sigvald, the Judas of this Nordic passion play, performed his double agent's role brilliantly. Cozying up to King Olaf, he found that Olaf's men were eager to leave. In order to buy time, Sigvald importuned and prodded and filibustered until he finally got the long-awaited, secret message that the Danish-Swedish force was in place. Now his mission was to guide King Olaf into the trap, near a creek called Svold, just west of the island of Rügen.

King Olaf had his own source of intelligence, however. He was soon informed of Svein Forkbeard's menacing mobilization. Earl Sigvald supplied the pomade.

"King Svein would never dare to oppose you and your powerful army with his Danish army alone," he said unctuously. "But if you have any suspicion that something is afoot, I will follow you with my force, manning eleven ships."

That seemed to assuage King Olaf's concern, since to have Jomsvikings in one's front line was a great honor. With his fleet swelled to seventy-one ships, a mellow and downright complacent King Olaf climbed to the quarterdeck of the *Long Serpent*. Earl Sigvald had another suggestion: that he lead rather than follow the fleet.

"I know where the water is deepest between the islands and in the sounds, and these large ships require the deepest," he said.

Olaf readily agreed. The flotilla sailed north, through the shoals of Peenemunde, toward the chalk cliffs of Rugen. In his overconfidence, given the presence of ferocious Jomsvikings on the point, Olaf dispatched his main fleet into the open waters of the Baltic. With his three colossal flagships, the *Crane* and the two *Serpents*, he followed Sigvald into the narrows west of Rügen.

Moving far ahead of the Norwegian ships, Earl Sigvald struck his sails once he got close to Svold and joined the three kings, who were discussing how they would carve up Norway among them after the fight and who should get the *Long Serpent* and all its bounty. On the latter point Earl Eric seemed to be the leading contender, since he had the best battleship. It was the *Iron Beard,* so called because it was fortified with iron plate and had iron spikes all around the gunnels to hinder enemy raiders from boarding.

Poised and cocksure, the heathen potentates watched the approaching enemy from a headland. "There comes a very large and very beautiful vessel," Olof the Swede shouted, pointing to the first Viking ship far in the distance.

"That will be the *Long Serpent!*" King Svein gloated.

"That is not the *Long Serpent,*" Earl Eric disagreed, with an air of superior intelligence. He knew his ships.

"Olaf Trygvesson must be afraid," Svein boasted. "Because he does not venture to sail with the figurehead of the dragon on his ship."

"That is not the king's ship yet," Earl Eric insisted. "I know his ship by the colored stripes of her sail. Let that one pass, it will be better for us if it is away from Olaf's fleet. It is very well equipped."

Three more ships followed, one very large.

"There comes the *Long Serpent,*" Svein Forkbeard said eagerly.

"They have many other great and stately vessels besides the *Long Serpent,*" Earl Eric said with a quavering voice. "Let us wait a little."

"Earl Eric will not fight and avenge his father," someone whispered. "It is such a shame that we lay here with so great a force and allow King Olaf to sail out to sea in front of our eyes."

At last Olaf's exquisite, gilded sea steed took shape on the horizon. Forkbeard was thrilled. "That dragon shall carry me this evening high, for I shall steer it," he boasted.

Others were merely aghast. "The *Serpent* is indeed a wonderfully large and beautiful vessel," someone remarked admiringly, "and it shows a great mind to have built such a ship."

Earl Eric seemed to have a temporary lapse of nerve. "If King Olaf had no other vessels but only that one, King Svein would never take it from him with the Danish force alone," he muttered.

Olaf's three ships entered the strait one by one and when the Norwegian commanders saw that Sigvald's ships had struck their sails, they did likewise, prepared to wait for their king. As the *Long Serpent* came alongside, the enemy fleet swung around the point, and Olaf understood his dire situation immediately. His fore-castleman pleaded with the king to back out of the narrow confines into open water and escape, but Olaf replied with a loud order: "Strike the sails!" he shouted. "I never fled from battle before. Let God dispose of my life, if that is the plan, but I shall never bolt! My men shall never learn from me from the dark weapon-cloud to flee."

As the battleships were lashed around the *Long Serpent*, the war horns sounded, and King Olaf, wrapped magnificently in a flowing red cloak, holding a golden shield, with his huge square head encased in a helmet of inlaid gold, barked his orders over his fighting platform.

"Who is the chief of the ships right ahead of us?" he roared, and when he was told it was Svein Forkbeard, he scoffed. "We are not afraid of these soft Danes, for they are cowards. Who are the troops on the right of the Danes?"

When he was told it was Olof the Swedish Lap-King, the suckling of the heathen bitch Sigrid the Haughty, he laughed. "Better for the Swedes if they stayed at home licking their sacrificial bowls. But who is that on the larboard side in the large ship?"

When he was told it was Earl Eric, the son of Hacon, whose severed head he had last seen when it was presented to him by the slave, King Olaf said, "He, I think, has good reason for meeting us. We can expect the worst from these men, for they are Norsemen like ourselves."

When the battle was joined, Forkbeard's soft Danes gave way like cheese, quickly retreating to a safe distance. Olof the Swede moved forward, but he took a licking as well, losing many men, and he withdrew. Then came Earl Eric and his *Iron Beard*. This was the test, *mano a mano*: Norsemen against Norsemen. Boarding the outer ships and thinning out their defenders, the earl's men cut the cables, clearing away the bark from a tree.

At last, it was down to the *Long Serpent* and the *Iron Beard*. Behind the pagan serpent, Danish and Swedish ships crowded in, leaving a safe distance, waiting to mop up, while in the *Iron Beard* itself, Earl Eric directed the close combat. A canopy of shields protected the heathen leader on his forecastle, as the axes and spears and arrows rained down. But more weapons and stones poured down on the *Long Serpent*. Some of King Olaf's men went berserk. They leapt over onto the *Iron Beard* and got sliced up. Some missed their leap and fell into the water, sinking under the weight of their armor.

For the greater part of the day, the hand-to-hand combat raged. King Olaf held his ground on the quarterdeck. He hurled axes and shot arrows, and when he reached for spears, it was said, he hurled two at once with both arms. Blood streamed out of his mailed glove, but his wound did not slow him down. As the day wore on, his hand-chosen troops fore and aft remained strong, but in the well of the long ship, along the gangways and amid the rowers' benches, the ranks thinned. Earl Eric saw his chance. With four men, he leapt onto the *Long Serpent,* but getting a "warm reception," he had to retreat to the *Iron Beard.* Still he had his soft point. On the second attempt, the heathen came with more men. They streamed onto the middeck at the central mast and, moving outward, separated Olaf's men fore and aft. "On to the charge again!" Eric urged on his men, as they pushed King Olaf and his few remaining soldiers toward the quarterdeck. "On to the charge again!"

And the charge was overwhelming. At last, King Olaf found himself nearly alone, shoulder-to-shoulder with only his brave marshal, a huge man named Einar the Bowman. Seeing that the Bowman was effective, Earl Eric shouted to his best archer, "Shoot the big man, there in the middle hold!" The heathen arrow was well aimed but hit Einar's bow, shattering it in two with a sharp clap. "What was that noise?" King Olaf shouted, and Einar answered, "That was the sound of Norway slipping from thine hand, O king!"

"So great a burst has not yet befallen," Olaf answered. "Take my bow and shoot with it." Einar took the bow, but was displeased. "Too weak, too weak is the king's bow." He threw it down and picked up his sword and shield instead.

They were pressed back onto the quarterdeck. To be killed there was noble but bad, and Olaf did not want to give Eric the satisfaction. To be captured and dragged before the hate-filled, heathen earl was worse, for Olaf could expect an end worse than Eric's father, worse than the torture he had meted out to Raud the Strong, worse even than the death of Ragnar Hairy Breeks in the worm close.

And so, at his last ditch, Olaf jumped overboard. The small sea bucks of the enemy that crowded around the *Long Serpent* rowed hard toward the place where Olaf sank. Only his gilded shield marked the spot. Eric's poet gloated:

> On Odinn's deck, all wet with blood
> The helm-adorned hero stood;
> The mighty mountain peaks shall fall
> Ere men forget this to recall.

While Olaf's poet wept:

> The Serpent and the Crane
> Lay wrecks upon the main.
> On his sword he cast a glance,
> With it he saw no chance.
> To his marshal, who of yore
> Many a war-chance had come o'er,
> He spoke a word—then drew in breath,
> And sprang to his deep-sea death.

Perhaps. As the news spread, many did not believe it. King Olaf was too clever, too strong, too powerful a swimmer simply to sink like a stone. Surely, he would swim, far underwater, beyond the heathen ships to the shore nearby. The legend of King Olaf grew from the day he sank beneath the surface, told and promoted by Hallfred, now his tragic, mournful scald. The Northlands were desolate at his fall, Hallfred wrote, but was everyone so sure that the raven had had his meal?

King Olaf lived? Could it be?

FIFTY YEARS AFTER THE BATTLE OF SVOLD, when Magnus the Good was king of Norway and William of Normandy had not yet come to England, a Norwegian mariner named Gautur plied his course through the Mediterranean, so says the legend, to Egypt and beyond. In Syria, his fortunes turned sour. After his companion took ill and died, Gautur himself became sick as well, wandering aimless and lost somewhere near Aleppo, without food or water. He came to a large river, probably the upper Euphrates, and across the expanse he saw a stone house, but he could not find a boat or a shallow place to cross. In time, he lay down and went to sleep and had a dream in which a large old man with a benign, time-worn face spoke to him of a spot nearby where he could find a small boat in the reeds. When he awoke, Gautur found the boat and crossed the river. When he came to the stone house, it was a monastery and, there, on its porch, and in prayer, was the same imposing, old man Gautur had seen in his dream.

The old monk made Gautur comfortable, giving him food and water and fresh clothes, and in due course they fell into conversation about Norway. The friar inquired keenly about the Norse kings after Olaf Trygvesson, and Gautur told of Olaf the Saint and his death, of Canute the Mighty, the son of Svein Forkbeard, and of his son Svein. The old monk inquired about Olaf Trygvesson's son Trygvi, and Gautur told of a battle between Trygvi and the son of Canute in which Trygvi had fought valiantly and had hurled spears with both arms and had shouted, "Thus my father taught me!" When Gautur mentioned the death of Trygvi in that fight, the old man grew sad.

"How is Olaf Trygvesson remembered?" the old man asked after a while.

"Honorably," Gautur replied.

"Why?"

"Because he achieved much glory . . . and because he brought Christ to the northern countries."

"Tell me, what do people think happened to King Olaf on the *Serpent?*" the old man asked.

"Some men say that he sank very deep to the bottom with his full armor and drowned."

"Why on earth would men think that?" the old man said, his pique showing beneath his smile. "Why would anyone think the king would want to kill himself? . . . that he was so frightened, too wounded and weak that he jumped into the water? Do people really think that he could not get away? He certainly would not have been the athlete he was said to be if war clothes would hold him down. Nay, men should not believe that."

"Other men think that the divine power took Olaf to God or put him in another place with a Great Light that many men saw appear over the king," Gautur said.

"That is very dubious," the monk replied. "He was not so holy, nor so worthy of the glory of God. King Olaf did a few good deeds, but he did many more sins. This should not be believed. No, he had to escape danger to his life in another way, with humility and with God's permission."

"Well, a few men think he was plucked from the sea by a boat that was near the battle."

"Yes, now there, men should believe that. That is what wise men here say, almost fifty winters after the battle."

After this, the old monk inquired about Einar the Bowman. Gautur's suspicion about the identity of this extraordinary monk now grew intense. Einar the Bowman still lived, he told the monk, and was highly respected.

"I saw him fight on the *Long Serpent*," the old man muttered vacantly. "He was equal to the strongest of the king's men."

With that Gautur could no longer restrain himself.

"Are you King Olaf Trygvesson, father?" he asked breathlessly.

"I do not seek stature . . . nor a king's title," the old man replied, and before Gautur could pursue the matter, a bell rang, calling the monks to evensong in the nearby village. The old man wrapped a threadbare red cloak over his simple monk's habit, and they walked together into town. As they entered the church, other monks rushed to him, treating him with great respect, and Gautur noticed that his benefactor was a head taller than all the other monks. After the prayer, he ordered other monks to take charge of Gautur and provide for his needs.

The following day after mass, Gautur, at last feeling considerably better, but with raging curiosity, was summoned again to the old man.

"When you get back to Norway, give my regards to Einar the Bowman. Tell him that I bear witness to this: no man fought better on the *Long Serpent* than he. To prove to him that you are telling the truth, I want to give you these things." The monk held out a fine knife and a well-made belt.

After three days, Gautur left in the care of several guides the old monk had provided to conduct the sojourner all the way to Greece. Sometime later, after he was back in Norway, Gautur sought out Einar the Bowman and told his story. When he presented the knife and the belt, Einar wept.

"It is true, Gautur," he said. "You have found Olaf Trygvesson."

CHAPTER SIX

AL MANSOR, the Avenging Moor

IN THE MIDDLE of the first millennium of the Christian calendar, the Spanish peninsula was in the grip of the Visigoths, a particularly brutal tribe of German barbarians who had crossed over the Pyrenees in the fifth century and overrun the Iberian provinces of the declining Roman Empire. Bold and fierce, they were nominally Christian, thoroughly corrupt, and profoundly superstitious. Among the icons of the Visigothic kings was an ark in which the gospels were kept. Whenever a king died, the ark was opened and the name of the king was inscribed inside, as if it were some sort of time capsule. This proved a good idea since the dynasty was about to drift away into history. Toward the end of their Spanish hegemony their domain was a model of tyranny: a small aristocracy, in league with the clergy, held vast estates and relied on wretched slaves to till the soil and satisfy the nobles' voracious appetites, while the middle class, such as it was, bore a heavy burden of taxation. The king's court was located in Toledo where the standards of barbarian grace and good breeding were savagely maintained.

The grisly rule of these Teutonic parasites lasted two centuries in Spain, but at the beginning of the eighth century they were losing their grip, holding on to power only through the swiftness of their sword and the helplessness of their victims. Their king was Roderick, a vigorous man who had begun with promise and ended with promiscuity. It was fitting that such a figure should bring down such a rule with such an act of personal corruption.

Across the narrow band of water at the southern tip of Spain lay the fortress of Ceuta, a strategic redoubt, the last of the far-flung Byzantine outposts. Ceuta commanded the entrance to the Mediterranean Sea but also guarded against an invasion of Spain from Africa. In 710 A.D. the governor there was one Count Julian, who, in storybook fashion, had a beautiful daughter named Florinda and who had made the mistake of sending her to Toledo rather than Constantinople to garner a little Gothic polish at the queen's court.

Instead, King Roderick ravaged her, and an eternal process commenced. The damsel in distress sent the news of her royal deflowering to her father by a swift, secret messenger, and the count plotted his revenge. For decades, his enclave had served as a kind of cork in the African bottle, the first line of Spanish defense against the rabid Berbers and the Arabs of the Magreb. But in recent times the pressure in the bottle had grown a lot greater. For North Africa was fermenting with the zeal of a new faith called Islam. Muhammad the Arabian prophet had begun to preach his message one hundred years before. Now it was sweeping west from Cairo, consuming Tunis and Morocco and Mauritania. The passionate believers were fierce horsemen as well, eager for conquest and plunder, all in the name of Allah. Count Julian no longer had a reason to hold them off; indeed, he had a very good reason to egg them on.

Upon a pretext, feigning ignorance of Roderick's crime, Count Julian traveled to Toledo. His purpose was reconnaissance as well as rescue. Roderick welcomed him unctuously, covering his shame as Julian covered his rage, and the king heaped praise and gifts on his vassal. As Julian prepared to leave with Florinda, Roderick importuned him with a final request: could he send the sporting king a brace of rare North African hunting hawks? Count Julian replied graciously: he would send hawks which would astonish and excite his majesty.

In the late summer of 711 A.D., hearing that Roderick was preoccupied with a revolt of the Basques in the north of Spain, Count Julian waved an army of eighteen thousand Berbers and Arabs through his streets and into their ships. The force was commanded by Tarik, the fierce general and governor of Mauritania, who soon landed at the massive rock then known as the Lion's Rock and later named Tarik's Rock (and still later called Gibraltar). Roderick reacted quickly. Within a few weeks, he faced Tarik across a stream the Arabs reverently called Wady Bekka, east of Cádiz, with a formidable army of mercenaries. At this awesome display of might, the invaders flinched. Seeing their hesitation, Tarik burned a few slackers alive as an object lesson and then went before his troops with a stiff proposition. "Men, before you is the enemy of infidels. At your back is the sea. By Allah, there is no escape for you, save in valor and in resolution." This, at last, was the Holy War the Koran had promised. If they fell, paradise awaited them. If they stood, all Spain was theirs.

And they did stand. The Visigoths were sliced up. Roderick was killed. The Christian infidels scattered. It would take another two years to complete the job. At Córdoba and Granada, Seville and Toledo, the intruders were successful after long sieges, largely with the compliance of the Jews, who had suffered mightily under the Visigoths, and even a few Christian priests, who led the invaders to the weak points in the wall.

As with the wild Magyars far to the northeast, the Moors were effective horsemen because they hailed from a nomadic tradition. They rode with incredible speed and were savage on the attack and unsparing in their cruelty. That they were dark-skinned and wore exotic turbans, carried curved swords, spoke in an incomprehensible tongue-and-throat babble, and prayed to an exotic god made them appear demonic to Europeans. That their leaders fancied the black

stallions of Arabia and that even their fair-haired leaders liked to dye
their hair black associated them all the more with the third horseman
of the Apocalypse. No wonder that their roots were said to be in the
land of Gog and Magog. Along with the Vikings and the Magyars, the
Moors represented the third prong of heathenism, as if toward the
end of the first millennium the devil had launched a pincer movement against Europe from three directions. If the prophecy of St.
John was flawed, it was that the great Dragon, the Great Beast of the
Apocalypse, the Great Whore of Babylon, had three heads rather
than seven.

Also like the Magyars, the Moors seemed to be the most dangerous to central Europe in the infancy of their conquest. Their tide
swept north. In 718 A.D., having overrun all of Spain except the
northwest Visigothic enclave in León, they crossed the Pyrenees to
go after the real prize, the land of the Franks. But in 732 A.D. at
Poitiers in western France, in an event that resounded with monumental significance, they were defeated by the French king, Charles
Martel. With the defeat of the Moors, the advance of Islam into
central Europe was checked forever. In the continent's heartland,
Christianity was saved. The Carolingian empire of the Franks was
also saved, and the groundwork for Charlemagne later in the eighth
century was laid. The Franks could turn their attention north, to
Scandinavia, and the Danes immediately felt the repercussions. In
737 A.D. the Danish Vikings built their seventeen-mile-long bulwark
across the neck of their peninsula. This formed the northern bound-
ary of the Carolingian empire and allowed the Vikings to build up
their power in relative safety, without much concern for their southern flank.

From 711 A.D. to 756 A.D., despite the ravages of the wild Moorish armies across Spain and France, the Moorish state wallowed in
anarchy. The Arabs' view of statehood was tribal, and yet they
paraded their own sense of superiority. In their arrogance, they
looked down on their Berber warriors as savages, driving them into
the barren, windswept central plateau known as La Mancha and trying to contain their repeated revolts. Spain was loosely administered
from Damascus by the Umayyad dynasty, but this absentee rule
ended in 750 A.D. when the Umayyad were overthrown by the Ab-

basid caliphate in Baghdad, and the sole surviving member of the dynasty fled to Spain.

This first Spanish emir, Abd al Rahman I, took firm control. He established the capital at Córdoba and set about to organize the bureaucracy. Brutal though he was, this fugitive prince, this son of a prince and a Berber slave, had one endearing quality: he amused himself by hiding among his people disguised as a leper and a tramp.

When Charlemagne came to power in 768 A.D. and saw his destiny as the evangelical Christian emperor of Europe, the presence of the Muhammadans in Spain was an insult. In 778 A.D. he invaded, conquering Pamplona and Barcelona and moving south in his crusade. But he was checked at Saragosa, forced onto the defensive. When he heard news of a Saxon revolt back home, he began his retreat. In the steep valleys of the Pyrenees, a force of thirty thousand Moors trapped his army in the Pass of Roncesvalles, on the pilgrims' route to Santiago de Compostela, north of Pamplona. His rear guard was cut off and wiped out. Thereafter, Charlemagne looked for glory elsewhere. But his valiant crusade became the stuff of popular song. "You Frenchmen had it rough, there in Roncesvalles," sang the Spanish. "The Saracens came and beat us up," sang the French. "God helps the bad, when they outnumber the good." It led to one of the most enduring of all romantic epics, *Chanson de Roland,* to references in Dante's *Divine Comedy,* and to monuments along the pilgrims' path. After the defeat, it is said, maidens thrust the spears of the fallen into the ground, accounting for the "forest of spears" near the battleground. Like the portrayal of the vulgar Vikings and the noble Englishmen in *The Battle of Maldon,* the Moors represented the wicked infidels; Charlemagne's cavaliers were the glorious fallen.

The first one hundred years of the Moorish caliphate in Spain featured a constant struggle in sorting out the relationship between the Muslims and the Christians. Across the peninsula Christian churches were appropriated and made over into mosques. No new Christian churches could be built; in those few remaining churches, no bells could be rung. Christians were restricted from bearing arms, and they were made to wear a distinctive belt, the forerunner of the Jewish star, to identify them as nonbelievers. The most severe penalty was reserved for slander against Islam, an injunction that was luridly violated in the mid-ninth century by several Christian prelates with martyr complexes.

Tolerance was deep within the Muslim sensibility, however. This tradition went back to the "covenant of protection," and it extended to conquered Christian territory in North Africa, partly to undermine resistance to the Islamic conquest. Such tolerance came at a price, however: a tax called a *jizya* was levied on any who rejected Muhammad's teaching. By the mid-ninth century in Córdoba, the Christian bells were ringing again on Sundays, and Christian funeral processions passed unhindered through Muslim neighborhoods. The inevitable intermarriage between the faiths led to further relaxations, and many Christians converted to Islam, if only to avoid the *jizya*. The converts included the ruling Visigothic family in Saragosa, which continued in power with the sanction of Córdoba.

After the massacre of Charlemagne's troops at Roncesvalles, the Moors acquiesced in the relative independence of the Christian provinces of Galicia, León, and Castile. Acquiesced, that is, until the fierce Al Mansor, the Avenger, resumed the Holy War toward the end of the first millennium. These northern lands are dry, rocky, and barren by comparison with the lush, fertile south, which is sweetened by African breezes, along the green valleys of the rivers Tagus, Guadiana, and, most important, Guadalquivir. (The name Guadalquivir is a later perversion of the Arabic Wady al Kebir.)

If the Moors acquiesced in the presence of Christians on Spanish soil, there was, however, no diminishing of their aggressive instincts. Throughout the ninth century Arab pirates and slave traders commanded the trading routes of the western Mediterranean. Genoa, Sardinia, and Tunis were their ports of call, and they operated from their base in the Rhone River delta on the island of Camargua. Occasionally they cruised up the Rhone River valley—in 840 A.D. they got as far as Arles—but beyond, the larger fortified towns discouraged their adventures. These brigands preferred smaller raiding parties, and thus small towns and isolated abbeys were more attractive targets.

In 890 A.D., a permanent Islamic warrior camp was established on an isolated outcropping of rock on the coast of Provence near Nice.

Called Le Freinet, for its cover of thorns and ash trees, this base grew to about two thousand soldiers and was the Mediterranean version of Jomsborg, the military base of the ferocious Jomsvikings in the Baltic. From this forward position, the Muslims organized small raiding parties. Avoiding the Rhone and crossing over the Alps—"real goats," they were called disparagingly—they attacked the abbey near Susa west of Turin in 906 A.D. and sometime later scattered the friars of St. Gall. By 940 A.D. they were operating as far north as the upper Rhine valley, burning the monastery of Saint-Maurice d'Agaune in the Valais. These incursions got the attention of Otto the Great, who sent a delegation to Córdoba in 962 A.D. with the demand that Le Freinet be evacuated. But the Moors were partial to their Frankish slaves. Otto's diplomatic effort failed.

The German emperor turned to military remedies. But he lacked the fleet to assault the nearly impregnable citadel, and its raids continued unimpeded. Finally, in 972 A.D. the Muslims made the mistake of capturing St. Majoulus, the famous abbot of Cluny, as he was returning from Rome through the Alpine route of the Great Saint Bernard. There, by the bridge of Ocieres, on the river Dranse, the great reformer, intimate of popes and potentates, was ransomed for a fantastic price. This unpardonable outrage mobilized the royalty of southern Europe, and, finally, this nest of Islamic bandits was cleaned out.

By 900 A.D. Córdoba had become, after Baghdad, the second city of the world. This luminous, teeming metropolis of 100,000, stretching twenty-five miles along the Wady al Kebir, was a fabulous polyglot of three continents and three faiths, populated by a handful of assertive ethnic groups. Oil-burning lamps lit its paved streets and narrow walkways. Its vigorous merchant class lived in neat, white-stuccoed houses constructed around charming pleasure gardens, filled with orange trees and jasmine, myrtle and bougainvillea. The opulent aristocracy had their grand haciendas in the elegant barrios of Rosafa, Balat Mughith, and al Qamari. Within the city walls, punctuated by seven gates, including the Gate of the Perfumers, there were hundreds of markets and thousands of shops, three hundred baths, an abundance of mills and weaving establishments. The Moors had a silk industry and practiced highly skilled agriculture.

With the wisdom of their Arabian experts, they had introduced cotton, rice, sugarcane, dates, lemons, and strawberries. Throughout the country, Moorish engineers built extensive irrigation systems. Silos were constructed to store grain. An aqueduct conveyed pure water from the mountains to the city, where scholars wrote authoritatively about agriculture and its economics and thought deeply about animal husbandry, botany, zoology, and psychology.

Córdoba was the "city of diverse hearts," a sophisticated but puritanical society where honor was as highly valued as discretion, where the concept of a transcendent soul was colored with distinct views of paradise and hell, where there were strict rules of law and justice. The wisdom of Allah, Omniscient and Omnipotent, was omnipresent. In the streets the story was told that a man came to Allah and said, "O Prophet, I have three terrible sins: drink, fornication, and lying. Command me which of these I should give up!" The prophet answered, "Give up lying." The man left and had the urge for a woman, but he thought to himself, "I will come to the Prophet, Allah, and he will ask, 'Hast thou fornicated?' If I admit, he will punish me as the law requires, and if I deny it, I will break my pledge." Lying, therefore, was the worst of sins, and the sources of all evil, in descending order, were said to be "the clacker, the rumbler, and the dangler." (The rumbler was an empty stomach.)

The emphasis on art and learning put Córdoba high above the rest of Europe. Christian Europe could boast of two universities in the tenth century; Moorish Spain had seventeen. Whereas no public libraries existed in Christian Europe, Moorish Spain had more than seventy. The central library of Córdoba, established during the reign of Al Hakkam II between 961 and 976 A.D., was the pride of the caliphate and possessed more than 400,000 books. In the mid-ninth century the Moors had introduced the first glazed pottery in the world. By the mid-tenth century they were experimenting with polychrome pottery, crafted into eighty shapes or more. Throughout the peninsula there was a kiln every fifty miles.

Of the sciences astronomy had a special place, since it was related to the Koran and to the formal process of conversion, to which the twelve signs of the zodiac were central. Rather than the solar reference of the Christian calendar, Muslim months were lunar and keyed to the latitude of Mecca. So chroniclers remembered events as happening in the moon of Safar, of Rebie Postrera, of *dylhagia,* or in the last *juma* of the moon, *dylcada.* This is not to say that the solar calendar was discarded, since both the harvests and taxation depended on an unchanging calendar. To serve heavenly observations, the Moors plied Arabic algebra and used Arabic numbers, calculated with the abacus, as they discarded the cumbersome Roman numerals. Just as *algebra* was an Arabic word, so was *chemistry,* and this science served the high art of medicine.

One of the most extraordinary figures of tenth-century Spain was a Jew named Chisdai ibn Shaprut. He was merely the best known of the flourishing Jewish community in the caliphate, which was encouraged and appreciated by the Arabic authorities. Shaprut might well have been a model for the Renaissance rather than the Dark Ages. As a physician, he had traveled to Navarre and had cured the grotesquely fat, deposed king there of his obesity and restored him to power. He had been instrumental in requesting from the emperor of Byzantium the Greek text of Dioscorides' *Materia Medica,* the most important pharmacological reference of the Middle Ages—six hundred plants were drawn and described in it—so that it could be translated into Arabic. As a counselor to two caliphs, he had successfully conducted the delicate negotiations with the emissary of Otto I in 962 A.D., turning aside the demand to evacuate the Islamic pirates' nest at Le Freinet. And as a rabbi, liberated and valued under the Moorish rulers, he advanced Jewish studies, undertaking a spiritual and intellectual quest to locate the lost tribes of Israel somewhere in the Crimea.

"Can you tell me," he wrote longingly to the king of the Khazars, "whether there is among you any knowledge concerning the final redemption which we have been awaiting so many years, whilst we went from one captivity to another, from one exile to another. How strong is the hope of him who awaits the realization of these events!"

In the tenth century this extraordinary culture bloomed into full flower under the caliphates of Abd al Rahman III and his son Al Hakkam II. Abd al Rahman III came to power in 912 A.D. at the age of twenty-one and reigned for fifty years. He was a stocky but graceful man, with a fair complexion and blond hair (which he dyed black), the result of his mother's genes, no doubt, for she had been a French slave. Abd al Rahman had inherited a state in disarray where rebellious chiefs throughout the country had scoffed at the weak central authority and where the prosperity of the people had disappeared amid the petty fighting between warring minor potentates. For nineteen years the new sultan fought across the breadth of Spain to consolidate his kingdom. One by one, he subdued the cities of Andalusia. Tribe by tribe, he tamed the unruly Berbers. In 929 A.D. in an important symbolic act, Abd al Rahman III became the first of the Spanish sultans to take the title caliph, an honor hitherto reserved for those who ruled over the holy cities of Mecca and Medina. Now the Spanish caliph accepted the holy duty as the "Defender of the Faith of God." Within the world of Islam, Córdoba was placed on an equal footing with Baghdad.

But the caliph's vision for Córdoba went beyond the mere consolidation of power and his own personal aggrandizement. He had a grand vision for a heavenly city, inspired by the description in the Koran of the imaginary place called Iram, the city of emerald columns and rivers of gold that had taken five hundred years to build and whose sultans had scoured the world for the finest tapestries, lamps, and golden utensils. In 936 A.D. construction began on a separate royal city just outside Córdoba, which the caliph named after his favorite wife, Ez Zahrâ, the Fairest. Over the next twenty-five years of his reign, the resources of the land were harnessed to this grand design: one-third of the state's revenues were expended on the endeavor. Ten thousand laborers toiled, cutting and polishing six thousand blocks of stone daily. When the city was completed in the reign of his son, Al Hakkam II, it was said to have nearly thirty thousand people, including more than six thousand concubines and their families, three thousand slaves and eunuchs, and twelve thousand attendants.

Situated at the base of a mountain known as the Hill of the Bride, the city contained palaces that surpassed even those of Constantinople and Baghdad. The mosque had a roof of gold, supported by walls of translucent marble. Extraordinary Byzantine mosaics and Moorish peristyles graced the Hall of the Caliph. Inside, surrounded by delicate filigree work, arches of ivory and ebony, and lamps of crystal, a circular fountain filled with mercury sparkled the light across the magnificent ceiling. In the throne, the caliph sat on a raised divan, surrounded by pillows, beneath the signature horseshoe design of red and white wedges.

When Al Hakkam II came to the throne in 961 A.D., the emphasis shifted to high learning, since this mild-mannered, cosmopolitan ruler preferred the company of his scholars and poets to that of his soldiers. Under him the library was established, and Jewish biblio-philes were dispatched across Europe to search for worthy volumes to add to the national collection.

"Córdoba is the Bride of Andalusia," wrote one citizen of the time about his beloved city. "To her belong all the beauties which delight the eye. Her necklace is strung with the pearls. Her poets gathered from the ocean of language. Her garment is made from the banners of learning, embroidered by the masters of every art known to man-kind."

FOR THE FIFTEEN YEARS OF HIS REIGN, Al Hakkam II was under the spell of his exceptional and beautiful wife, Subh. She was Basque, born into slavery and raised a Christian; she converted to Islam when she was brought to Córdoba. As a *belleza capturada*—the Moorish caliphs seemed to prefer Basque, Frankish, and Galician women to their own—she was sold to the harem. There she was given the name Aurora, or the Dawn.

That the caliph's consort was originally a Christian slave was un-remarkable, for within the caliphate of the tenth century there ex-isted a complicated and fascinating relationship between masters and slaves. Slaves were more prized when they were well educated, and they made up a powerful bloc within the royal palace. Among the gentry, generally, they were central to the life of the household. Many are the stories of slaves dominating the life of a family, and many a heart was broken by a slave who rejected the overtures of the master. The "free women," who bore the heavy burden of protecting a family's honor, were veiled and sequestered behind the mansion walls, whereas the slave girls were free to sing and play the lute and recite poetry, not to mention to flirt openly with their masters. In a society where Platonic love was idealized and where the lovers exchanged locks of hair, perfumed with ambergris and rosewater, to serve as a souvenir when they separated, an air of gamesmanship hovered over the master-slave relationship. Falling in love with a beautiful and passionate slave was a common occurrence, just as common as was the unhappy ending of an elegant lover being spurned by his slave. But in his doldrums, the forlorn lover might have an old chewed toothpick as a reminder of past love . . . and even a poem to go with it:

> Her spittle, as I verily
> Believe, is Life's own fount to me,
> Yet she destroys my heart entire
> In flames of passionate desire.

Among the slave girl's most envied privileges was her ability to move freely about the town. A famous story is told of a well-known poet who is strolling purposefully and piously toward the mosque when, near the Gate of the Perfumers, he spies a lovely girl who captures his heart instantly. He follows her a long way, across the bridge and far into al Rabad before she turns on him and demands, "Why are you walking behind me!"

He declares his fascination for her, but she is sharp in her reply: "Stop this talk immediately! You will expose me to shame. You have no prospect whatever of achieving your purpose."

"I am satisfied merely to look at you," the poet exclaims.

"That is permitted," she softens.

"My lady, are you a free woman or a slave?" he asks.

"I am a slave," she replies.

"And to whom do you belong?"

"By Allah, you are more likely to learn what inhabits the Seventh Heaven than the answer to that question," she says.

"Where may I see you again?" he asks.

"Where you saw me today, at the same hour, every Friday," she replies.

For many Fridays thereafter the poet goes to the gate at the same hour, but the slave girl never appears again . . . perhaps because she is not a slave at all, but a "free woman" disguised as a slave only so that for one brief afternoon, hoping she would not get caught, she could taste the freedom of the streets.

Subh, then, was a slave with high ambitions. She combined the most sought-after qualities of the concubine: the lustiness of the Casbah, the gentle piety of Mecca, and the education of Baghdad. To rise to the top, however, she would need ministerial discretion and magisterial wisdom. For her beauty and her energy that was almost masculine, Subh stood out among the others. And when she showed her fertility by giving the aging caliph two sons, she became the first among all others. During the last twelve years of Al Hakkam II's reign, he never made an important decision without consulting her.

If Al Hakkam II loved the cultural life of his palace, it was largely because of Subh. He doted on her, and he hated the hardships of the battlefield; once, when he was forced reluctantly into a tour of his kingdom, he wrote his farewell to her in verse:

From thy sweet eyes, in that sad hour of parting

There fell hot tears: they bathed thy cheek,

And lay upon thy loveliest neck, a circle

Of pearls beyond all price

I know not how it chanced that the fierce flame

Of that atrocious grief consumed me not.

Maddening I asked, "Where is my light of life?

My heart's sole treasure, where?" yet there in truth

There didst thou lurk! aye, in my heart of hearts,

Where thou art ever; Pole-star of my life.

Soul of my soul! mine own! mine own Subh.

As genuinely touching and sincere as were these sentiments, the old caliph had other romantic interests, primarily an erotic interest in young boys. In his historical reputation, he is remembered as much for his pederasty as for his library.

In the waning years of Al Hakkam's reign, he grew increasingly anxious about succession. His eldest son had died mysteriously, leaving only the small boy Al Hishâm, known as the Assisted One, Protected by God. The child would not reach the age of maturity until 982 A.D., many years off. Not surprisingly, the palace was rife with intrigue. Several eunuchs in the inner circle, one the Keeper of the Wardrobe, the other the Grand Falconer, exercised considerable influence, for they not only shared the intimacy of the caliph's bedchamber, but they also controlled the caliph's personal guard. These guardians in turn controlled a group of more than a thousand eunuchs who formed the backbone of the palace staff.

Outside the palace, these beardless men were resented, for they were arrogant and cruel toward the local population. To these complaints, the caliph turned a blind eye. "These men are the guardians of my harem," he would say. "They have my full confidence, and I cannot be forever reprimanding them." Should the aging sultan die before his son reached the age of responsibility, the eunuchs would not countenance a regency, for there was no precedent for such a thing in Umayyad tradition.

Beside this inner circle, there was a triumvirate of important advisers. The vizier or prime minister was named Musafy. The son of a Berber and a poet, he controlled the administration. This made him the most powerful man in Córdoba. Then there was Ghâlib, the acclaimed general, who had won great victories in North Africa and squandered a great fortune in the process. He returned from Africa, chastened but triumphant, in September of 974 A.D.

And finally, there was the one who would later be called Al Mansor.

His name was Ibn Abi Amir. His roots were in a minor noble family of Arabian extraction which had come to Spain in Tarik's army and had maintained its station, as one chronicler put it, as nobility of the gown, not of the sword. From his earliest days, his ambition, his initiative, and his single-mindedness were extraordinary. After a university training in the classics, with a fondness for stories about poor outcasts who rose to great positions of power, he set up an office outside the palace gate. There he transcribed legal documents for the laymen and the illiterate, all the while plotting how to get inside the walls. As he was gifted and cunning, so he was handsome and suave. He used these attributes shamelessly to ingratiate himself to the ladies of the harem, where the sublime arts of poetry and calligraphy were interspersed with gossip and court intrigue and the study of the Koran.

Once he was introduced to Subh, his career was launched. He pampered and flattered her, lavishing her with gifts, including a silver model of the royal palace. The sultana, in turn, leaned on her husband to promote Ibn Abi Amir rapidly upward, into posts where the young upstart had his hands on the purse strings. From steward of her children's property to master of the mint (where he put his face on Moorish coins) to the comptroller-general of finance in North Africa with a mandate to control General Ghâlib's excesses, Ibn Abi Amir handled his missions brilliantly. He controlled the generals without alienating them; he dispensed gifts generously to those he wanted in his debt; and most of all, he wooed the sultan and the sultana indefatigably.

"I cannot conceive how this young man gains the hearts of the ladies of my harem," the caliph told his wife on one occasion. "I lavish on them everything they can desire, and yet no gift that does not come from him is to their liking. I scarcely know whether to regard him as an extremely clever servant, or as a potent magician. But I am never quite easy in my mind about the public money which passes through his hands."

By the age of thirty-one, Ibn Abi Amir held six lucrative posts at once. In the elegant barrio of Rosafa, he built a luxurious manor, made of marble imported from the valley of the Euphrates. At this seignorial hacienda, he entertained poets and generals, powerful counselors and scholars, pressing expensive gifts on them made of gold or silver. One of his most famous gifts was a magnificent bridle studded in jewels. Whenever an important personage found himself in distress, Ibn Abi Amir was always there to help. His reputation for generosity became legendary.

In 975 A.D. Al Hakkam II grew ill. This intensified the power struggle in the palace. Musafy remained in control of the administration, and Ghâlib was in control of the army. But Ibn Abi Amir had added the palace guard and the city police to his list of posts. And he had something else of value, it seemed. The sultana had become his mistress. Still, so long as the caliph lived, the eunuchs remained in charge of the sickbed.

In his delirium the caliph was given to high anxiety over his successor, worrying not only about the fate of his son, but also about the future of the Umayyad dynasty. It was prophesied that if his successor strayed from the direct line, the dynasty was finished. To make matters worse, the Christian enclaves in northwest Spain were taking advantage by attacking Muslim outposts.

On February 5, 976 A.D., sensing the end, the caliph called his counselors together and made them swear allegiance to his ten-year-old son as the next caliph. Musafy was charged with carrying out the transition, and Ibn Abi Amir was made his chamberlain. His affairs thus in order, Al Hakkam II died a few months later.

Immediately, the palace eunuchs plotted to cast the child-emir aside and offer the throne instead to his uncle, Mughira, on the condition that he name the Protected One as his successor. Mughira was an attractive alternative. Twenty-seven years old, gentle and learned, he could be easily sold to the people as an upright transitional figure. The conspirators approached Musafy with their plan, and he humored them, seeming to approve. But once the eunuchs were out of sight, the prime minister convened a council of state. It settled on an extreme measure: Mughira was too attractive. He would have to be eliminated, with extreme prejudice. The generals and the police were horrified at the notion of ruthless murder of this innocent royal personage, and they balked. Ibn Abi Amir stepped forward.

"Our policy cannot fail," he exclaimed. "We must support our leader. His orders must be obeyed. Since none of you has the courage to carry the matter through, I will undertake it myself." And he rode off to Mughira's palace with one hundred men.

Mughira appreciated his danger at once. He cowered before this awful messenger, as Ibn Abi Amir explained the necessity for the regency to go forward. "But the viziers fear that this plan may not meet with your approval, and they have sent me to inquire about the matter." His tone was measured and cold, weighted with sinister meaning.

"Words fail me to tell thee how much my brother's death grieves me," Mughira sputtered. "But I rejoice to hear that my nephew has succeeded him. May his reign be long and prosperous. Please inform those who have sent you that I will obey them in all things. I shall keep the oath of allegiance to Hishâm which I have already taken."

At this Ibn Abi Amir softened. Perhaps they had overreacted. Could not there be some accommodation? In a message to Córdoba, he announced that Mughira had expressed no objection to the succession of the boy and was fully in agreement with their goals. In short order, a ferocious answer came back from Musafy. "Your scruples will ruin all, and I begin to suspect you of playing us false. Do your duty or we will find another." With that, Mughira was strangled. Ibn Abi Amir took no pleasure in the awful deed. Instead, he vowed revenge on his superior for forcing him into so odious and unnecessary an act.

Festive days followed. The boy-caliph was paraded joyously through the streets of Córdoba, as Ibn Abi Amir rode, beaming, beside him. Toward his rival Musafy, Ibn Abi Amir presented a courteous and even deferential face, displaying no displeasure or awkwardness. With Mughira eliminated, loose ends needed to be tied up, and that would take time. The eunuchs were soon driven from the palace. But Christians from the north represented a more serious threat, for they had continued to press their advantage during this period of disarray in the caliphate. In the late fall of 976 A.D., they were threatening the very walls of Córdoba itself. Subh was terrified, and she implored her ministers to do something about the threat. This time, Musafy lost his nerve. Once again Ibn Abi Amir stepped forward to do the hatchet work. "I will lead the troops," he said brazenly, "on the condition that I select them myself and that I am accorded a subsidy of a hundred thousand pieces of gold." At this enormous price there were grumbles. "Very well, take two hundred thousand and command the army yourself—if you dare," Ibn Abi Amir taunted. He got his command.

In February 977 A.D., this parvenu crossed the eastern border, attacked the Christians at Los Baños, and proceeded to Saragosa. What he lacked in military training, he made up for in bluster. To his cheering troops, he invested this first campaign with histrionic significance. Their effort was merely the first skirmish in the Holy War on Christianity, the jihad. From now on, war against the Christians would be perpetual. They would not cease until every Christian had been killed or driven from the Iberian peninsula. His commanders should be ready to make two incursions into Christian territory every year.

This hot, passionate rhetoric departed dramatically from recent history. The campaigns early in the reign of Abd al Rahman III had been straightforward conflicts over territory between secular authorities. Since then, there had been peace between Christian and Moorish Spain for nearly fifty years. An air of tolerance allowed both sections to prosper. Now the clarion call to jihad changed everything. Its shrill sound was as different as it was popular.

For Ibn Abi Amir, the significance of this first incursion was more political than military. His quest for power had a breathtaking single-mindedness about it. In April he was returning to Córdoba as a great war hero, the savior of Córdoba and Islam, the favorite of his troops, and he meant to make the most of it by September. He had renewed the old tradition of a great feast for his troops after victory, where he handed out gifts and medals and then distributed the gold of his government subsidy throughout his army. Before his columns, several thousand prisoners were driven. Behind came the bursting wagonloads of plunder. The victor accepted the adoration of the people and the embraces of the sultana and plotted to supplant his rival Musafy. The following year he marched north to Galicia, this time with a more formidable army, fortified with a Berber cavalry and flying the banners of Andalusia and Mérida.

Upon his triumphal return from the second incursion, he took a new title and a new name. He was now Al Mansor, the Illustrious Victor, Defender of the Muslim People, Protected by God. Before the year was out, Musafy was in prison, his property confiscated, his family name disgraced. In prison he wrote doleful poetry, railing at "the fox," who had disgraced him. How fickle was fortune. Lions had once been in fear of him, but now he trembled before a fox.

"Aghh! how shameful is it," he moaned, "that a man of worth should be driven to sue for pity to a peasant!"

For five years he languished in the tower, sick and pathetic, until the Illustrious Victor had him strangled.

IN HIS STRUGGLE TO DEPOSE MUSAFY, Al Mansor had allied himself with the third member of the Andalusian triumvirate, the formidable general of the army, Ghâlib. At a critical juncture in the power struggle, Musafy, in an effort to shore up his desperate position, had proposed that Ghâlib's lovely and cultured daughter Asma be given in marriage to his son. To this Ghâlib had readily agreed, but when Al Mansor heard of the proposed match, he shot off a long, plaintive letter, warning the general that Musafy's marriage proposal was a sham and a trap and putting *himself* forward as Asma's prospective groom. Ghâlib saw this as a better deal, and a new marriage contract was promptly drawn up.

Under Islamic law a man could have four legal wives, and Al Mansor was to stretch the limit, eventually taking two Christian wives of his enemies, the kings of Navarre and León. But this first match, though conceived in political expediency, was his best. Genuine affection grew between them. Not that marriage undercut his special relationship with the sultana, Subh. That affair continued apace (just as Subh kept a second lover, the mayor of Córdoba). The affair with Al Mansor, however, was the butt of street lampoons. "The end of the world draweth nigh!" the street urchins sang. "Destruction impendeth, for abominations are rife! The Caliph plays in school, while a brace of lovers share his teeming den."

Not surprisingly, these jokes did not amuse Ibn Abi Amir. Nor did he appreciate, vain as he was of his splendid physique, that he was occasionally called a hunchback in the streets or, worse, "the fox," that dastardly label that Musafy had affixed to him. Once a slave girl, thinking she was amusing the hajib, made the mistake of auditioning her voice with one of these amusements and was strung up for it. Nor, by this time, did it pay to offer any criticism of Al Mansor's policy. One official of the treasury said loosely that the "expeditions of the Hajib, far from being as glorious as his friends would have them, are of little value to the state. All we obtain from our outlay is the loss of our soldiers and horses. Our good king, Al Hakkam, understood much better the duties of a ruler." For that, the official was deprived of his property and found himself in the tower.

With Musafy dead, Al Mansor turned his attention to his father-in-law. It had become nearly as dangerous to be Al Mansor's friend as his enemy, for in his passion for power he had evolved an interesting technique of allying himself with a rival in order to supplant others, raising his "friend's" stature until he had outlived his usefulness, and then killing him. Since Ghâlib's position was based in the army rather than the court, however, he was a more formidable adversary. After his glorious victories in Africa and across Spain, the general swaggered about with two curved swords strapped to his belt. He was an idol to his troops.

To combat this, Al Mansor set out to change the very nature of the army itself. He began to recruit foreign mercenaries by the thousands, offering high pay and lavish benefits. The Berbers from Mauritania streamed across the strait. They came dressed in rags and rode sorry nags. "But in a little while," wrote a scribe, "they were to be seen clad in the richest attire, gallivanting through the streets on high-spirited chargers. Never could they have beheld, even in their dreams, such splendid mansions as these in which they now lodged."

His other source of soldiers was, ironically, Christian Spain. From León, Navarre, and Castile, the very lands against which he had launched his jihad, he recruited disgruntled soldiers. Once these traitors came to the caliphate, he coddled them and ensured that their religious practices were respected, just as he mobilized them to expunge Christianity from Spain altogether. Their allegiance was to Al Mansor alone.

In the short term, this was a cunning strategy. It helped Al Mansor in his power struggle with Ghâlib, and his newfound power gave him the upper hand. But the long-range consequences were profound. With his powerful personality, only Al Mansor could control the Berbers. The influx of Christians into the caliphate and into the army undermined the ethnic and cultural identity of the state. The Arabic tradition of tribal loyalty was diluted when the regiments ceased to be named after tribes as these foreigners were assimilated. What about the time when he was gone?

Ghâlib, of course, understood Al Mansor's game very well, but he was scarcely powerless. He put himself forward as the protector of Arab traditions, of the youthful caliph, of the caliphate itself. Nor was he above expediency: he allied himself with the Christian king of León.

In 981 A.D. this struggle of titans came to a head. In a place called Torrevicente the factions clashed in mortal combat. For a time, Ghâlib seemed to have the upper hand and appeared to be on the verge of a rout. But in an unlucky charge, his horse lurched, his head hit against the saddle's pommel, and he fell to the ground mortally injured. Seeing their champion thus incapacitated, his soldiers fled the battlefield. No doubt with Al Mansor's approval, Ghâlib's head was severed and transported to Córdoba, where it was presented to the general's daughter, Al Mansor's wife. According to Moorish lore, she did not flinch or evince any sadness, for in the tradition of that culture, her first loyalty was to her husband.

With Musafy and Ghâlib gone, Al Mansor stood unchallenged as El Señor de al-Andalus, the supreme leader of the caliphate, the master of Spain. And yet he was sensitive to the point of paranoia about the illegitimate nature of his rule. The Illustrious Victor on the battlefield was also the hajib of the court, and yet there was no rest for him. He had to win greater and ever greater victories on the battlefield, lest idleness in the army breed new rivals. No doubt he had kept in mind a conversation he had had with one of his commanders.

"How many true and valiant cavaliers do you account us to have in our host?" Al Mansor had asked ebulliently.

"You know the number well, sire," the general had replied.

"Do you believe them to be a thousand?" Al Mansor prodded.

"Not so many, sire," the commander replied.

"Are there five hundred?" asked the hajib.

"Not yet five hundred," the general replied.

"Do you count them at a hundred—or perhaps fifty?" Al Mansor said with increasing annoyance.

"Not as many."

"How few, then, do you esteem them to be?"

"I could not be sure of more than three," the general replied.

From that time forward, he redoubled his vigilance against any dissension or indiscipline within his own ranks. This could result in the cruelest measures. Once at a muster of his legions, he noticed the glint of an unsheathed sword and instantly had the offender dragged before him.

"How dare you draw your sword before the command is given!" Al Mansor fumed.

"I only wished to show it to a comrade," the soldier stammered. "I did not mean to draw it from its scabbard. It slipped out by accident."

"Lame excuse!" exclaimed Al Mansor. And then, turning to his lieutenant, he shouted, "Let this man's head be struck off with his own sword, and let his body be taken along the ranks as a lesson in discipline!"

Within the court, subtler measures were required. There he had to create perpetual tension and crisis, lest comfort among the cavaliers encourage fresh adventures.

In succeeding years, he went to war every summer, and every winter he built ever greater monuments to glorify his rule. The original mosque of Córdoba had been built by the immigrant caliph from Damascus in the eighth century and had been extended twice by subsequent caliphs: Al Mansor doubled its size. To accomplish this gargantuan task, he had to appropriate the tightly bunched houses that crowded around the mosque. One by one, he called the house owners into his presence:

"My friend, I intend to enlarge the mosque, that sacred shrine where we address our prayers to heaven, and I wish to purchase your house for the good of the Muslim community. Our treasury overflows with riches, thanks to the booty which I have seized from the unbelievers. Tell me then the value you set upon your property. Don't be shy. Boldly name your price!"

Whereupon the property owner would name what he thought to be an outrageous price.

"That is far too little!" Al Mansor bellowed. "Your modesty is excessive. Come, come, I will give you twice as much!"

When he had the land he needed, Christian slaves, in ankle irons, cleared it to make room for the greater glory of Allah. From time to time, well advertised in advance, Al Mansor appeared at the work site, took up a pickaxe, and toiled briefly beside the slaves. When his extension was complete, this Fortress of the Faith was a wonder of the world. Beneath its gabled roofs and minarets, its magnificent gate was embroidered in intricately woven leaf and floral designs, for the Koran forbids the representation of the human form. Past the purification court, one entered the glorious space of the vast prayer hall. There a forest of columns supported the distinctive red and white horseshoe arches which had become the symbol of Moorish culture. In this place of light and color, shape and mystery, the worshipers were drawn toward the holy core, the Macsura, where the *kibla* wall faced Mecca.

Buildings alone, however, did not satisfy him. Since the Great Caliph Abd al Rahman III had built the magnificent city of Medina Al Zahrâ outside of Córdoba and made it the throne of royalty and the seat of the administration, Al Mansor set out to build a totally separate city in honor of himself on the other side of town. There he moved the administration, thereby removing the presence of generals and politicians and troublemakers from the vicinity of the boy-caliph. For a name he deliberately chose a sound so close to Al Zahrâ that they were easily confused: Al Zahira.

His new city was built in two years. When the administration came, the tradesmen followed, and before long the tentacles of the new town reached the outskirts of Córdoba. Al Zahira was his political masterstroke and the pride of his life. His city was magnificent, and yet in time it instilled in him an anxiety, as if there were something ephemeral about his creation.

"Unfortunate Al Zahira," he mused one day. "Would that I knew who it is who will soon destroy thee."

At this dark brooding, his councilor expressed astonishment. "You yourself will witness the catastrophe," Al Mansor continued. "I see this fair palace sacked and in ruins, and I see the fire of civil war devouring my country."

Al Zahira was costly, both in gold and in historical destiny. His last rival, as Al Mansor saw it, was the child-caliph himself, Al Hishâm. The child had become an adolescent and would soon be a man. And once he was a man, his mother might want him to act like one. By 983 A.D. he was seventeen, already the age of discretion. For seven years, he had been pampered and cloistered, his mind softened with scholarship, his spirit with piety, and his body emasculated with every conceivable carnal pleasure. In the harem he was molded to be weak and effeminate; in this training, Al Mansor and his mother, Subh, were conscious co-conspirators. No one could see the boy without the permission of his wards and jailers. He seldom left Al Zahrâ, except on high holy days when he was surrounded and out of view in the Macsura, hooded like all the others in his entourage. He did not leave the mosque until it was empty of the other worshipers. With the administration moved to the other side of town, the caliph lived in hedonistic isolation. The only proof of his existence was his image on the coin of his realm.

If the caliph was weakened, so was the caliphate. The royal office was transformed into a place of remote hubris, of flowers, of dark light flickering off mercury, of lovely formal gardens. Al Zahrâ was a museum, with the caliph as its most prized *objet d'art*. Meanwhile, the cult of Al Mansor brought the caliphate to its pinnacle of power. But what would happen after him?

In his new palace, Al Mansor paraded himself as the impresario of high Moorish culture. His poets were a fixture of the court, where they competed with one another in spontaneous wit, in eloquence, in hyperbole about the ruler's most admirable qualities. Their highest challenge was to compose a *casida* whose verses, sometimes more than a hundred in number, had to conform to strict rules of form and rhythm. When the Illustrious One liked the verse, he showed his pleasure with gold doubloons. Not only the literary men but others wrote poetry. Once, as winter receded, a general sent roses together with a fawning poem. How could he send roses when the bite was still in the air . . . because "the power of the Great Al Mansor turns all our life to Spring!"

Such sonorous flattery was pleasing to the hajib, but beware the critical poet, for Al Mansor appreciated the concept of poetic justice as well. Once when a talented poet was found to be part of a conspiracy against the young caliph, Al Mansor condemned him to perpetual silence in the streets of Córdoba, where the punishment for speaking to him was severe.

Meanwhile, the hajib promoted education. On his frequent visits to the colleges and secondary schools, he sat himself attentively among the students and listened to the lectures. At term's end, he personally handed out the academic prizes, not only to the students but to the teachers as well. In his new palace, he established a scholarly academy where men of learning came together to debate. This laudable activity had an ulterior motive, of course. On the one hand, he wanted to identify the most brilliant students and the best minds and to recruit them into his service. On the other hand, he listened keenly for any hint of dissent or disapproval among the intellectuals.

The law and the mosque and the universities were the natural breeding grounds for trouble. By his past indifference to religion, his Holy War notwithstanding, he was open to criticism from the imams, who made up a powerful lobby in the capital. He would now show, by deed as well as word, that he was more pure in his faith than the purest, that he was the most zealous in its defense.

With fury, he turned on the new theories that were sweeping through the Islamic world from Baghdad to Cairo to Seville. Embraced by the learned classes, this new wave was Mu'tazilism. Its doctrine rejected predestination, asserted the primacy of reason, and argued that the Koran was not received directly from God, but created by inspired men. This notion of free will—that the acts of men were not determined by God—was dangerous and much feared among the puritans and fundamentalists of the established order.

For strictly political reasons, Al Mansor tried to root out this heresy with one of the most horrendous acts of his reign. Summoning several of the most orthodox imams, he commissioned them to examine critically the catalogue of books in Al Hakkam II's great library. In particular, works of philosophy and science were targeted as forbidden, especially those dealing with astronomy (although this did not prevent Al Mansor from ordering a horoscope upon the birth of his children). Once identified, these books, about one-tenth of the entire repository, were ceremoniously thrown into the streets and burned. In this witch-hunt, many intellectuals were silenced and expelled. Among the victims was Abd er Rahman Ben Ismail, a Jewish mathematician widely known as the Euclid of Spain.

After his crackdown, Al Mansor was often seen at the mosque, listening sanctimoniously to the long and tedious sermons of clerics. He ostentatiously carried a copy of the Koran on his military campaigns and made a display of transcribing portions of it in his own hand during idle moments.

Between his harsh measures and these public displays of personal piety, he became *el grand creyente,* the great believer.

THROUGH THE DECADE OF THE 980S, Al Mansor rode out of Córdoba every spring on his black stallion, resplendent in his flowing robe and golden sombrero, ever passionate in his perpetual war against Christianity. His first stop was often Gormaz, the mighty fortress atop a high butte which commanded a vista some forty miles in every direction in the upper Douro River valley. Gormaz was the largest fortress in western Europe, some four hundred yards in length, and the tabby walls on its western facade were considered magical. This daunting place was Al Mansor's staging area for his northern raids. From here, he would follow various routes north, along which an elaborate system of watchtowers had been constructed by the brilliant Moorish military engineers.

León, that formidable citadel to the north, drew his special attention, since the king of León had aided Ghâlib in his revolt and must now pay for his treachery. With its massive towers, its twenty-foot-thick Roman walls, and its impertinent king, the city seemed to taunt Al Mansor. In its literature, it saw Al Mansor and the entire Córdoban culture as alien, not simply the intrusion of Africa onto the Iberian peninsula but the intrusion of the lower depths. In contemporaneous illuminated manuscripts of León, the Whore of Babylon was depicted as seated on a divan of stacked cushions, and the Feast of Belshazzar in the Book of Daniel takes place beneath a horseshoe arch of alternating red and white wedges, the design so distinctive of the great mosque of Córdoba. So the profanity of Belshazzar was associated with the pronouncements of the Muslim leaders. In the illuminations of Beatus of Liebana's commentary on the Apocalypse, Córdoba was portrayed as the evil symbol of both wealth and heathenism, next to the text for Revelation 18:

"Mourn, mourn for this great city; for all the linen and purple and scarlet that you wore, for all your finery of gold and jewels and pearls; your huge riches are all destroyed within a single hour."

For Al Mansor this slander was a red cape before an angry bull. Livid and bent on destruction, he camped his troops on the banks of the Estola River south of the city. But the Christians fell upon them in a peremptory strike, and the bewildered Moors scattered in disarray. At a critical point, with defeat near and his own personal ruin as a certain antidote, Al Mansor threw his golden sombrero to the ground and squatted down in despair. The pathetic sight of their despondent ruler rallied the Moors. They regrouped and pressed the Christians back into their fortress. But despite the mayhem, León held.

Four years later, Al Mansor returned to subdue León once and for all. This time he came with a larger army, and the Christian rulers promptly lost their nerve. Before the enemy arrived, they exhumed the bones of their ancestors and transported them north across the mountains to Oviedo where the remains were reburied in the cathedral there. This defeatism soon got its due, as the wall was breached and Al Mansor himself rushed through the opening with a banner in one hand and a sword in the other. The place was sacked and left as a pathetic pile of rocks among half-torn-down towers and one marble gate, facing the Big Dipper, as a stern reminder to any nonbeliever who might defy the Defender of Islam.

These attacks on León were punctuated with a campaign against Barcelona in 985 A.D. Before Al Mansor, in the halcyon days of accommodation between Moorish and Christian Spain, the caliphs had stayed away from Catalonia, regarding it as the province of the kings of France and fearing that a Muslim incursion would draw Christian armies over the Pyrenees. Moreover, the powerful and popular Count Borrell, the patron of the future pope Gerbert, ruled the city. (To call the Barcelona of the time a city is an overstatement. The walk traversing the center from wall to wall was about four hundred yards.) But Al Mansor brushed the concerns of his craven predecessors aside. The Carolingian dynasty of France, he knew, was on its last legs and incapable of foreign adventure. Besides, this was jihad. His ambition was no less than to expunge Christianity from the entire Iberian peninsula.

On the thirteenth day of the moon, *dylhagia,* in the Muslim year 377, his columns departed Córdoba and marched east to Murcia, where the viceroy of Tadmir entertained the Illustrious One and the forty poets he had brought with him. There were great feasts and at night a bath of rosewater for the conqueror. Upon his departure after two weeks, Al Mansor showed his gratitude by presenting his host with an exquisitely beautiful slave. In Valencia, Tortosa, and Tarragona, the hajib reinforced his army with fresh troops before he reached the plains west of Barcelona.

Count Borrell met him with a massive army, perhaps twice that of Al Mansor's horde, and armored in the European fashion. But Al Mansor knew that these soldiers, beneath their breastplate and their colorful ornament, were "rude hill people," unaccustomed to disciplined combat on a wide plain, who had been impressed into duty and wished only to survive in the face of the fierce Berbers. As he suspected, Borrell's troops broke at the first engagement. Before long, Borrell himself slipped away in a simple boat under cover of darkness.

As usual, Al Mansor withdrew from the city after it was pillaged and after the slaves were rounded up. His purpose, here and across the northern provinces, was not merely to defeat and to plunder, but to harass, degrade, and dishonor Christians and Christianity. He had no interest in occupying infidel territory. Count Borrell was to return unhindered to the ruins of Barcelona two years later, as Al Mansor was busy humiliating Christians far to the west in León.

Barcelona was the hajib's twenty-third drubbing of the Christian north in just nine years. By no means had he tired of his jihad—there would be twenty-nine more campaigns before his demise. But he was prepared at any moment for a hero's death. On all his campaigns he carried his coffin with him. After each battle, he returned to his tent for a personal ritual: he had the dust shaken from his battle clothes and carefully gathered. These treasured granules were placed in a decorative vase which was guarded as sacred. The dust was to be scattered on his casket if he should be killed. To Al Mansor this holy dust would serve him well at Judgment Day, for it was written in the Koran that "God will save from the fires of Hell him whose feet are covered with the dust of His Highway." In addition, his burial clothes, sewn and stitched lovingly by his daughters from the cloth of his native region, were always pressed and ready in his trunk.

If one eye was on the horizon, looking toward the next battlefield and the next triumph, the other eye never strayed from the domestic front. The hot pots of rebellion bubbled all around him, and he could never be sure when one might spout into a geyser. No sooner had he returned in triumph from León than he discovered his eldest son, Abdallah, in a conspiracy with his best field commander, a general known as the Flint-Heart. This was a serious matter. The son was twenty-two years old, dashing, headstrong, and bitterly resentful of his father's inattention. That was family business, almost to be expected. But Flint-Heart had been rewarded with the governorship of Toledo. That was different.

It would take Al Mansor several years of careful maneuvers to undermine this plot. For his erstwhile commander he fell back on the tried-and-true charges of financial malfeasance and personal corruption. In time, Flint-Heart fled into the arms of the king of Castile. This generosity brought Al Mansor's armies to the gates of Osma. Eventually, the general was handed over. Al Mansor paraded him through the streets of Córdoba on a camel, chained and ragged, preceded by a herald who barked: "Behold the Flint-Heart who forsook Islam to join the enemies of the faith!" After the plot was snuffed out, poor Abdallah was summoned one night by Al Mansor, but he was waylaid on the road and murdered. Al Mansor had never loved him. He even had doubts about the young man's true paternity.

In 991 A.D., fifty-four years old and increasingly interested in his immortality, Al Mansor turned his title of hajib over to his younger, more compliant, less flamboyant son Abd al Malik. For himself he invented the new and stately title of "noble king." This was meant to be close in eminence to "caliph," but not in lieu of it. At yet another turn, Al Mansor was destroying Moorish tradition.

Meanwhile, as if fate were simply playing out the inevitable, Al Mansor and Subh came into conflict. The sultana's son Al Hishâm was now in the prime of his life. Dissipated though he was, the marionette was now suddenly supposed to undergo a miraculous metamorphosis into a bold prince. Subh looked at her son and saw that it was too late. In this wan creature she divined her own fatal handiwork. And so she turned on her co-conspirator. Her love for Al Mansor was transformed to hate. Abandoned and ignored, she saw that she had only been his instrument to gain power. She began to doubt whether he had ever loved her, and felt like so many other aging castoffs of the harem. With bitterness she was reminded of the old Moorish saying "Women are like aromatic herbs . . . if not well tended, they lose their fragrance." How much she had risked! The scandal, the damage to her son and the caliphate itself! She saw it all in a flash.

With all her cunning, she set out to crush Al Mansor. First, she soured Al Hishâm's relationship with his surrogate father, and cross words began to pass between them. Meanwhile, the message spread through the harem and through the land that the caliph was ready to step forward but Al Mansor stood in the way. Gossip was not sufficient, however. The sultana had only one real source of power, the purse, for the treasury still resided at Al Zahrâ. In Africa there were warriors eager to invade Spain, but they lacked the resources to mobilize an army. Subh conspired to get them the help they needed. She ordered that 80,000 pieces of gold be packed in jars and covered with honey. Then one by one, in the arms of trusted women, these jars of sweet nectar were conveyed to a rendezvous outside the city, from whence they were dispatched south.

Al Mansor found out about this treachery only after the gold was gone, but before it reached its destination. Moving quickly, he informed his council that the woeful caliph, devout and upright as he was, had become so preoccupied with his religious practices that his harem was stealing him blind. To keep the treasury safe from further theft, the remaining six million pieces of gold should be removed to his own city of Al Zahira. This was agreed. When the porters arrived, however, Subh barred the door, stating that the caliph himself forbade the transaction.

This challenge tested the limit of Al Mansor's guile. Through elaborate subterfuge, unbeknown to Subh, he gained access to the caliph alone, and the way was made easy from there. Within minutes the caliph was persuaded to give up this destructive game, as Al Mansor forced Al Hishâm to admit that he was incapable of ruling

Spain, much less of pursuing a religious war against the Christians. A document was produced acknowledging Al Mansor as the sole leader. The caliph dutifully signed it beneath the gaze of the principal cavaliers of the court. This formal declaration was promptly announced to the people with much fanfare, whereupon a parade through the streets of Córdoba took place, with the caliph in his ceremonial headdress riding grandly next to his noble king.

And as they passed into the shadow to the royal palace, the Alcazar, one might have heard the poet whisper:

> Palace of royal state, proud Alcazar:
>
> What rich delights within thy walls are found:
>
> May thy good star preserve thee from all harm!
>
> How many powerful monarchs have thy roofs
>
> Seen pass beneath their splendors. Yet the stars
>
> Now calmly look upon the silent graves
>
> Of kings and heroes who have there abode.
>
> Tell to the world then,—whose admiring eyes
>
> Look on thy seeming steadfastness—that all
>
> Is but deceit. Say, that of earth's delights
>
> Not one hath permanence; and bid all know
>
> That Time holds ever on his measured course.

AS THE MILLENNIUM APPROACHED, it seemed sure that Al Mansor would sweep Christian faith from the Iberian peninsula altogether. On July 3, 997 A.D., the Moor embarked on the cruelest and most notorious of his raids. His target was the very heart of Spanish Christianity. Again, his purpose was not to conquer but to humiliate. At the head of his cavalry, he went northwest across the desiccated, unforgiving plains of the Extremadura, through Mérida, Coria, and Viseu. At Oporto, his army made a rendezvous with his fleet, which had sailed from Alcácer do Sal in southern Portugal. These ships were lashed one to another, stem to stern, to form a bridge across the river Douro. Once the columns crossed over these pontoons, they rode north over the rugged defiles of the Galician coast, past Vigo and over the Sierra of the Cat's Tail, until they arrived at the marshes below the most holy of all Christian shrines in Spain, the city of Santiago de Compostela.

In Christian legend, its sanctity had been discovered only two hundred years before, around the time that Charlemagne suffered his catastrophe at Roncesvalles. A bishop known as El Padron had seen a brilliant light emitting from a distant thicket, in a place called Iria Flavia. After three days of prayer in which he prepared himself for a miracle, the prelate entered the sacred copse to find a shimmering marble tomb. Through inspiration, the bishop divined that this was the final resting place of the apostle St. James. After Christ's crucifixion, the apostles had scattered to the far corners of the earth to preach the gospel, and James had apparently come to Spain in 38 A.D., landing first in Andalusia and then traversing the peninsula in search of souls. Few responded to him, and he returned disconsolate to Palestine, where Herod caught and beheaded him. The body was thrown into the streets outside Jerusalem's walls, and it was gathered up by the faithful and brought to Spain in a granite boat.

When the facts of El Padron's discovery reached Rome, the pope, Leo III, confirmed the verity of the bishop's intuition. For two centuries afterward, pilgrims streamed across the Pyrenees, past Roncesvalles, past the monuments and shelters of Rioja, to León and Oviedo and on to the holy shrine.

Now the Antichrist came to disgrace and destroy this home of the Spanish patron saint. (He would not be the only heathen drawn to this Christian holy place. Only seventeen years before, in 980 A.D., the Vikings had come here with the same purpose, the same motive, the same result.) When the Muslim forces entered the town, they found it deserted, except for a solitary, aging monk who knelt praying before the apostle's shrine.

"What are you doing here?" Al Mansor demanded, peering down, astonished, on the old man.

"I am praying to St. James," the monk replied serenely.

"Pray on!" Al Mansor bellowed, and he set a guard round the tomb, while he systematically went about razing the town. The apostolic church was demolished so efficiently that, as an Arab chronicler put it, "No one would have supposed it ever existed." But before this work began, the handsome iron bells of the church were removed, and after the work was over, they were hoisted on the shoulders of the captives and carried back to Córdoba. There they were transformed into decorative lamps for the courtyard of the new mosque.

Upon the crusaders' return, the great deeds of the Illustrious Victor were proclaimed from the rooftops and the minarets of Spain. The fortresses of the infidels had been destroyed and their churches burned: *Allah, Hu Acbar!* God is the greatest, the most powerful!

But the Christian chroniclers wished to record this history differently.

"As he [Al Mansor] went into the holy place of Santiago," one was to write, "he was frightened by a lightning bolt that nearly struck him. Later, as he and his company were leaving, they were infected with a punishment from God for the obscene sin committed at Santiago. They were visited with diarrhea. Al Mansor and his entire army were consumed and wasted and most died except for a very few."

If so, they revived and multiplied, for each year thereafter the Moorish host was somewhere else rampaging in Christian land as usual. In the year 1000 A.D., however, a new and dynamic Christian king, later called Sancho the Great, had come to power in León, and, through him, the rulers of Navarre, León, and Castile finally gathered in an alliance to oppose the Antichrist. In 1002 A.D. their combined force moved south to block Al Mansor's advance at the arid plain separating northern and southern Spain. At the end of a sluice-like valley, in a tiny fortified village called Calatañazor, the Christian army deployed itself and braced for the onslaught. Arriving with the regularity of the night moth, Al Mansor came with a formidable force of two divisions: one of Berber cavalry, the other of Andalusians. The armies faced one another across the upper reaches of the river Douro. But it might as well have been the river Styx.

Never before had Al Mansor confronted so disciplined and well arrayed an infidel foe. During the night before, he seemed to know that this would be the critical battle of his life. In the morning the armies clashed with terrible fury. The Christians fought like "famished wolves," the chronicler said, the Moors like "raging panthers." Al Mansor himself dashed amid his ironclad warriors and plunged into the thickest of the ardent fight, enraged at the unusual tenacity of the resistance. Only with darkness did the armies break off. Late into the night, Al Mansor waited in his pavilion for his commanders, so they could consider their next steps. But no commanders came. Only then did the Moor realize the extent of his loss. He gave the order to retreat.

By morning, he began to feel the pain of the injuries he himself had sustained in the fight. Dispirited and remote, as if he knew that in his first defeat he would die, he disregarded his wounds, and they became infected. Within a day he was being transported in a litter. At the border town of Medinaceli, fourteen miles from Calatañazor, he died. In that desolate place he was buried, as the dust of his highway over Christianity was reverently sprinkled on his coffin. On his sepulcher the following words were inscribed:

> Such as he shall we not see again
>
> Through all the coming ages. Never more
>
> Shall so great a leader arise. Ever conquering,
>
> Of Ismail's people he increased the empire,
>
> That well he knew to guard. Alas, our father,
>
> Our shelter, and our shield.

The Christian world was more cryptic. "Al Mansor died in 1002," a monk from Burgos wrote. "He was buried in Hell."

Rapidly, the story raced through both Christian and Moorish Spain that a man had been seen on the seashore, dressed like a fisherman, and wandering about proclaiming eerily:

"In Calatañazor Al Mansor lost his drum."

From Córdoba people raced out to find this prophet, but he had disappeared, only to reappear in the mountains, repeating over and over, through his tears:

"In Calatañazor Al Mansor lost his drum."

In the Christian chronicle, the meaning of this apparition was clear. This was the Satan incarnate, lamenting the defeat of the Moors and the mass destruction they would suffer from then on.

And thus, Al Mansor, Hero and Villain, Savior and Antichrist, passed into legend. "The Lord selected the arm of Al Mansor to avenge Islam," wrote one Muslim historian. If so, once avenged, Islam withered away in Spain after him.

CHAPTER SEVEN

Little Sancho and Sancho the Great

IN THE YEAR 1002 A.D. the apotheosis of both the dream and the nightmare of Christianity passed away into the ether of the new millennium. After a passionate, poignant, and brief life, Otto III, the visionary emperor of the Holy Roman Empire, died tragically in Italy. Within months, his collaborator in the Vatican, Gerbert, Pope Sylvester II, was also dead. Meanwhile, in Spain, Al Mansor, Islam's avenger, also went to his final calling, in defeat and in disappointment, and with the good riddance of the Christian north. After him, the fate of the Moorish caliphate, so iridescent as the high culture of Europe, was uncertain.

Toward the end of his life, Al Mansor pondered the

continuation of his family's personal rule and found the prospects bleak. To his heirs the Moor would leave a Córdoba seething with factional strife, a North Africa primed for invasion, a Christian Spain eager to redress the humiliations of the jihad, and a weak, childless caliph whose very weakness was Al Mansor's own doing. After the execution of his eldest son, an execution in which Al Mansor himself had connived, the next in line was Al Malik. He was the son of Al Mansor's Leónese wife, but Al Malik and his mother competed for power and stature with the progeny of a third wife, a son known as Little Sancho. Thus, Al Mansor did not need to look beyond the confines of his own family to see the germs of destruction. By taking multiple wives, he had set up multiple wife-and-son power centers which would compete for the spoils of his tyranny after he was gone. At its core, Al Mansor's rule had been illegitimate. To pass illegitimate rule on to the next generation as if it were a royal birthright involved enormous, and maybe insurmountable, obstacles.

In the last year of his life, Al Mansor took pen to paper and tried to pass on the method of his governance to his successor. His last testament came in the form of a letter to Al Malik, his intended, and it provided instruction for exercising effective rule, for navigating through the political wilderness of Córdoba, for avoiding calamity to their "dynasty." The document began with encouragement to his son. He must be confident and bold. "You know how to be the Señor de Palacio," the father wrote. Above all, his son should guard the money in his mother's possession, for that was the foundation of his power. "If you can solve problems in the capital, that is what you should do," Al Mansor wrote to his son, "but do not forget the aspirations of the Umayyad and their partisans in Córdoba." Above all else, his advice was to respect the legitimacy of the caliph, regardless of Al Hishâm's weakness. For the issue was not about the caliph but about the caliphate. It was easier said than done. Since Al Hishâm had no children, the Umayyad dynasty would end with him unless something was done. After Subh died in December 999 A.D., pretenders to power from various royal bloodlines emerged at every corner, some wishing to use Hishâm for their own purposes, others wishing to replace Hishâm with another, more virile prince of the Umayyads.

"Beware not to manhandle any Marwarid," Al Mansor wrote of

one Córdoban faction, "although you have the power to do so, for I know too well the crime I have committed against them." At this late stage, having virtually destroyed the institution of the caliphate, Al Mansor's contrition seemed a bit empty.

Al Malik was no Al Mansor. The son enjoyed his father's jihad against the Christians and pursued a similar policy without interruption. But beyond the battlefield, he had no talent or taste for the subtle politics of Córdoba, nor did he possess any sophistication in cultural matters. As Señor de Palacio, he was a cad. Eventually, he fell in love with a passionate cheesemonger's daughter, who after his death was passed on to a Berber chief.

On one front, however, he followed his father's advice precisely. He befriended Al Hishâm and invited the caliph to travel (anonymously, through back streets, always cloaked) from his elegant prison at Al Zahrâ for festivities at Al Zahira. Gullible and easily manipulated as he was, the caliph rewarded Al Malik with the grand title of Al Muzaffar, the Victorious.

"The heavens look on you," the caliph's proclamation read, "because of the highest levels in which God is well-disposed to us, because of the preference he shows us, because of the success which he presents us, and with which he honors our kingship, because of the confidence he has placed in all the people, because of the affection which he feels for us, because of the joy which he has left in our rule."

Neither elegant words nor pomp nor foreign adventure could cover up the internal rot. In the first four years of Al Malik's rule, hunger and pestilence visited the caliphate. As Al Malik caroused with his generals, the luminous city of Córdoba began to decay. Even among the devout there was a sense of drift. Strange, heretical sects began to flourish in the capital, to the dismay of the puritans, whom Al Mansor had tried so hard to satisfy. One such cult had an original but rather precarious cosmology. It believed that the earth rested on a fish; the fish rested on a bull's horn; the bull stood on a rock; and the rock rested on the shoulders of an angel.

On October 20, 1008 A.D., as the hollow warrior prepared for a winter campaign against Castile, Al Malik abruptly died. The official explanation was a heart attack, but the real reason was more sinister.

Al Malik had been poisoned by his brother Little Sancho, who cut an apple in half with a knife, poisoned one side, and ate the safe half while Al Malik, without suspecting, received the poisoned half.

If Córdoba was shocked, there was no sign of it, for the capabilities for treachery there were nearly unfathomable and almost expected. In this case, there might have been foreign involvement as well, and that was a new element in the mix. Little Sancho's mother was a Basque Christian, the prize of an Al Mansor raid. In the land of the Basques, Sancho the Great, king of Navarre, had increased his power and prestige with each passing year since his accession to the throne in 1000 A.D. The advantage of this turmoil in the Córdoban court to the Christian north was obvious: first to encourage strife and then in the ensuing chaos to recapture lost territory.

If Al Malik had been a misfortune, Little Sancho was an unmitigated disaster. If Al Malik had died of a poisoned apple, Little Sancho was the poison apple for the caliphate. "Little Sancho inaugurated his government with licentiousness and buffoonery," the chronicler wrote, adding disdainfully, ". . . and he drank wine." More than the occasional goblet seemed to be involved here. Drink was not his only vice. Soon his sacrilege became the butt of street talk. He was said to have remarked, when he heard the muezzin call the faithful to prayer from the minaret:

"Hasten to prayer! Why not hasten to a bacchanal! That would be much better."

In his drunkenness and debauchery and impiety, Little Sancho puffed himself up with delusions of grandeur. Like his late brother, he ingratiated himself to the caliph, inviting him to parade full-face in full regalia through the main streets to celebrations at Al Zahira. Finally, in a fit of bonhomie, Little Sancho declared to the caliph that they were . . . cousins! Was it not true that the caliph's mother had been Basque? Never mind that Subh had been a captured slave, whereas Sancho's mother was a Basque princess. They were related through the proverbial maternal uncle!

Abruptly, Sancho appropriated the name of the great caliph of the mid-tenth century, Abd al Rahman III. Two and a half months after that, he announced to the caliph, at spear's point, that he, Little Sancho, must be named the successor to his "cousin's" throne.

This did not go down well with the people. Though they might have lusted for the prize, neither Al Mansor nor Al Malik had dared to tamper with the legitimacy of the Umayyad throne. For this little Andalusian señorito to assert royal lineage was more than Córdoba could take. "The people reproached Sancho and his Caliph in naming Sancho with this caliphal name," wrote a chronicler, "and he was deprived of the support of the country's nobility who were disgusted."

Four days after his demand to be named caliph, Sancho sent troops to the gate of the Al Zahrâ, entered the caliph's throne room with his ministers, and laid before Al Hishâm a declaration of succession. The proclamation was a remarkable document for both its content and its style. The prince of the believers, in his piety and chastity, had surveyed the far corners of the land as well as the nearest streets of the capital, "knowing that no action is worth more to God than pious deeds," and he had met no one more worthy of being honored with the rank of heir-apparent than Abd al Rahman, son of Al Mansor—"God Bless Him." The prince of the believers had studied and tested his successor's personality, and the son of Al Mansor had emerged "without detriment to the path of righteousness. . . . Given the goodness of his spirit, his nobility, his famous ascendancy, his great dignity, energy, and intelligence," Little Sancho was the man, as the prophet said, "to lead the Arabs with his staff."

The proclamation was signed, witnessed by the councilors, approved by several hundred observers, and finally sealed outside the gates of Al Zahrâ with the ceremonial fist and handshake. In the streets it was lamented and deplored, secretly at first.

The people entered the palace grounds to offer their hollow congratulations, each "holding back a tear as befits a flatterer," and they left, according to an observer, "with their hearts filled with hate for him." Thereafter, Little Sancho paraded in the streets wearing a caliph's robe, as if he had already replaced Hishâm. Swiftly, he appointed his own son as prime minister, conferring upon him the title of the brother he had murdered: Al Muzaffar, or Sword of the State. On the heels of these many outrages, Sancho added one final atrocity: he insisted that the visitors to Al Zahira and even its servants discard their traditional Andalusian dress and don the Berber turban. He would impose the odious uniform of the wild and alien African barbarian on the cultured Moors.

With Córdoba in a state of shock, and the little señorito overeager for the battlefield laurels of his father and brother, Sancho mounted a great stallion and led his turbaned columns north for a holy campaign against Christian Castile. On both the political and the military fronts, he was the very picture of stupidity. He gave himself no time to consolidate his outrageous rule at home, and, leaving in February, he was marching out of town during the rainy season. By the time he hit the mountains, the snow was heavy, and the usurper failed to find an enemy to attack. Only when the mud became knee deep and his columns were nearly unable to move did he give the order to retreat.

In Toledo, he finally got word of the catastrophe he had left behind. His legions had scarcely passed over the horizon when the rebellion against his silly reign began. The conspirators put one of the few remaining Umayyad princes at the center of their revolt. He was Muhammad Ibn Abd al Jabbar. This Jabbar, aged twenty-seven, blond and blue-eyed, was brutal, determined, and most of all impatient, for he was the presumed successor to the caliph's throne, should Al Hishâm remain childless. Jabbar now took the name Al Mahdi, or Guided by God. He would need all the divine guidance he could get, for he was taking a fateful step. Within the Muslim theocracy, to rebel against established authority was a dire act. It was sure to begin a civil war, a *fitna,* and the word *fitna* had all the resonance of a jihad, except that the former portended a death struggle between Muslims. By definition, any who participated in a *fitna* were branded by God, either for sainthood or for evil. Their faith was being tested. If they lost, their punishment would be unspeakable. Al Mahdi did not intend to lose.

Ignoring the settled and comfortable nobility (except for the mother of the late Al Malik, whose champion he was), Al Mahdi found the core of his support in the professional classes, in the imams who deplored Little Sancho's behavior, and in the riffraff of the marketplace. The opposition quickly turned into a mob. Only nine days after Little Sancho's departure, Al Mahdi ordered an assault on Al Zahira. The raid began with Al Mahdi and only thirty men. They attacked the gate and killed its defenders.

News of the raid spread quickly through the city as thousands gathered in excitement and anticipation. Al Mahdi appeared before them as their savior. His men distributed arms to the mob. The horde poured into Al Mansor's second city. As the residents fled from their palaces and offices without resistance, a rampage began that would last four days. A force had been unleashed that Al Mahdi could not control. The Berbers joined in the looting. When all the wood was carted away and all the valuables were gone, the looters dug up the floors in search of buried gold. When the structures and the grounds were so picked over that nothing of value was left, the pride of Al Mansor was burned to the ground. So complete was the devastation that no trace of the city was apparent within a few years.

Soon enough, Al Mahdi entered the royal palace of Al Zahrâ itself. Searching the buildings and the gardens, he finally found the caliph hiding among the women of the harem. Al Mahdi demanded that Hishâm abdicate, and of course the feeble caliph agreed at once.

Meanwhile, in Toledo, Little Sancho insisted that his followers awaited his triumphal return to Córdoba. He must ride to the rescue of the state. As he set out for the capital, his troops melted into the countryside. His Berbers, concerned about their property, now saw that they were on the losing side. Before long, Sancho's retinue was reduced to a few Christian soldiers, a few slaves, a troupe of musicians, a harem of seventy women, and a stouthearted Christian called Count Gomez. Somewhere, outside Córdoba, this motley band encountered the troops of Al Mahdi. Little Sancho was invited to dismount, and Al Mahdi demanded that the son of Al Mansor kiss the hooves of his horse. In this sport of humiliation, Count Gomez chimed in, but it did him no good. His hands were soon tied along with those of Little Sancho. Then they were beheaded.

The following day, on the moon of Regeb, Little Sancho's corpse was thrown into the streets of Córdoba, and Al Mahdi made a public spectacle of trampling over it with his horse to the hysterical shrieks of the crowd. The body was then perfumed, its head reunited with its trunk, and the assemblage was pinioned on a cross outside the great mosque. Next to this hideous sight a dazed man exclaimed, over and over:

"Behold Little Sancho the Blessed. May God's curse light upon him . . . and myself."

The poor devil was the captain of Little Sancho's royal guard.

IN THE NEXT YEAR AND A HALF the great Umayyad caliphate of Moorish Spain collapsed into a swamp of anarchy and
internecine warfare. Al Mahdi's revolution had ousted the family of
Al Mansor, but it was short-lived itself. Al Mahdi himself turned out
to have the worst qualities of Little Sancho and Al Malik combined:
he was a cruel, reckless, and bloodthirsty tyrant, and he too was
devoted to the grape. In the streets he was known as the "wine-sot."
With breathtaking speed he alienated all his natural supporters: the
common people, the professional classes, and, most important of all,
the wild and unpredictable Berbers upon whom his rule depended
and upon whom he now heaped his scorn. Within six weeks of Little
Sancho's death, a combined force of Berbers and disaffected Christians was pounding at his palace gates. Within a year he had fled to
Toledo, where he was tracked down and killed in July 1010 A.D. Al
Mahdi, "guided by God," had been guided right into his premature
grave. In Córdoba his head was paraded on a pole in the streets and
then presented as a gift to the Berbers.

The kings and counts of the Christian north watched this amazing
spectacle with surprise and awe. At first they reacted tentatively, for
the horrors of the past thirty years were still fresh in memory and
encouraged a cautious approach. It was hard to imagine an impotent
Córdoba, left to an odd collection of petty competitors from the remnants of the once prominent families. Gradually, the Christian rulers
began to take advantage. First, the Castilians and then the Catalans
united forces with the Berbers to join in the pillage.

In September 1010 A.D., a new ploy proved even more effective
than a frontal assault. The count of Castile threatened to put his
entire army in league with the Berbers in an invasion unless a large
complement of fortresses, previously captured by Al Mansor, was
returned to Castile. Having no choice, the rump government of
Córdoba agreed, and thus, without a single arrow fired in anger,
some two hundred castles including the great fortress of Gormaz,
were handed over. Another Christian count soon followed suit.
Just like that, the spoils of the jihad were being given back wholesale.

Even without Christian allies, the Berbers could not be contained. For too long, they had been used and abused, derided as barbarians, discriminated against as second-class citizens, and exploited by one Arab faction or another. Now the masters were gone, and it became a mad scramble to save their property and snatch whatever else they could lay their hands on. In October 1010 A.D. they put Córdoba under siege. On November 3, 1010 A.D., they rode the few miles downriver to Al Zahrâ where a disgruntled slave let them through the royal gate. An orgy of looting and massacre followed in which the entire royal garrison was liquidated. When everything of value was carted away, even the mercury in the fountain, this magnificent monument of Moorish culture was set aflame. Then the rebels turned back on the capital. It too was overwhelmed, and there was terrible slaughter in the streets.

When the news of this conflagration reached the north of Spain, there was rejoicing in the cities and in the farthest reaches of the Christian provinces. Along the sacred road of the pilgrims to Santiago de Compostela, it was as if a terrible scourge had been lifted. Somewhere in the dark and dank scriptorium of a far-flung monastery outside Burgos, a monk dusted off the old illuminations of Beatus, turned to the colorful folios, and nodded with satisfaction. There were the crude drawings of Córdoba's horseshoe arches, the rich traders in their turbans and their kaftans, and the Whore of Babylon seated upon her soft oriental pillows. Next to these pictures were words of Revelation 18: Babylon was burning; the kings and the merchants were mourning, especially the kings, since they had "fornicated with the whore" and now they wept at the loss of their gold and silver and precious stones, their fragrant wood and vessels of ivory.

The tight and elegant script read:

"I saw the angel come down from heaven, having great authority, and the earth was lighted up by his glory. And he cried out with a mighty voice, saying, 'She is fallen, Babylon the Great' . . . and the kings of the earth who committed fornication with her and who grew rich will weep and mourn over her when they see the smoke of her burning. They will stand far off for fear of her torments, saying, 'Woe, woe, the great city, Babylon, the strong city, for in one hour, your judgment came!' "

IN THE SMOKE and the torment of Córdoba, Sancho Garces III, also known as Sancho the Great, became the supreme figure of northern Spain. He had been crowned in the year 1000 A.D., had gathered his Basques together in an alliance with the kingdoms of León and Castile, and had led this united force in victory over Al Mansor at Calatañazor. In 1011 A.D. this Christian king stood before the very gates of Córdoba itself. He was, however, in no position to conquer the city permanently, for his small northern kingdom did not have the resources to sustain a prolonged occupation. Moreover, he was deterred by a plague which suddenly swept through the streets of Córdoba in June of that year. Instead, Sancho installed a friendly Moorish figurehead before he departed for the north.

With the Moorish caliphate collapsing on itself, Sancho the Great asserted his control one by one over the larger but weaker northern Christian states. In León and Castile, he ruled through his family vassals. In time he was able to claim dominion over the county of Barcelona as well, where he created a Christian empire that spread across the north of the peninsula. Inevitably, this empire expanded south militarily, as the territories of Sobrarbe and Ribagorza were retaken from the Moors. By the end of his reign in 1035 A.D., Sancho the Great claimed the formal title of Rex Dei gratia Hispaniarum.

In millennialist terms, Babylon was burning, and the kingdom of a Christian God was restored. The dream of the Christian reconquest of the entire Iberian peninsula grew more powerful in the north. Once again, reconquest was revived as a Christian duty, although the dream had none of the passion of a jihad. The seeds of this vision extended back to the very beginnings of Moorish rule, from the resistance to the caliphate in the eighth century, to the Christian martyrs of Córdoba in the mid-ninth century, to the endless religious conflicts between the two halves of Spain through the tenth century. The prophecy of reconquest had been a constant theme and fervid hope of the Spanish Christian. He looked to the themes of the Book of Ezekiel for inspiration, as the Moors became synonymous with the wicked. The quest was to destroy the army of an Africanized Gog, to take revenge against his infidels, to destroy his cities, and to displace his pharaoh . . . and once this was accomplished, to restore the kingdom of the believer. Even the date for the reconquest had been set:

"By November 11, 884 A.D., our glorious lord, Alfonso, will rule all Spain," predicted the prophetic chronicle of Alfonso III. But November 11 came and went, and the Moors were more powerful than ever. If the date was wrong, it did not undermine the apocalyptic fervor of the north. If not now, someday soon, the promise of Ezekiel and the promise of Revelation would be realized. Ten thousand saints, clad in white, riding upon white horses, would sweep the Antichrist from the peninsula. In more than twenty references to white robes and blood in the Book of Revelation, the vision of white robes in a field of blood was evident.

In Sancho the Great the Spanish Christians, at last, had their champion. After the desecration of Santiago de Compostela, the Christian emperor moved to restore its glorious sanctity. The town was rebuilt from the ruins of Al Mansor's horrible raid in 997 A.D., and now Sancho the Great did his utmost to encourage pilgrimage to the holy shrine. He altered the path through the mountains to make it easier on the devout traveler and merged the paths from Toulouse and Bordeaux at Puente La Reina, where he built a bridge and named it for his queen. To the pilgrims he extended royal protection from highwaymen and provided food and lodging at points along the road. And he promoted the lore and the romance of Galicia, as the proud and stubborn enclave of Christian resistance to the Muslim infidels over the decades of tribulation. "When I hear the Galician mandolin played, I don't know what's happening. Tears come into my eyes," a poet of the time wrote about the sanctuary. "I see Galicia in my mind, beautiful, pensive, and alone, like a lover without a love, like a queen without a crown. In my soul is desolation, sad and deep. I cannot tell if this is singing or crying."

The mystique of Santiago de Compostela spread over the Pyrenees. Pilgrims streamed in from France. This brought the north of Spain out of its isolation. The region was becoming part of Europe, welcomed proudly into the young family of newly Christianized nations. Sancho the Great reached out to Cluny, accepting Cluniac monks as his principal advisers. With this overture, he initiated a boom in the construction of fortress-monasteries like the beautiful Canigo, while existing monasteries like Oña, Leire, and, most important, San Juan de la Peña, were reformed.

As the pilgrims, including kings and princes, came, so the cult of St. James grew. How close were the Christ and the Antichrist! How close was the poetry that surrounded them! When Al Mansor destroyed the holy shrine of Santiago, his poet wrote an elegant tribute to him:

> Today the Devil has recoiled.
>
> In Santiago you arrived with your white swords
>
> Like the moon
>
> Which passes through the night between the stars.
>
> And the force of Islam rides
>
> Rides like a brilliant planet
>
> Which revolves around your pole
>
> You have uprooted
>
> The foundations of the heretics' religion.
>
> As you have defended the faith of Allah.

In the north the Christians of Sancho the Great had their counterpoint. Once the humble fisherman from the lake of Gennesareth, the apostle St. James was transformed in legend into a great Christian warrior, clad in armor, astride a magnificent white horse, clutching a sword in one hand and a white banner with a red cross in the other. This wondrous metamorphosis was manifest in a mythical battle of the ninth century that was suddenly remembered and was said to have taken place not long after the sepulcher of St. James had been discovered. In 842 A.D. a Christian king of the Asturias named Ramiro I had come to power and abruptly had to contend with a raid of heathen Vikings from the North who found Galicia "the best realm beneath the sun's path" and who gloried in giving "the war ravens food." Worse, several years later, in 845 A.D., the infidels from the south came across the central plateau once again, and Ramiro met them in the Rioja, at a hallowed place called Clavijo.

Anticipating the customary defeat and humiliation, Ramiro fell asleep the night before the battle. In a dream St. James appeared to him, cheering the king on with the prophecy of victory. In the morning, Ramiro rallied his troops with this divine apparition. They rushed at the formidable army of the Moors with the battle cry *"Santiago! y cierra, España."* (Santiago! Protect Spain!) As the armies clashed, St. James, the protector, appeared in the clouds, magnificent in his full battle regalia. Then, as the story was whispered along the pilgrims' road, the apostle himself personally slew seventy thousand Moors. Many were beheaded as if in revenge for the apostle's own beheading in Jerusalem. From that time forward, through the time of Cervantes, St. James became Santiago, Matamoros, the Moor-Slayer.

One battle alone, it seems, is not sufficient for a cult. At yet another terrible battle against the Moors, this time at Simancas, on July 19, 939 A.D., the apostle had appeared again, the pilgrims were told, when defeat seemed certain. This time he appeared with different weapons, a miter and a crosier, and he was accompanied by another knight of God, St. Millán. Again a miraculous victory resulted; many Moors were slaughtered. And, inevitably, a poem was written:

> White horsemen who ride on white horses, O fair to see,
> They ride where the rivers of Paradise flash and flow.

In propagating the faith, in promoting holy pilgrimage, in announcing the miracles of Santiago, and in consolidating the Christian north, Sancho the Great was pivotal in Spanish history. With the disintegration of the caliphate it was as if Christian Spain were emerging from a long night. The expansion of Christian territory was huge. The devil, it seemed, had been cornered. If he was not entirely put back in his cage, his dominion was in tatters and he was on the defensive. True, it would be centuries before the Moors were driven from Iberia and the reconquest of Spain for Christianity was complete, but in the years after the first millennium, the seeds not only of the reconquest of Spain but of the crusades were planted. Combining evangelical zeal with military action, the myth of Santiago underpinned the events that were to come later in the century. In 1065 A.D., the Moorish town of Balbastro was attacked by a French force in the first mini-crusade that was more noteworthy for its rape and pillage than its militant piety. In 1085 A.D. the city of Toledo fell to Christian soldiers, and in 1095 A.D. Pope Urban II issued the first broad call for the first crusade against Palestine.

The reign of Sancho the Great was the turning point. Sancho had united the provinces in the north, Castile and Aragon, and had created the nucleus of the modern Spanish state. This union was ultimately cemented, more than four hundred years later, with the marriage of Ferdinand of Aragon and Isabella of Castile. Under these monarchs, in the year 1492 A.D., not only did Christopher Columbus sail to America to advance the work of Leif Eriksson, but the Catholic kings finally entered the city of Granada, ending forever the Muslim dominion in Spain.

If Al Mansor the Victorious did not fit the exact description of the Antichrist, Sancho the Great did not fit the exact description of the Christian savior. Though his armies might easily have swept over the caliphate in 1011 A.D., he had been content to approach the walls of Córdoba and install a Muslim puppet before he withdrew. Though he might have invoked St. James in a Christian crusade against the forces of darkness, his cavaliers were more preoccupied with Christian competitors in León and Castile. Though his northern empire might have begun a Christian dynasty, he treated his patrimony instead as personal property and upon his death splintered it into three parts among his sons, who proceeded to act out a Spanish version of *King Lear*.

Even Sancho's death is ambivalent. The Christian saga writers put the king on the pilgrims' road at the end of his life, struggling to get to the cathedral of Oviedo to visit the relics of the saints and the bones of the Christian kings who came before him. But, say the Christian chronicles, he died sadly just short of his goal.

There is another account. He was on the road to Oviedo to be sure, but he was on the run. And on a lonely road in the mountains of Pajares, not in piety but in fear, he was assassinated, felled by the sword of an offended and cuckolded husband.

Let us not demystify him. In Spanish history, he is Sancho the

Great, more for the forces of history that swirled around him and for the accident of having reigned at the turn of the first millennium than for his achievements. To live at that calendrical hinge exaggerates both accomplishment and fault, it seems, and it did so with Sancho. On his sepulcher in the monastery he built at Leire was written:

Here Lies Sancho
King of the Pyrenees and of Toulouse
Catholic Ruler
Prince of the Church

CHAPTER EIGHT

Forty Thousand Horsemen of the Apocalypse

IN THE CENTRAL CITY OF BUDAPEST, there is a venerable old lady of a hotel called the Gellert, situated on the banks of the Danube, next to the dramatic, craggy hill where St. Gellert—St. Gerard of Csanad in the Catholic annals—the Christian martyr and educator of King Stephen's son, was thrown to his death by pagans in 1046 A.D. With its Turkish minarets and its marble, becolumned Roman bath and a cadre of smart red-suited porters who snap to attention when a taxi is needed, the hotel is the remnant of a past era. From her glory days as the meeting place for comfortable bosses, she is threading a bit around the fringes now in the new order, but the old style is still apparent beneath the plastic and Formica of the new epoch.

The grand staircase of the Gellert Hotel is graced by a large stained-glass window of rose and yellow whose central motive is a stag and two hunters in pursuit. This is a portrayal of the central origin myth of the Hungarian people, a people so mysterious and unique in central Europe that they are still to this day trying to figure out who they are, where they come from, why they settled here, in this basin surrounded by the Carpathian Mountains.

In the Myth of the Magic Stag, the deer appears and then disappears, luring the two hunters farther and farther west. The hunters are brothers who stem from different stock: one from Attila's race along the Volga River, the kingdom of Gog and Magog, the other from the Magyar, a tribe that had lived among the Khazars and the Turks in Asia Minor and whose name means "the man who can speak." Once the hunters are tantalized into the Carpathian basin, they find a home, but it may not be their last, for the nomads by nature are restless. They are without women until they come upon a covey of dancing girls, daughters of King Dal, from the ancient Scythian peoples of Iran. The hunters ravage the dancers, and out of the violent unions springs the race of angry and militant Hungarians.

In the Danube valley there are dueling origin myths, one just as violent as the next. As affectionately held is the notion of a superior race of people which sprang from the loins of a woman and a hawk. This is the legend of Almos, the central origin myth of the Arpad dynasty, which conquered Hungary in 896 A.D., ruled at the turn of the millennium, produced the great leaders of Geza and Vajk, and reigned until the thirteenth century. In this myth, the leader of ancient Scythia marries a woman of the Russian steppes, and she has a dream in which a hawk flies onto her and makes her pregnant. From this remarkable couple comes the tribe of the Arpads. All over Hungary, including one that hovers over Budapest, are statues of a hawk, wings spread and fecund, ready to embrace the people and presumably to impregnate them with predatory instincts.

The magic stag and the impregnating hawk are powerful pagan images, but the holy menagerie was far larger among these migrating tribes from the east. Each of the fifty clans that rode into the Carpathian basin in 896 A.D. had a sacred totem. Birds of prey were the most common, but the lion, the snake, the fish, and the wolf were also revered symbols. All had magical powers, to attack and to defend, but mainly to attack and move on.

Naturally enough, because these nomadic tribes depended totally on the horse, the steed also had a cult, especially the white horse. The horse was the most important creature on earth—the conveyance for wandering, the engine of war, the beast of the field—and the white stallion was its most perfect and beautiful incarnation. The leaders of the clan always rode the white steed. (It was a tradition for Hungarian leaders lasting into the twentieth century.) This sacred symbol was the object of the most somber sacrifice in the holiest of rituals, especially in the burial of a chieftain. Then the magnificent beast was slaughtered, partially eaten, and buried with its master.

It could also be the most prized of gifts. In the conquest of Hungary by the eastern tribes, the defeated party were the Moravians, and in the surrender, after the disconsolate prince of Moravia had presented the conqueror, Arpad, with a clump of grass, a handful of earth, and a vial of water—symbols of the land he was surrendering—he received in return a magnificent white horse. The gift was meant to be consolation but also to certify the transfer of land.

Beyond the totems of the tenth-century clans and tribes of Hungary, there was a vibrant sense of higher beings. The tribes originating in Siberia had the concept of the Highest Creator, the father-God called Atyaisten. He did not create the world from nothingness, but rather shaped and transformed it from the existing chaos. Atyaisten was assisted by a working god, Torum, the Man Who Takes Care of the World. There was also a female goddess, clothed in a resplendent gown that illuminated the world as the blue sky. The emotional hold of this goddess over the Hungarian sensibility was great, and easily adapted to the cult of the Virgin Mary later. Below these prime deities, the Hungarians worshiped the sun and moon, fire, winter, summer, rain, wind, forests, horses, water, day, the night sky, and the earth. If Atyaisten was the god of the steppes, Ordog was the devil, the incorporation of all evil.

Among the Hungarian tribes, there were neither churches nor priests, but shamans. They were the living link between the real and the supernatural world, and to them fell the duty to bring rain or to heal or assure victory on the battlefield. The chief shaman was known as Taltos, and he (or she) could either be elected or chosen at birth. If it was the latter, there was usually a visible sign of different-ness like an exposed tooth at birth or a sixth finger. Once chosen, the shaman-novitiate went into a seven-year training, and after this ap-prenticeship he could fall into a trance that had real meaning.

In 896 A.D. ten wandering tribes arrived in the Carpathian basin and found themselves protected on three sides by impenetrable moun-tains. They came as conquerors, but from a long tradition of defeat and humiliation. Nomadic not so much by instinct as by necessity, they had been driven out of Siberia and the Urals, out of the Khazar empire and Crimea, out of Iran and Turkey and finally Bulgaria before they moved north through the valley of the Danube. Always fighting, always looking over their shoulder, they had developed into rough but disci-plined warriors. For this was the age of slavery and anywhere along their journey from southern Siberia through hostile and uncharted ter-ritory, one false step could have put their wives and children into bond-age. Along their path across Eurasia they had acquired tales and beliefs and languages that blended into a unique brew, unconnected to any of the traditions of Europe. Add to this combustible mixture the rage of the outcast. Their belligerence was the natural outgrowth of a dis-placed people, that strange combination of fear and aggressiveness that the world has known in many incarnations among exiled people. As the ninth century slid into the tenth, the Carpathian plain was not so much a basin as a cauldron.

For the next seventy-five years, the heathen horsemen of Hungary poured out of the Pannonian plain and rampaged across the Chris-tian countries of central Europe more than fifty times. Proud and brave warriors, they could endure any hardship, and they liked to think of themselves as "rich in blue squirrel, white silver, yellow gold, golden millet, black sable, and brown horses." But they were restless and rootless wanderers. Perhaps the Carpathian plain was not meant to be their final resting place, but we do not know for sure. They left no memoirs. We do know their movements, however. Finding quickly that they were superior fighters to the Moravians and the Bavarians, the Slavs and the Italians to their east, they stormed north to Bremen and south to the boot of Italy and the Greek isles, west as far as Spain and the Loire valley, east to Constantinople.

Unlike the Vikings, booty was not their chief object, although their greed can certainly not be discounted. "What is gotten in a dog's way will also be lost in the manner of dogs," ran an old tribal taboo. Rather, they loved to fight, especially on horseback. And they had their own code of honor. They might kill nuns, but never rape them. They had no marriage ceremonies, but they were monogamous. In the first few years in their new homeland, an uncertain accommodation with the emperor of Bavaria constrained them, but when he died and his successor, Louis the Child, under the sway of the church, disapproved of this unholy alliance, the horsemen poured into Bavaria. They burned castles, destroyed churches, massacred, and even drank the blood of their victims.

The terror they spread was unimaginable. From Germany one observer put it this way: "Seeing the cruelty of these enemies and the havoc they were making among his own people, so fired the hearts of all with apprehension that any one by chance failed to serve in the war which he proceeded to wage against them, there was nothing left to do but hang himself. Against Louis's great army an innumerable multitude of the villainous Hungarians hastened to advance. No man ever more ardently desired a drink of cold water than these cruel savages longed for the day battle. Indeed their only joy is in fighting." Their terrible reputation grew with the news of their ravages. It was gossiped that as soon as a barbarian child was born, his mother cut his face with a sharp knife, so he would learn to bear the pain of wounds before he received the nourishing pleasure of his mother's milk.

In the winter of 899–900 A.D. the hordes were in northern Italy, defeating the forces of King Berengar I, slaughtering twenty thousand Italians, and plundering Pavia, Brescia, and Milan. A formal Italian surrender netted the horsemen regular tribute and, in the years afterward, the well-traveled road between the Carpathians and Lombardy was given the imperial name of Strata Ungarorum. Perhaps the Magyar tribes contemplated northern Italy as their next resting place.

Peace and easy plunder on the southern front allowed them to turn their attention north. In 906–7 A.D. they were riding through

Saxony, catching the Germans at dawn, sleepy-eyed near Bratislava. "The Hungarians, thirsting for murder and eager for the fray, fell upon the Christians, while they were still yawning with sleep. Some indeed were awakened by arrow points before they heard the cries of battle, others were transfixed in their beds, and were not roused either by the din or by their wounds. . . . On both sides a furious battle started, and the Turks retiring in feigned retreat caused great havoc by the fierce fire of their arrows." So wrote a Christian bishop, adviser to the German emperor, and it is no doubt from his later poetry that he saw these Hungarians as the horsemen of the Apocalypse.

When great Jehovah veils the golden light
Of Phoebus with his clouds and draws dark night
Athwart the heavens, swiftly all around
The Lightnings play and fast the thunders sound.
Then tremble they whose trade it is to turn
Black into white and fear themselves to burn
In levin fire, conscious of their sins.
So swift, so fast, when once the fight begins,
The foemen's arrows hurtling in the air
Pierce breastplates through and leave each quiver bare
And as the cruel hail on cornfields falls,
Or rattles on the roofs of lordly halls,
So fall the sword strokes on the helms beneath,
So arrows send the brave to mutual death.

How clear did the mark of the Antichrist have to be? The eyes of these heathen invaders were deep-set; their oily hair was braided and their skin was yellow-brown. Their language was the scrambled sounds of Babylon. Their seven tribes reflected the seven-headed beast of which St. John had spoken in his Revelation, and upon each head was blasphemy. And their blasphemy was revolting. In their pagan rites, they even slaughtered the white horse, the symbol of the purity of the apostolic Christian church which St. John had mentioned in the first of his seven seals. And the origins of these tribes! They hailed from the tribes of the distant east, perhaps the tribe of Dan which the Bible had proclaimed as the source of the Antichrist. It was also said that they came from the kingdom of Gog and Magog. They were surely the wicked issue of the Great Whore of Babylon.

As much as the good bishop liked to think of these invaders as savages from hell, the Hungarian army was no rabble. To put forty thousand horsemen on a field of battle and to have them move with speed and coordinated purpose took great skill. It was possible only because the nomadic tradition had created a warrior class among the Magyars, a strata of professional soldiers with distinct and defined privileges and duties. Like the Leidang system of the Vikings, each clan in Hungary was required to outfit and train a certain number of cavalry and to contribute them to the larger national force. The training began at youth as well-supervised hunting became a young man's preparation for the battlefield.

The horses of this daunting force were small and strong, with the speed of a sprinter and the stamina of the marathoner. Pack horses rather than battle wagons carried supplies, so the army could move through the mountain passes and along the bridle paths of the Carpathians or the Alps or the Pyrenees with relative ease. Each rider had three or four horses which he spelled, so he always had a fresh mount. Compared to the heavy-laden knight army of feudal Germany, which moved at the snail pace of only twelve miles a day for only a few days before it needed rest, the Hungarian light cavalry could move twenty-five miles a day almost indefinitely.

On the field of battle, the cavalry was lightly armed. Their armor was lightweight leather: a leather helmet, leather body plates, high knee-length boots. Only the Hungarian princes wore metal breastplates. The bow, made of horn, and the arrow with an iron tip was the principal weapon, and while the enemy could expect the sky to rain with arrows at the beginning of any battle, he would also find that in close combat, the Hungarians used their arrows as daggers. The use of the bow and arrow in the hands of the Hungarians was doubly effective because, unlike many of their opponents, they had stirrups, meaning that they could swivel in their saddle and shoot to the rear (undoubtedly, the result of being run out of so many places over the previous decades and trying to make a safe getaway). Of secondary importance was the spear, to which the Hungarians attached small colorful banners and streamers. These small flags were no mere decoration, but had a military purpose. Multiplied by many thousands, the flickering colors of these streamers created a blinding, mesmerizing effect from a distance, complementing their terrifying battle cry of "Hooy, Hooy, Hooy" and the thunder of hoofs and the glint of steel. The battle streamers completed the picture of devil-inspired terror. The effect was unsettling not only for man but for opposing beast, which had to be blindfolded.

The light cavalry moved fast and cleverly, in concentric, interlocking circles with the leaders of the individual clans forming the center. On the point were the latest recruits from the last conquered people, and these brave and well-motivated men formed the charging brigades. The newest Magyars were the most expendable, but also the most heroic, and they stood to capture the most valuable booty to furnish their new homes.

Their tactics were cunning and well considered. They chose their moment to engage their enemies intelligently, never attacking on the spur of the moment, always choosing their high ground carefully. Their hallmark was the feigned retreat and the well-planned ambush. "By this time Phoebus was sinking in the sky marked one hour after noon and the war god was still smiling upon Louis's side," an account of one engagement runs, "when the Turks with their wonted cunning set an ambush and feigned to retreat. As the king's men, deceived by the trick, rushed boldly forward, the troops in ambush fell on them from every side and the victors found themselves in a moment vanquished and slain. The king himself, conquered now instead of conqueror, was filled with dismay, the reverse being all the more serious because it was so unexpected. You could have seen the woods and fields strewn with corpses, the rivers and water channels running red with blood, while the neighing of horses and the blare of bugles increased the terror of the fugitives and cheered the assailants to fresh efforts."

The rout of the German force at Bratislava (known in German as

Pressburg) drew the Hungarian horde farther and farther north in Saxony. To their victims in central Europe, however, it seemed as if these heathen horsemen were everywhere. After a few years, since there was no one in the east or southeast of Europe able to resist the Hungarians—for they had by this time forced the Bulgarians and the Greeks to pay them tribute—they took the opportunity to visit the peoples of the south and west and try their strength upon them as well. They got together an army so huge that it defied calculation. Now it swooped down upon hapless Italy. They pitched their tents, or rather the miserable rags that served them as shelter. "The Chevy Chase fled and the heathens pursued them savagely," wrote a chronicler. "The flight became butchery, and the whole realm was scoured by the Hungarians' merciless fury. No one ventured to withstand their approach unless he was behind strong walls. Indeed at this time their valor was so irresistible that while one section of them was plundering Bavaria, Swabia, France and Saxony, another host was laying waste all Italy."

Finally, in 913 A.D., this scourge got its first check. In that year, a Bavarian prince known as Arnulf the Angry defeated the raiders on the banks of the River Inn and captured a Magyar prince. This led to an armistice, formalized in 917 A.D. with an agreement that Hungarian forces could pass unimpeded through Bavaria on their way to wicked deeds farther west. Farther north, in 924 A.D., the Magyars approached the kingdom of Saxony, but the German king there, Henry the Fowler, rallied his forces with a moving exhortation that invoked the Saxon struggle with Charlemagne 150 years earlier. The Saxons of old were lions in battle, Henry told his troops, who fought for Christian salvation. And now they faced the heathenish "Turks," men who knew nothing of Christ, who hated God's church and asked ransom to march away.

"Up then, my heroes, and enter the fight!" he cried. "Show to the foe your invincible might. Pay them no tribute, but let the knaves know that Death is the gift they shall carry below. Tell them to count their doubloons in the red fires of hell!"

In an inspired fight, the Saxons captured another Magyar prince and, with this prize hostage in irons, immediately sued for peace.

Nine tranquil years followed on the northern front. Henry the

Fowler put the time to good use by developing a formidable castle system and a strong army, as he begrudgingly paid tribute to Hungary. During the years 924–933 A.D., the Hungarian empire also flourished. A buffer zone was created, stretching five hundred kilometers wide from the North Sea to Lombardy, and this protected Hungary from invasion. While the Magyar horsemen avoided Saxony in the north, they continued their annual predations in the south.

In 927 A.D. they turned up in the villages of eastern Switzerland. The intruders were drawn to St. Gall. The monastery there had been built at the confluence of three rivers to honor the Holy Trinity, and already had a certain apocalyptic mentality. Over one of its chapel's arches, an inscription about the Last Judgment had been cut as a decoration:

> Lo the trumpets blare forth which dissolve death's rule
>
> The cross gleams in the heavens; cloud and fire go before.
>
> Here the exalted saints sit down with Christ the Judge
>
> To justify the devout and to damn the wicked to Hell.

The Magyars fulfilled this apocalyptic wish. The news spread that the barbarians were coming, burning and plundering villages as they came. The monks gathered up the treasures of the monastery and fled to a nearby fortification . . . all except a half-wit named Heribald. Heribald declined to accompany his terrified brothers in flight because the master of the monastery had not issued him his annual allotment of leather that year, and therefore he lacked shoes in which to flee. When the heathens burst into the monastery, they found poor Heribald sitting, alone and melancholy, in the courtyard, but not in the least afraid. This confused and, ultimately, amused the Hungarians, who spared the monk on account of his idiocy. Idiot and barbarian were soon frolicking through the deserted monastery in a vain search for booty. When they came to the wine cellar, one rowdy lifted his axe to destroy the cask, but checked his swing when Heribald blurted out, "Leave it, good man. What shall we drink when you are gone?"

In the frenzy there were two accidents. One raider was convinced that the rooster on the spire must surely be made of gold. But when he climbed the belfry and reached with his lance to flip the rooster off, he fell to his death below. Another invader climbed the eastern face of the monastery to desecrate God's sanctuary, but when he pulled his pants down to defecate, he fell backwards off the wall. These heroes were placed between two doors, and toasted in a Taltos sandwich.

Eventually, a great feast was held in which the Hungarians drank from buckets of wine that were placed around the courtyard. They roasted sacrificial lamb, gnawed at its meat, and then threw the bones at one another. They wrestled one another, and then they forced Heribald to lead them in butchered Christian hymns. Heribald took this all in the spirit of good fun. At an opportune moment the half-witted monk pled for his release. "He prayed for help from the holy cross, and between tears, threw himself at the feet of the chiefs," the later account read. "But they, hissing with excessively wild emotions, with awful grunts indicated to their henchmen their desires, and they, in a fury rushed up to him with drawn knives. Before they would kill him, they placed a crown of hair on his tonsured head." But luckily for Heribald, spies turned up just then from a reconnaissance, telling of the fortification nearby, and the Magyars rode off, leaving Heribald to tell his brothers later about the "wild morals" of the heathens.

In 933 A.D. Henry the Fowler had completed his castle system and was ready for pitched battle. At Merseburg the Saxon prince once again exhorted his troops to holy war. "The deeds of Kings of old and the writings of the holy fathers tell us we must do," the king proclaimed. "It is not hard for God to defeat a great host with a small company . . . if the faith motivates them, a faith not of words but of deeds, not of the lips but of the heart. Let the heresy of simony, hated by God and condemned by the blessed Peter, be banished from our realm. Love of unity will bind together those whom the devil's cunning has separated!"

In the sentimental account of the ensuing battle, the Christian chronicler spoke of the battle lines coming together as the Germans chanted "the holy and wondrous cry 'Kyrie eleison'" while "from the heathen came the foul and diabolical shout 'Hooy, Hooy!'" An epic battle took place in which the Hungarian forces received more than a check or a repulse, but their first disastrous defeat. In the carnage, it was reported that 36,000 Hungarians were killed. This ended the flow of Saxon blood money, and there would be only one more northern campaign for the Hungarians afterward.

The lines of nationhood were appearing, however indistinctly.

IN 936 A.D. an event of supreme importance to Hungary took place far from the battlefield. In Aachen, the city of Charlemagne, Otto I was crowned as the king of the Franks. He would become a huge and commanding figure in central Europe, the first great leader of Germany since Charlemagne, and it would be his role in the coming two decades to unite the disparate, independent principalities of central Europe and to mold these duchies into the German Holy Roman Empire. In placing the crown upon his head and presenting him with the king's sword, the archbishop of Mainz signaled the religious basis of Otto's rule: "Receive this sword with which you will drive off all the enemies of Christ, barbarians and bad Christians, and by which God gives you power over the Empire of the Franks." In true feudal style, the various dukes of the far-flung realm approached the throne, put their hands between Otto's, and swore allegiance to their new king.

By the description of his chronicler, Bishop Widukind of Corvey, Otto was a born leader, a man of iron will, great loyalty to his friends, and even great charity toward his vanquished foes. Illiterate in youth, he learned to read and write in middle age. Strong as a lion and possessed of a violent temper, he hunted all his life and loved all sports on horseback, even as he loved chess no less passionately. Describing him in his later years, Widukind wrote: "From his sunburnt face shone light and lively eyes. Sparse gray hair covered his head and his beard, after the Saxon manner, blowed long and mighty over his chest which was very hairy like a lion's mane. He wore Saxon dress and shunned foreign splendor. He spoke his native Saxon tongue, but had some knowledge of Roman and Slavic speech. He slept sparingly, and as he talked in his sleep, seemed always awake."

For a strong leader suddenly to rise in the center of Europe was ominous for the Hungarians; for that strong leader to be a zealot was truly dangerous. The mission to destroy heathenism and to save Europe for Christ as the millennium approached was the very basis of Otto's rule. Against paganism he burned with a "monstrous fury," and he meant to be Christ's great champion. But the vision was grander than that. Otto revived the dream of the Roman Empire and the quest of Charlemagne. He imagined that a great Christian state would rise in the center of Europe, melding the papacy with an empire, bonding pope and emperor, the scepter and the sword. This holy dominion would stretch from Denmark to the boot of Italy, cover France and most of Spain.

Diligently, he set about organizing his holy domain. His administration was not always pursued under the soundest principles, however. In 940 A.D., for example, upon hearing that the episcopal chair had become open in Regensburg, he traveled there to install the new bishop. The night before, he was advised in a dream to appoint the first person he saw at the monastery the next day. Rising early, he went to the church, and the first person he saw was a monk who was the night porter.

"Brother, what will you give me for the bishopric?"

"My shoes," the crusty old monk replied. His shoes were soon exchanged for the bishop's slippers.

Despite such charming lapses, the emperor's personal life and demeanor reflected the depth of his commitment. "He divided his days between work and prayer, matters of state and the service of God," Widukind wrote. "Of his royal and imperial dignity he was ever conscious and ascribed it to God's favor. He never placed the crown upon his head without having first fasted and prayed. In those who rose up against his majesty he saw offenders against God's law." Seven years before he was crowned, Otto had married Edith, the daughter of the Anglo-Saxon king of Wessex, Edward the Elder. She was the most devout of noble ladies, a woman of serene disposition, who was a great calming influence on the volatile king. In language and court manners, this was no exotic match, since Anglo-Saxon England spoke the same language as Saxon Germany and the royal lines had long been intermingled. Nor was there any disagreement about

Christian evangelism. If anything, Edith was more religious. She wore her charity on her sleeve. Otto would have to restrain her habit of giving away the jewels of the crown to the poor, once disguising himself as a beggar and accosting her, only to have the queen cry out, "The king has left me nothing but my clothes," whereupon she tore off her gold-embroidered, gem-studded sleeves and gave them to the beggar. The king produced the evidence at dinner.

For this pious couple, the first order of business was to annihilate the terrible scourge of Hungary. The reign of Gog in Europe needed to be short, and its end needed to be swift.

In the first few years of taking power, Otto I beat off several probing attacks by the Hungarians in Saxony, but it was more important at first to subjugate the other German dukedoms, then the Czech lands on the northern border with Hungary, and finally northern Italy, Hungary's last ally in Europe. By 951 A.D., the last passage to the rich western lands open to the pale horsemen was blocked.

Combining all these lands with the old Frankish lands to the west, Otto shaped a powerful empire of Franconia, Burgundy, Swabia, northern Italy, and Bohemia. The probes by Hungarian raiders, who were back again in 948–49 A.D., this time in Bavaria, helped Otto to consolidate his vast realm further.

In 954 A.D., however, the situation brightened briefly for the Hungarians. Otto's own sons, concerned about succession and discontented with their father's high-handed management in northern Italy, rose against him in rebellion. In short order, Bavaria and Swabia were in full-fledged revolt, and Otto's vision of a strong confederacy of Christian states was in danger of dissolving into tribal warfare. Otto's sons Liudolf and Conrad turned to Hungary for help. This was the proverbial invitation to the fox into the chicken coop. Hungarian horsemen poured once again into the heartland of Europe, guided by the rebels across the Rhine and led as far as Burgundy by the rebels, who heaped gold and silver on them.

Ironically, this renewed invasion of the wicked heathens from the east was Otto's salvation, for the presence of Hungarians yet again on German soil lost the people's sympathy for anyone in league with them. Through the fall of 954 A.D. Otto moved relentlessly on the forces of his rebellious sons, picking up popular support as he went. By December, Swabia was back in the empire, and the Hungarians were out of the country. By the following March, Bavaria was subdued, and two sons had lost their dukedoms. Peace and union had returned to Otto's far-flung realm, just when he needed it most. Otto I was stronger than he had ever been.

The usually clever Hungarian warlords, blinded by greed and drunk with overconfidence after their easy pickings in 954 A.D., failed to perceive the change of circumstance in Germany that the emperor's rebound had wrought. When spring came, they again mounted up and rode west. To the Germans they boasted: "There is no one like us! The earth will not open up to swallow us. The sky will not collapse to crush us. We cannot be stopped!" This was the army of eastern Hungary, led by a general known as Bulcsu, also known as the Man with the Bloody Hand. Ironically, Bloody Bulcsu had been baptized a Christian in Constantinople five years previously and had a Christian bishop, named St. Wickert, preaching the Christian gospel to his pagan troops. But the message of Christian charity had eluded him.

South of the Danube, only the fortress town of Augsburg was still under Otto's sway, and Bulcsu decided to dispatch it first, before he attended to the main body of Otto's army somewhere to the north. Full of a sense of their own superiority, bolstered by the memory that forty-five years before, in 910 A.D., they had crushed Augsburg, the Hungarian force of forty thousand set up camp on the east bank of the Lech River. They put the town under siege, surrounding it completely and raining their arrows down upon it. In this operation, however, all their tactical advantages of the past availed them nothing. Their fast and numerous horses were of no use whatever, and the invaders were not equipped with ladders for scaling medieval walls. The town's dilapidated walls were far from impregnable, but the defenders put up a stout defense in the first day of the siege, and they were cheered on by their leader, Bishop St. Ulric. Sensing that Otto's forces could not be far away, the bishop stalled for time. On the second day of the siege, he rode out of the town into the Hungarian horde, unarmed and in his pontifical robes, a move so reckless that it threw the astonished Hungarians into total confusion. When the invaders regrouped, they stormed the east tower of the town nearest the riverbank, attempting to scramble up the walls with horse whips, but this technique was easily repulsed.

When Otto learned of the fresh invasion several weeks before, he was north in Saxony, with only a small force. As he moved south, he acquired eager battalions along the way, and by the time he approached Augsburg, he had a formidable army of Saxons, Bavarians, Franks, and Czechs. In another of Bulcsu's careless strategic mistakes, he allowed Otto's army to cross the Danube unimpeded, and in yet another incredible blunder, he enabled the defenders of Augsburg to slip out of the town and join Otto's army. While Otto was still badly outnumbered—25,000 to 40,000—his soldiers were heavily armored. Suddenly, it did not matter that the Germans were slow and heavy-laden, because Bloody Bulcsu had forgotten, in his conceit, what had made Hungarian armies so terrifying in the past. On the night before the battle, Otto gathered his troops, and, standing before them holding his Holy Lance within whose iron point was embedded a nail from Christ's cross on Calvary, he exhorted them to holy war.

"Up until now I have gloriously used your energetic hands and arms, and they conquered everywhere in the world and in my kingdom," the emperor proclaimed. "Now, in my country, in my own kingdom shall I turn my back? We are outnumbered, I know, but not in bravery, nor in arms. What is our great solace? Our enemy is stripped of the help of God. For them there is boldness alone before the wall. For us there is hope and divine protection. Let the masters of Europe be ashamed to surrender to these enemies! Better if the end lies near, my soldiers. Let us die gloriously rather than be subjected to this enemy and lead our lives as slaves in the manner of wicked beasts. I might speak more, my soldiers, if I thought that words would increase your bravery and daring. Better that we begin our discourse now with swords than with our tongues!"

The following day, August 10, was the feast day of St. Lawrence, the martyr who had been burned on a gridiron and who was known as the Vanquisher of Fire. Appropriately enough, it was raining. In the woods between the Lech and the Wertach Rivers the Christian forces gathered in orderly phalanxes, eight legions in all. Bohemians formed the first line of defense, heavily mailed and clutching strong shields, spread in a formation four kilometers long. They were backed up by an even longer line of Swabians and, behind them, two divisions of Franks and Saxons who surrounded the emperor himself. Standing erect, clutching his Holy Lance in his left hand and a sword in his right, protected by his personal guard of young, handpicked commandos whose symbol was the banner of St. Michael, Otto awaited his enemy.

The heathen horsemen crossed over the Lech near the east tower of Augsburg, turned south, and spread out in two lines, two kilometers across, their tiny banners limp in the gray rain. Bloody Bulcsu planned to attack the front and the rear simultaneously, but the timing was off, and the attack on the rear began prematurely. Against the Czechs his mounted troops had initial success. They penetrated the German line and put some soldiers to flight. But Bulcsu's rear force was not large enough to penetrate deeper into the German core, and the attack stalled.

Then the frontal assault commenced. All craft and generalship seemed to have left Bulcsu, as if he expected the mere sight of his cavalry to terrify the Germans and send them running. But the Germans did not run, nor did they race forward when the Hungarians tried, yet again, their old and now familiar tactic of feigning retreat. In desperation, Bloody Bulcsu ordered his light cavalry to turn and charge the line of heavily armored Teutonic swordsmen. In the ensuing hand-to-hand combat, the Hungarians were slaughtered by the thousands. They fell back in disarray. For the first time in the tenth century, there was the amazing spectacle of Hungarians fleeing their enemies in terror. The stragglers clamored into the swift-moving Lech River and were cut down on the riverbank. A well-timed counterattack by a Frankish battalion finished off the remaining Hungarians and turned the day into a total rout. They had been outfought and outgeneraled.

In the aftermath of the battle, fifty years of vengeance was compressed into two days. Bloody Bulcsu was captured, along with another Hungarian warlord named Lel, who had been pinned to the ground beneath his dead horse. They were taken to Regensburg and, as their bedraggled and defeated army watched from the field below, they were hanged from the east tower of the town. Then thousands upon thousands of Hungarian prisoners were mutilated and tortured, before they were buried alive. By all accounts, from a cavalry of forty thousand, only seven individuals were allowed to survive. They had their ears and noses cut off before they were sent back to Hungary to tell the story of Lechfeld. The menace of western Hungary had been completely annihilated (although the tribes of eastern Hungary were unaffected and continued to harass Byzantium in the following years).

In the crusade to transform Europe, the Battle of Lechfeld in 955 A.D. stands with the Battle of Poitiers in 732 A.D. when the French king, Charles Martel, defeated the Moors in southern France and removed the Muslim menace from the south. The triumph of Lechfeld was a profound turning point. Europe's nightmare of the pale horsemen from the east was fleeting away forever. But crushing the Hungarian military machine was only half the solution. The other half awaited a messianic king, born with the name Vajk, who could transform Hungarian society at its core.

Otto, meanwhile, was exalted as the Defender of Christianity and the Father of his Volk and Vaterland. In the chronicles, the spoils of victory were described. Ambassadors from Rome and Constantinople came to pay homage, bearing elaborately engraved vases of gold and silver and bronze, vessels of glass and ivory, magnificent oriental rugs, balsam, pigments and paints of endless variety, exotic animals never seen before by Saxon eyes, lions and camels, apes and ostriches, "for in Otto all good Christians saw their best hope."

He was now Otto the Great. And he proceeded to convert his kingdom to Christianity in the spirit of the old German verse:

> And wilt thou not a Christian be,
> I'll smash thy skull, just wait and see.

OTTO THE GREAT was drawn inexorably to Rome, by the ghost of Charlemagne and by his own equally strong dream of the ecclesiastical state. The Eternal City was the ultimate prize, the

Apostolic See, residence of the universal pope, object of a tenth-century monk's ardor.

> O Rome, noble mistress and world ruler,
>
> All other cities in glory surpassing;
>
> Reddened with the roseate blood of martyrs,
>
> Aglow with the white ness of virgin's lilies,
>
> Hail to thee we sing, now and forever,
>
> For all eternity be saluted and blessed.

But the Rome of 955 A.D. did not quite live up to this romantic idyll. In that year the overlord of Rome forced his teenage son Octavian upon the Roman nobles, and they elected him pope. Octavian was a wild, undisciplined eighteen-year old, "a youth and given up to the vices thereof." Upon his unmerited elevation, he took the name of John XII, a name that would become infamous in the annals of the papacy. Among the first acts of the new pontiff was to take up arms against his competitors in southern Italy. Marching south at the head of the papal army, he found himself opposed by local princes who had gone into an alliance with a ferocious Muslim warrior. This frightened the papal soldiers, and John XII was driven back to Rome in humiliation. The pontiff then turned his attention to the north, where the unpopular king of Lombardy, Berengar II, stood in the base tradition of his ancestral benefactors. Marozia and Theodora, the vampire queens of the early tenth century, had appointed, then bedded, then murdered popes. The women controlled Roman politics in a "pornocracy." Now Berengar II was raging through northern Italy. To deal with him, the young pope turned to Otto I, inviting him into Italy to subdue northern Italy and then to come triumphantly to Rome.

This squared handsomely with Otto's own ambitions. Free at last from the scourge of Hungarian horsemen, he had consolidated his power within his vast empire. Across his empire, he put into practice his vision of Christian state where the king was the senior partner in an association with the church. He organized the episcopal regions into the "Ottonian system," whereby the archbishops of the church were strong but subservient to secular authority. Thus, he strengthened the church as he exerted his control over it. On the personal level, an invasion of Italy would exact a measure of revenge as well. Otto's devout first wife, Edith, had died. He had then married Adelaide, a French princess, whom the Italian king had previously imprisoned in Lake Como after she had refused to marry his son.

Most important, this was, at last, the chance to realize the ancient idea of a Christian empire in Europe. To subdue Italy and then to be coronated as the sacred ruler of Europe was to achieve Otto's ultimate quest: he was to be the new Caesar Augustus, commander, prince, and high priest, the first in the line of many Christian emperors. In a reprise of Caesar Augustus's Pax Romanus, Otto the Great would now impose his own Pax Germanus.

Along the old Roman way, he marched through the Brenner Pass and into the Veneto. As he did so, Berengar II shut himself up in his castle at Montefeltro and his soldiers fled. The German legions marched farther south unopposed.

Otto must have felt keen disappointment upon meeting the callow young pope. If only John XII, *his* pontiff, were a truly holy man, a philosopher of vision and learning, a man of sincerity and culture, then he would have a worthy partner in his grand and pious design. But such a man would not dignify the papacy for forty years, until Gerbert of Aurillac would come from France and become Sylvester II at the turn of the millennium. Instead, Otto's pope was a lecher and a reprobate, the grandson of the vampire queen and seducer-killer of popes, Marozia. Completely given over to hunting, hawking, wenching, gaming, and wine, John XII had fathered a number of children and had given away the church's treasures to his concubines. The Lateran Palace had been turned into a brothel, and John XII did not seem to care in what shape his women came nor from what station. "Witness the women he keeps," one report stated. "Some of them are fine ladies who are thin as reeds, others are everyday Bulcsu wenches. It is all the same to him whether they walk the pavement or ride in a carriage and pair." The absence of women in the churches was explained, as one report to Otto put it, by the fact that women "fear to come and pray at the threshold of the holy apostles, for they have heard how John a little time ago took women pilgrims by force to his bed, wives, widows and virgins alike."

When Otto first heard these rumors, he was indulgent. "He is only a boy," the emperor said, "and will soon alter if good men set him an example. I hope that honorable reproof and generous persuasion will quickly cure him of these vices: and then we shall say with the prophet: 'This is a change which the hand of the Highest has brought.' " But it would be Otto who quickly changed his mind. John XII would not change his ways. The pope had allowed the churches of the papal realm to fall into disrepair, with rain leaking onto altars and holy relics. He hunted publicly, meted out punishments of blinding and castration, accepted bribes for episcopal appointments. It was said that when he drank wine he invoked the devil and when he played dice, he asked the blessing of Jupiter, Venus, and other heathen deities. "There cannot be a doubt," one Christian account says blandly, "that John XII was anything but what a Pope, the chief pastor of Christendom, should have been." Still, it was Otto's idea that the grandeur of what they were doing transcended the personalities.

On January 31, 962 A.D., Otto the Great arrived in Rome. John XII received the German conqueror unctuously and ceremoniously, but Otto had no illusions about his host. Shortly before his coronation, he turned to his sword bearer and issued a wary caution: "When I pray before the sacred shrine of the Apostles, hold your sword over my head all the time. For my ancestors had good reason to suspect the good faith of the Romans. And the wise man of forethought anticipates difficulties while yet they are afar, that they may not overwhelm him unawares." As yet, Otto I had no earthly concept of how many difficulties lay ahead of him.

In a glorious spectacle in St. Peter's Cathedral on February 2, 962 A.D., the pope bestowed "the glory of the imperial crown" upon Otto and Adelaide. The Holy Roman Empire of the German Nation thereby came into being. The pope swore allegiance to the emperor in an oath "over the most precious body of St. Peter," while Otto in turn lavished the pontiff with precious gifts of gold and gems. "To thee, the Lord Pope John, I King Otto, promise and swear, by the Father, Son, and Holy Ghost, by the wood of the life-giving cross, and by these relics of the saint, that, I will exalt to the best of my ability the Holy Roman Church and you its ruler," the emperor swore. "Never with my will or at my instigation shall you lose life or limb or the honor which you possess. And without your consent, never, within the city of Rome, will I make any regulation which affects you or the Romans. Whatever territory of St. Peter comes within my grasp, I will give up to you. And to whomsoever I shall entrust the kingdom of Italy, I will make him swear to help you as far as he can to defend the lands of St. Peter."

Officially now, Otto the Great restored to the church the "Donation of Charlemagne." These were lands originally given to the Holy See in 754 A.D. but lost in the subsequent political chaos of the Italian peninsula. The gift consecrated the boundaries of a formal papal state, from Naples in the south to Parma in the north. This temporal state, under the control of the pope, would last for another nine hundred years.

This great moment of glory in the history of Christendom lasted a very short time. Given the jealousy and the debauchery of John XII, the situation quickly disintegrated into chaos and rivalry and bickering. No sooner had Otto turned his back on Rome than Pope John XII, feeling constrained by the power of Otto over him, violated his solemn oath of allegiance and fell back into league with the infamous Berengar II.

Berengar was having his own problems with women, as it turned out. He was being cuckolded by a short, hairy, swarthy priest named Dominic. Dominic had found his way into the queen's bedchamber, to the certain knowledge of the king's chamberlains. The king himself remained ignorant until one night a royal dog intercepted him, barked and bit the priest, and brought out the entire neighborhood. Berengar promptly had the priest castrated. As a contemporary observer, the bishop of Cremona, remarked:

"Those who turned the priest into a eunuch declared there was good reason for the love his mistress bore him: his tool, they discovered, was worthy of Priapus himself."

In Rome, meanwhile, the pope fomented a rebellion against the German conqueror. When the German emperor in Pavia heard of the pope's treachery, he rushed back to Rome. And in the coming several years, he would have to rush back four times, as John XII was alternately exiled, restored, deposed, excommunicated, and reinstalled. His last restoration to the papal scepter came, according to one report, after "the women, with whom the so called pope John was accustomed to carry on his voluptuous sports, being many in numbers and noble in rank, stirred up the Romans and brought John back again into Rome."

Finally, on May 14, 964 A.D., John XII mercifully died. Appropriately, he breathed his last *in flagrante delicto*. As the bishop of Cremona described it, "One night when John was disporting himself with some man's wife outside Rome, the devil dealt him such a violent blow on the temples that he died of the injury within a week. Moreover at the prompting of the devil, who had struck the blow, he refused the last sacraments at his death bed."

Thus, this noble melding of sword and scepter did not have an auspicious beginning. If the wretched John XII was a disgrace, Otto the Great was petty and brutal in his suppression of the Roman rebellion. On one occasion, just to make a point, Otto had a rebellious prefect thrown in the dungeon in the Lateran Palace and then hanged him by his hair from the equestrian statue of Marcus Aurelius. After he was cut down, the wretch was forced to ride naked on a donkey through the streets of Rome. In trying to deal with the birth pangs of this new holy empire, Otto the Great spent only two of the last fourteen years of his reign in the German principalities. He was the quintessential itinerant emperor, forever on the move.

Eventually, both emperor and pope earned the disgust of the Romans. "Woe to Rome! Oppressed and downtrodden by so many nations!" wrote a Benedictine monk. "Thou are taken captive by the Saxon king, thy people are judged by the sword. Thy strength is become as naught. Thy gold and thy silver are carried away in their purses. Thou, who wast a mother are now become a daughter. What thou didst possess, thou hast lost. In the might of thy power thou triumphed over nations, has cast the world into dust, has strangled the kings of the earth. Thou wast so beautiful! Thou hast borne the scepter and the great power. Now thou has been plundered and ravaged by the Saxon king."

The ideal of a true marriage between church and empire would have to wait another forty years. Then, at the turn of the millennium, the grandson of Otto the Great, Otto III, followed his ancestor in triumph to Rome to be coronated as the third emperor of the Holy Roman Empire of the German Nation. But his partner would be Pope Sylvester II, one of the most devout and most cultured men ever to sit on the papal throne.

CHAPTER NINE

Vajk the Saint

KING STEPHEN OF HUNGARY was born with the name Vajk in 970 A.D. The given name was Turkish and meant "rich" or "master" but the year of his birth was scarcely a rich or masterful one for the Magyars. For the last time the tribes of eastern Hungary stormed out of their horseshoe plain as raiders and thieves. Twenty thousand strong, they crossed the mountains and joined the tribes of Transylvania and the Slavs of the eastern steppes, the Bulgarians, Pechenegs, and Russians, to form an army of sixty thousand, commanded by the prince of Kiev, Svyatoslav. They went with their customary greedy expectations, but this time the barbarian alliance challenged a Byzantine Empire that had grown stronger with each passing year and had already closed off the Mediterranean to Viking raiders of the North.

The eastern army crossed into Thrace, and the great pearl of Constantinople seemed in danger. But at Arcadiopolis, near Adrianople, well within the Greek lands that had long been a source of lucre for the Hungarian horde, the barbarians were crushed in a decisive battle. As the defeated soldiers stumbled home in anger and humiliation and shock, they turned on their Russian commander, killed him, and made his skull into a drinking bowl.

The disaster at Arcadiopolis was the death knell for Hungarian expansionism. Just as Lechfeld had liquidated the menace of western Hungary for Germany, Arcadiopolis eliminated the threat of the eastern Hungarian clans to their southern neighbors. After this campaign half of Bulgaria was absorbed into Byzantium. The terror of the horsemen had passed. Further foreign invasions were hopeless, even in alliance with other tribes. Suddenly, the country found itself sandwiched between two powerful, expanding empires. In 972 A.D. these empires formed an alliance between themselves which made Hungary's strategic position all the more desperate.

The son of Otto the Great, Otto II, married a Byzantine princess of legendary beauty and sophistication named Theophano, and warmth spread between the two empires and the two forms of Christianity. Finding itself squeezed like a pea in a vice, Hungary was forced to compromise or be squashed. It chose the former.

Unhorsed and detoothed, Hungarian society shifted now, under the leadership of Vajk's father, Geza, to a strategy of survival. Before the Carpathian plain could be truly safe from invasion, it needed to change the very nature of its culture, to expunge the source of its former aggressiveness, perhaps even to give up its prized uniqueness, for the two imperial giants that pressed in east and west were not only large but evangelistic. The aggressive instincts of the Hungarians were bound up with their pagan myths and practices, and these were also the basis of the tribal folklore. Geza saw that these tribal traditions had to be broken down, if he was to consolidate his people into a national unit and thereby save them from being overrun. Paganism needed to be removed as an excuse for foreign invasion.

In 972 A.D., in an act of pure expediency, Geza announced his intention to convert to Christianity. He sent an envoy to Otto the Great with this startling news, and the German emperor did not care to question the sincerity of the conversion, for he was now old and infirmed, less than a year away from death. For this soldier of Christ, the military taming of Hungary was empty unless it was followed by conversion. To Otto, the bulletin from Estergom was as much political as religious. In short order, the first bishop was dispatched to Hungary, as Otto sent a wary message to Pilgrim, the bishop of Passau:

"Otto, by the grace of God, Holy Emperor, to Pilgrim, honored bishop of the Passau church: Our greetings and mercy. We are sending to you Bishop Bruno and commending him to your favor, so that you should afford him all the help possible, in whatever he needs and should most cautiously guide him, supplying him with men and horses and other needs for the road, as close to the border of Hungary as you can. We delegate him there so that he should bring our power into contact with their king, Geza, as soon as possible. You should take the utmost care that this envoy should reach his destination safely, because our intent should meet with success. It will be of benefit to you and to your people. God be with you."

The first episcopal see was established near the royal palace in Estergom, high above the Danube, facing west to Slovakia. Several years later, Pilgrim ventured east to Pannonholma and baptized five thousand Hungarians during a single ceremony. The event had the air of a cattle roundup.

During this period of phony conversion, Geza's son Vajk had been born and baptized. According to church legend, his mother, Charlotte, had something of a Virgin Mary experience during her pregnancy. In a miraculous dream, St. Stephen the Martyr appeared to her, saying, "Woman, be of good courage, and put thy faith in Christ. Know that thou shall bring forth a fortunate son, unto whom this kingdom shall be given. Such a wonderful man as he shall be Pannonia has never seen, nor after his death shall ever see again. After his departure he shall be numbered among the saints."

"Who are you, sir?" Charlotte asked in wonderment.

"I am Stephen, who was the first to suffer martyrdom for the name of Jesus. Give him my name."

And so Vajk became Stephen. All of this, however, is according to later sanctified accounts. The reality was something a little less pure. Charlotte was a decidedly earthy woman. A princess from Transylvania, she was lusty, tomboyish, temperamental, and domineering. While she was known for her beauty as the "white lady," she loved to drink and cavort with the rowdiest boys in the roughest games. An accomplished rider, she was said to have killed a man in a fit of temper. St. Stephen the protomartyr may have visited her in a dream, but she was no martyr herself, for she salted her beer and her Christianity with pagan rites. Upon her husband, Geza, she exerted a heavy influence, somewhat in contravention of the wariness among Hungarian men of bossy women.

"Beware of the bearded woman," runs the old Magyar proverb.

Since her husband saw Christianity chiefly for its political usefulness, Geza too practiced an odd brand of religion. And yet before the new religion could take hold, the old ways had to be crushed. With relentless brutality and against fierce resistance, Geza set out to destroy pagan temples and idols and to loosen the grip of the shamans, for his purpose was to undermine the power of local chieftains. He raved among his negligent subjects, killing recalcitrants in fits of temper, and abolished godless habits with bloody hands. From each household he extracted the tax of a marten pelt: in every betrothal, a horse for the king was the price of a marriage license. This deprived the petty chiefs of wealth and authority. "He mobilized all the great part of his army for the sake of true fear of God," says one account, "and those who he found on a different way, he subjugated with threat and terror." Like Charlotte, however, he could not part with his pagan gods in his private chambers. He believed in witches and gnomes and expected to be a prince in the next world where his slain enemies would be his henchmen. When his bishop confronted him with this apparent hypocrisy, he replied blandly:

"I am so rich and powerful that I can afford to worship both gods!"

This drove his bishops to distraction. One said that this religion, part Christian and part heathen, was "worse than barbarism itself." These priests were foreigners, however, and they had little sway over Geza. He had set out upon an independent course, bowing to the strength of the empires without accepting their control. In this delicate balancing act, he was compliant enough to deflate any hostility from abroad while he insisted upon the uniqueness of his land. He listened attentively to the teaching of his bishops while he denied any obedience to Rome. In this transitional period, Hungary was to be part of Christian Europe in name only, certainly not part of any fold that implied subservience to the Greek or the Holy Roman Empire. To become an "apostolic king" held no attraction for Geza.

In reporting about this strange new convert to Otto and to the pope, the bishops gave a mixed report. "Geza ordered that every Christian who should want to move into his lands should be greeted with hospitality and granted security. He gave permission to the priests and monks to appear before him and listened to them with pleasure. When the time, ordained by the Powers Above came, he was baptized, with his family and became one of the faithful, taking an oath to convert all his subjects to the Christian faith. He took excessive pains to put down the rebels, abolish ungodly rites, and set up bishoprics to establish the Holy Church." If that were the only account, Geza must have sounded like a model Christian . . . but it was not. Of the mission to Geza's Hungary by the saint and martyr Adalbert, it would be written later: "He was able to cast only the shadow of Christianity on them as they changed but little in their straying."

His parents' failings as model Christians notwithstanding, Vajk was raised in a vibrantly religious atmosphere. In affairs of the royal court, he was instructed by an Italian count called Teodata de San Severino. His spiritual director was Adalbert, the Czech bishop who would be killed by pagans before Stephen became king. For daily moral instruction, the prince was schooled by a humble monk called Radla, who set out to groom the young man to be a Christian (and a Roman) king. Vajk's fate, Radla taught, was not only to be monarch, but to be high priest to his nation. If Geza and Charlotte were still attached to their raunchy pagan deities, they kept their vices to themselves. The boy grew to be slender and diminutive, almost fay, and he was intense and earnest. He smiled seldom, for he was taught that playfulness was unmanly and unkingly. This dour expression was Radla's doing, since he had taught the prince from Scripture:

"Laughter mixes with pain and at the end, joy turns into sadness."

By 995 A.D. Geza was old and worn out. For over ten years, he had been harassed in the western marches by an aggressive Bavarian prince called Henry the Quarrelsome, but Henry died in that year, and a serene and much relieved Geza prepared to meet his maker. Several years before, Geza had gathered his war council and addressed the question of his succession. In an announcement shocking to some, he pronounced Vajk to be the next king of Hungary. The youth, still an adolescent, was lifted triumphantly upon a shield, as was the custom, and paraded ceremoniously through the stone castle at Estergom.

But the king's decision sowed the seeds of rebellion, for it broke a cherished tradition. Within the Arpad dynasty, given its tribal rather than feudal traditions, succession was supposed to pass not by primogeniture but through the principle of "seniorate"; that is, the next in line was the next oldest in the ruling family. That was Koppany, Geza's younger brother. To choose Stephen was to circumvent the rightful heir to the throne. In addition to seniorate, there was also the legal custom of "levirate," whereby the younger sibling inherited the widow of his deceased brother as his wife. By rights and by tradition, therefore, Koppany was supposed to get both Geza's crown and his wife.

In Geza's diminished state, Charlotte took the reins of power, for she, at age forty, was still vigorous and fiery as ever. She prepared her son to become king. In 995 A.D., as a symbol of improving relations with Bavaria after the death of Henry the Quarrelsome, Vajk was betrothed to Henry's daughter, Gisela. Far from quarrelsome, the bride was pious and ethereal, almost to the point of otherworldliness, for she had been educated by a saint, Wolfgang, and raised to be a nun. She was also proud, like all the Bourbons, an estimable woman who had to be reckoned with. Accompanied to Hungary by German knights and priests and deposited in the castle at Nyitra, she was a gift to Vajk, a gift to Hungary, and a gift to the church.

In 997 A.D. Geza finally died. Vajk became king. His uncle Koppany promptly revolted. It was a conflict of principle: between the old and the new, between seniorate and primogeniture, between levirate and a woman's right to choose or reject a husband. In the last, it might also be considered a conflict between the Old and the New

Testament, because in the Old Testament levirate was sanctioned as a method to maintain the purity of the bloodline in a simple society, whereas the New Testament regarded the practice as lechery. It was a blood and power feud between the dead king's son and his brother, but it was also a struggle between paganism and Christianity, between the "black" and the "white" Hungarians. Having been baptized with the rest of the family several decades before, Koppany was officially Christian, but now the black heathens rallied to his side, for to kill the Christian king was to wound his faith.

Ironically, Koppany marched on Charlotte's castle in Veszprem, as if to gain a wife he had to lay siege to her. His army was formidable, its elements drawn from southern Hungary and those Slavic regions south of Lake Balaton which made up his suzerainty. Within his force were also ferocious Viking elements whose origins were Swedish and who had migrated south and west through Russia as guards and mercenaries to various potentates. In Estergom, meanwhile, Vajk mobilized a modern force. His master of the horse reinforced the royal light brigades with the heavy German cavalry from Gisela's personal escort and with the colorful mounted units from far-flung Bulgar and Transylvanian tribes. He too had his Viking mercenaries. These foreign elements were to provide the margin of victory, a fact that would not be forgotten or forgiven, as many later accounts of the clash would depict a battle between Germans and Hungarians. As he prepared to march on his uncle, Vajk convened his German bishops and dedicated the campaign to St. Martin, the fourth-century saint who had been born a heathen in western Hungary and who went on to be a great fighter against heathens. If his army was victorious, Vajk promised, he would grant Koppany's domain to the abbey of Pannonholma and found a great church there dedicated to St. Martin.

North of Lake Balaton, the forces clashed, and Vajk was victorious. A German knight took credit for killing Koppany, and the rebel's body was quartered, the sections sent to castles in the four quarters of Hungary where the meat was nailed to the castle gates at Gyor and Gyulafehervar, Nyitra and Bihar as a warning to rebels and heathens alike. This ghoulish practice was in accordance with the traditional punishment for lechery, but it also symbolized Vajk's unification of his country.

The Christian chronicles later put a gentle spin on Vajk's cruel suppression of his uncle's black rebellion:

"The king attacked the blacks with force, intimidation, and love, bringing them to the true faith."

WITH KOPPANY'S REBELLION greeting his accession to the throne and with the enormous problem of consolidating the disparate elements of his country after such chaos, it is understandable that Vajk might have had little time or interest in ceremony. But something more profound was at work. The new king was intensely aware of the Christian calendar. The turn of the millennium approached, and for Vajk it was a time of rededication, of judgment, of epiphany. He might have been coronated in 998 A.D., and there were good political reasons to do so in the short view. But coronated as what? With its bizarre language, its pagan traditions, its militancy and menace, Hungary was still estranged from the rest of Europe and from the Roman church. To his own people, Vajk was king, but to the rest of Europe, he was chief of an exotic land, governor to a dangerous and barbarian people, ruler of the once terrible mounted bowmen.

In his reflections during the year 999 A.D., Vajk faced two choices. He needed to decide between Rome and Byzantium. If he chose the western brand of Christianity, he had to choose between pope of Rome and the lesser bishops of Germany. In the first choice, sheer survival was the issue. Given its precarious situation between the two great engines of Byzantium and Germany, Hungary would have to turn to the west or to the east, if it was to continue to exist.

For Vajk this first choice was relatively easy. Hungary had been tilting toward the west for a generation. His father had maintained hostile relations with Byzantium throughout his reign, whereas the relations with Bavaria had been steadily improving. The second choice was more subtle. Vajk had begun the formal organization of the Hungarian church into ecclesiastical districts and parishes on his own, but he could not carry the formal conversion of his country further without sanction from the eternal church. But where to turn? Saints of the German church like Wolfgang and Adalbert had evangelized the Hungarian people ever since Geza's "conversion" in 972

A.D., and Wolfgang had been central to the education of Vajk's Bavarian wife, Gisela. Though the German emperors asserted supreme authority over all the pagan lands of Europe, Hungary recognized no such claim by the German church. Indeed, Geza had stoutly resisted any such claim from the beginning. To associate his country with the church of the German Empire might hold great peril, whereas an association with Rome might counterbalance the German influence in his country.

In 999 A.D. an event of great importance eased Vajk's dilemma. On Palm Sunday, April 2 of that year, the tiara was placed on the head of a new and glorious pope. In contrast to the disasters and scandals of the previous years that had brought the papacy to its lowest ebb in dignity and prestige, the new pope, Gerbert of Aurillac, was a man of immense power and breadth. The first French pope in history took the title of Sylvester II.

From the beginning Gerbert saw the opportunity of the moment. Christianity was sweeping the continent, perhaps for fear of the impending apocalypse at the turn of the millennium. Vast territory throughout Europe was ripe for formal entry into the Catholic domain. King Boleslav of Poland was petitioning Rome for the ecclesiastical organization of his church. Presenting himself as "Christ's Athlete," the Polish ruler washed his hair in a sacred font, then cut it all off, and sent it to Rome to show the sincerity of his petition. To the north, overtures had come from Olaf Trygvesson of Norway, and the new pope responded by demanding that the Viking lands discard the stick figures of its runic script and proclaim Latin as the formal written language. Even as far away as Kiev, Vladimir I sought the dignity of the Roman church. And now Hungary. It was for Sylvester II to make the most of these propitious circumstances.

Vajk wanted to be part of the new fashion that was sweeping Europe. To appeal to this learned pope was a privilege and a joy. In the spring of 1000 A.D. he dispatched a loyal and experienced envoy named Astrik to Rome. The ambassador carried an application to the pope to confer upon the Magyar ruler the noble title of King by the Grace of God. Only in this manner could he become a true Christian ruler, and only the Holy Father could confer upon him the title of an apostolic king. In the style of the German emperors he longed to be both king and, simultaneously, a canon of the church. When Astrik arrived at the Lateran Palace, there seemed to be some disingenuous confusion about Hungary. Where was the country? certain prelates asked. It was a land almost unknown to Catholic fathers, they professed. But by the time Astrik was ushered into Sylvester's presence, the pope was effusive in his welcome. Astrik, after all, was a pupil of St. Adalbert, the martyr, who three years before had been killed by pagans.

"I am but apostolic," the pope exclaimed, "but the master who sent you here is, in truth, the apostle of Christ himself!"

In the weeks that followed, the Vatican prepared the formalities for Hungary's entry into the Christian family of nations. A papal bull had to be written; the organization for the episcopal districts had to be discussed, and a proper crown had to be made. In fact, the Vatican already had a crown on hand. It had been made for the duke of Poland, whose ambassador had come to Rome with an identical request to the pope only days before Astrik arrived. But Poland was only technically independent from the German Empire, having discarded its vassal status only weeks before. Details were still to be worked out, and the church was in no hurry to consecrate the independence. Moreover, Gerbert had an awful dream in which an angel warned him of evil rulers who would succeed the current leader of Poland, Boleslav the Brave. The angel ordered the Holy Father to spurn the Poles and to confer this holy crown on the Hungarians instead.

In the early summer of 1000 A.D., Astrik set off for home. As the priest neared Estergom, Vajk rode out to meet him in great anticipation. The prince stood somberly at attention as Astrik read to him the papal bull: "Wherefore, glorious son, all that you have asked of us and of the Apostolic See . . . the crown, the kingly title, the metropolitan see at Estergom and the other bishoprics, we gladly grant. By the will and authority of Almighty God, and by that of the holy Apostles Peter and Paul, and with the apostolic blessing, we allow these things to you. You offer to St. Peter yourself and the present and future people of Hungary, and therefore, we place your country under the protection of the Holy Roman Church, returning to your wisdom and to your heirs and lawful successors to have and to hold, to rule and to govern. These thy heirs shall be bound to testify to us and to our successors due obedience and respect." And then Astrik presented a cross, embedded in the seal of the Hungarian nation . . . and the holy crown: "We pray Almighty God who directed us to give to you the crown we had prepared for the duke of the Poles, to preserve the kingdom for you and you for the kingdom."

On August 15, 1000 A.D., a Sunday to mark its sacred significance, Vajk was consecrated as the king of Hungary. In accordance with ritual, he was roused from his sleep by Astrik and two archbishops from Germany, and at his bedside they delivered a prayer:

"Almighty and eternal God, who have deigned to elevate your servant on the summit of the kingdom, grant to him, we ask you, that he may decide everything for the benefit of all. In the course of this work, may he never depart from the path of your truth." Vajk dressed and was brought to the royal chapel. At the threshold of the church, the king-in-waiting paused to regard the assemblage of knights and priests and chosen representatives of the people. The archbishops took their place at the altar in front of the empty throne.

The order of service for the coronation was the Mainz Sacramentary, and the assemblage waited with great anticipation for the blessed and exorcised oil of catechumens to be brought forward in the holy ampulla. In the presence of this holy oil the king made his solemn promise to the church, to his nation, and to his people: he promised to seek peace, justice, and mercy in the land. After the Te Deum, the ampulla was brought forward, and the king was anointed, on his bare chest, on his forehead, and on his shoulders.

"Ungo te in regem," the archbishop proclaimed. By this act the sacred power of the church was conferred on the king, as the bishops sang the antiphon "Sadoch, the priest, and Nathan, the prophet, anointed Solomon king of Zion, and coming to him, they said, joyfully, May the king live forever."

Then in succession, the king was presented with the ring of the holy church, the royal sword to defend the church, the scepter of righteous rule, and the cane of virtue, the last of which was "to encourage the gentle and scare the reprobate, to show the way to those who go astray and reach your hand to the fallen ones, to disperse the proud and help the humble."

And at last, the papal crown. When the crown was brought forward, Vajk knelt at the altar as the priests and nobles gathered round. Raising the crown aloft, the archbishop blessed it. It was elegant in its simplicity: two intersecting gold hoops upon which were engraved colored images of twelve apostles; on the top, at the point where the hoops were joined, there was a small globe, topped with a cross; the hoops were joined with a headband of simple Romanesque designs. With this crown on his head, and after the papal benediction, Vajk, son of Geza, heir of the Arpad dynasty, ruler of the Magyar tribesmen, became King Stephen I of Hungary, namesake of Stephen the protomartyr, and Rex Apostolicus. As the young king took his place upon his throne, the strains of Kyrie Eleison filled the stone chapel, and after a high mass, the bells rang jubilantly over the Danube.

From a distance Sylvester II viewed this pontifical event with satisfaction. He had the power to dignify a rough and once pagan nation, and it was a strong message to those who were still outside the Christian family. In the capture of Hungary for Christendom and western civilization, the Roman church had done more than merely add another pagan land to the dominion of the devout. Geographically, the land of the Magyars held a strategic position in Europe. Now there was a converted and vibrant land, lying astride the Carpathians, which could be a bulwark against the infidels of the east and a safe route to the Holy Land for pilgrims. But it might also be more.

In his imagination Sylvester envisaged more than merely the safety of the pilgrims to the Black Sea. Hungarian lands might also provide the route of Christian soldiers marching to Jerusalem to rip the holy places away from the heathens. Sixteen years before, when he took up his position as the bishop of Rheims, Gerbert had meditated on the enslavement of the Christian church in Jerusalem.

"Arouse thyself, then, soldier of Christ," he exclaimed. "Take your standard and fight for Him! and what you cannot effect by force of arms, bring about by your counsels and by your money. By me, God will bless you, so that you may become rich by giving." This was one of the earliest calls for a Christian crusade against the infidels.

The preparation for holy war began benignly. In the years after his coronation, Stephen took measures to make the passage to Jerusalem safe and comfortable for the pilgrims. Over the mountain paths through the Transylvanian Alps and downriver along the Danube, soldiers were stationed to protect the faithful from bandits, and hostels were built to shelter and feed the travelers. The word of this service began to spread quickly through the Christian world. St. Odilo, the abbot of Cluny, wrote his thanks to Stephen. "Almost the whole world speaks of how great your soul's passion is in honor of our divine religion. Especially those who returned from the tomb of our Lord bear witness to you."

The conversion of Hungary laid the groundwork for the crusades a century later.

I N THE FIRST YEARS of the new millennium, King Stephen devoted himself to the organization of his church and to the foundations of his young nation. His royal seat remained at Estergom. Also there, he established the primatial see of the Hungarian church. A royal chapel was built on high ground above his castle, on the bluff above the Danube, just as the abbey of Pannonholma was on high ground to the east. Later in his reign, after a successful war with the Bulgarians, Stephen transformed the spoils of victory into the stones of a third church, the cathedral at Szekesfehervar. This royal church was dedicated to St. Peter and St. Paul, and to the Virgin Mary after various relics of saints were deposited there. The king also had Geza reinterred in the same place. Szekesfehervar was meant to be for Stephen what the sacred capital of Aachen was to Charlemagne.

With these three churches as the jewels in the tiara, the apostolic king divided his country into dioceses, demanding that every ten villages band together and construct a church. If any family were so fortunate as to have ten children, the tenth was obliged to become a monk at the abbey of Pannonholma. To aid in this division of the country, as well as to establish his control and authority over his people, Stephen developed a system of castles and royal residences. In the lands around Budapest alone, there were residences at Csepel, Arad, Buda and Pest, Visegrad, Domos, Cinkota, and Taksony.

Queen Gisela inherited Charlotte's castle at Veszprem. More than a third of the entire population was employed in maintaining these royal residences in a variety of roles from cup bearers to grooms to store masters, from armorers to the distinguished keeper of the metal seal. By regulation these castles had the same layout. The chapel was always built outside the castle walls on higher ground; and the marketplace was encased in the lower substratum within. There was a connection between the two: market day was on Sunday, and it was a festive, fun-filled time. But when the church bells rang, the people were herded together and marched to the church to receive the word.

The network of royal residences and castles had another profound consequence. Abolishing clan estates broke down arcane tribal ways, and homage to the national king undermined the authority of the old chieftains. Stephen introduced private landownership, which was an additional blow to local chiefs.

To organize his Christian kingdom in this way, Stephen wrote laws and established royal courts. In general, an air of compromise marked this first rudimentary code, but criminal penalty was the stiffest when it affected private property. If a servant was killed, damages were paid to the servant's master. If a husband killed his wife, he was obligated to pay blood money to his wife's family. A man who abducted a woman was obliged to pay the woman's family ten steers. The church was charged with punishing moral offenses like revenge for murder. To break a fast meant an automatic week's imprisonment on bread and water. If a sorcerer or a shaman cheated a family, the cheat was handed over to the cheated to do their worst. Later, in making pagan practices illegal, a formal law was pronounced as follows: "Anyone making a sacrifice next to wells or giving offerings to trees, fountains, and stones according to heathen rites shall atone for their offense with an ox."

The irony of Stephen's legislative efforts is that they established an ecclesiastical basis for a Christian state at the same time as they prevented Hungary from turning into a vassal state of the Roman papacy.

Early in the new millennium, internal and external strife threatened these nascent steps toward nationhood and Christianization.

No sooner had he dispatched and dismembered Koppany, his uncle on his father's side, than Stephen found himself attacked by his uncle on his mother's side, who sparked a rebellion in Transylvania. Once again the frayed banners of St. Martin and St. George took their place at the head of Stephen's army, and the rebellion was crushed. Then, in the Lower Danube, the chieftain of the black Hungarians took up arms against the king, as pagan remnants flocked to their latest hope. In this case there was allegedly divine intervention, for the commander of Stephen's forces was awakened by lions who warned the general that he must attack at once. This he did, crushing the resistance and cutting out the tongue of the rebel chieftain as a prize.

The foreign threat lay to the south and east, where the Bulgarian tribes separated Hungary from the Greek lands of the Byzantine Empire. Alliances seemed to shift as often as the wind. In 1001 A.D. the Bulgarians and the Greeks were at war, and in 1004 A.D. the Greeks seized Skoplje in Croatia, which shrank the Bulgarian territory considerably. Inevitably, Stephen was sucked into the conflict, first on the side of Bulgarians, who provided him with a needed buffer against Byzantium. In 1014 A.D. there seemed to be a reversal of fortune. The Bulgarian army defeated the Byzantine army by driving the Greeks into a narrow Macedonian valley and pulverizing them with stones. Soon after, however, the tide shifted back to the Greeks when the Byzantine emperor captured a Bulgarian force near Strumica. According to legend, Basil II exacted a terrible revenge on his fourteen thousand Bulgarian captives: he blinded ninety-nine out of every one hundred captives and had the lucky few lead their maimed comrades home. When the Bulgarian leader saw this gruesome sight, he died on the spot.

In the face of this volatile situation, Stephen's policy was to back the winning side. When the Bulgarians were down, the Magyar leader, with a hint of irony one hopes, began to refer to his eastern neighbors as "barbarians." He sent a separate force against them, defeating the Bulgars and cashing in his war loot for the stones of his cathedral at Szekesfehervar. With the Bulgarians crushed once and for all, he formed an alliance with the Byzantine Empire, and, inevitably, the friendship was sealed with a royal marriage when King Stephen's only son, Emeric, married a Greek princess.

Prince Emeric was actually the king's second son—the first, Otto, having died at an early age. Thus the entire future of Stephen's line rested on Emeric's vulnerable shoulders. In his son's education the king had invested much. The boy's spiritual adviser was St. Gellert (who, like St. Adalbert before him, would be killed by pagans). When the prince grew to manhood, Stephen personally instructed his son on the high calling of the Christian king. The true king must be both leader and high priest, the servant of his people and the servant of God. Stephen committed his "admonitions" to writing, compiling a book, as his legend writer later says, "in the heat of love," in which he taught his son "above all [to] be painful to the Catholic faith, strengthen order in the church, respect the dignity of high priests, love the nobles and the warriors, administer justice and exercise patience in all his deeds, be hospitable towards immigrants, do nothing without asking advice, revere his ancestors and take them as his models, and fulfill his duty to pray and practice the virtues of piety and mercy." If the king became proud, spiteful, or restless, Stephen warned, he would lose his throne to another.

With this careful preparation for kingship, Prince Emeric became Stephen's partner in power. When in 1030 A.D. the Hungarians faced an ambitious German emperor, Conrad II, who had overstepped his bounds, Prince Emeric assumed the command of the royal army, and the Hungarians defeated the German force, pushing it back beyond Vienna. His son was ready for the throne, Stephen concluded, and the king prepared to step aside, making Emeric the regent and allowing him to rule Hungary by himself, while the king receded into prayer.

But then, in a hunting accident, a wild boar killed Emeric. Hungary was plunged into crisis. Devastated, falling into a permanent state of melancholy, Stephen now stood without a successor. All his Christian accomplishments were exposed and in jeopardy, and his nation still strongly inclined toward heathenism. By the old method of succession, the next in line in the house of Arpad was his cousin Vazul, who was stupid, reckless, and half pagan. King Stephen was now sixty years old, six years away from death. Increasingly, he was confined to his sickbed. In his mysticism and his delirium, he was preoccupied with the parallels between his life and that of Christ. His consciousness of the millennium was intense. He had been coronated a thousand years after the birth of Christ, and now he faced death a thousand years after Christ's death. Was this his fate— to die childless and to be succeeded by pagans?

In sacred scholarship, it was said that Christ began his teaching at age thirty and died at age thirty-three. Perhaps the millennium was dated not from Christ's birth, but from his death. By this construction, the second coming was nigh. Anxiety, foreboding, preparation became the mood of the royal household. Queen Gisela turned her castle at Veszprem into a royal workshop, producing crosses and altar ornaments for Hungarian churches and turning out clerical vestments as if her priests all needed to be properly dressed for the apocalypse.

In this royal atelier, the seamstresses also worked on a magnificent red and gold silk mantle for the king. In this "bell chasuble," Stephen the Protomartyr and King Stephen were portrayed together in a series of panels depicting kings, popes, and saints together, beneath the outstretched hands of God. It was as if Stephen were imagining his place in heaven after Judgment Day. The Roman numerals MXXXI were embroidered into the fringe, and in one panel a halo dissolved into the figure for omega.

With the royal household in this grip of anticipation—of Stephen's death and of the apocalypse—the king performed acts both sacred and profane. He formally dedicated his basilica at Szekesfehervar to the Virgin Mary, and as he drew near to death he "presented" his country to the mother of Christ. This act was meant to appeal to heathens as well as Christians, for it gave the believers in a heathen goddess (whose gown was the blue sky) a figure with which they could identify and to whom they could transfer their loyalty. His action established the cult of the Virgin Mary in Hungary.

At the same time Stephen proclaimed his nephew Peter Orseolo to be his successor. This was a shocking decision, even to the most loyal of Stephen's followers, for it challenged both Hungarian traditions and independence. Though he had been a fixture in the Hungarian court for thirteen years, Peter Orseolo was the son of the doge of Venice, a virtual foreigner with foreign attachments. Predictably, the rightful successor, Vazul, impetuous and dull-witted though he was, responded with an attempt on the king's life. As Stephen lay immobile in his sickbed, Vazul's assassins snuck into the palace, but they were apprehended outside the bedchamber.

Vazul was dragged before the royal court and proclaimed to be the culprit. Then in an act downplayed by the subsequent biographies of Stephen, Vazul was blinded and hot lead was poured in his ears, rendering him, at the very least, unfit to rule.

On August 15, 1038 A.D., thirty-eight years to the day after his coronation, King Stephen of Hungary died. Not long afterward, pagans threw the pious educator of his son, Bishop Gellert, off the high hill above the Danube at Old Buda. And not long after that, Vazul's sons returned to Hungary to reclaim the country for the house of Arpad. That dynasty would last another two hundred years.

But in the centuries to follow, the stature of King Stephen as the founder of Hungary soared. Sainted by the Catholic church and lionized as the father of his country, this figure of the millennium took on mythical proportions. Through the invasion of Genghis Khan's Tartars in the thirteenth century, through the Muslim occupation of the Turks in the fifteenth, even in the Communist era including the uprising of 1956, St. Stephen is invoked and summoned whenever the country finds itself in crisis. In times of travail, a hymn is sung:

> Ah where are you, resplendent star of Hungarians?
> Ah where are you, King Stephen? For you Hungarians long
> In remembrance of you their tears overflow
> Their sad meadows bedewed with sorrow.

CHAPTER TEN

Gerbert the Wizard

DURING THE TENTH CENTURY, the papacy lurched from ignorance to debauchery to violence without pause or shame. From the harlot's reign of the vampire queen Marozia early in the century, to the lechery of the boy-pope John XII in midcentury, to the papal assassinations of the 980s and the struggles between the popes and antipopes at the end of the century, the Holy See was a swamp of chaos and scandal. Its dignity and authority was at its lowest point since St. Peter first sat on the papal throne. Only the crimes of the Borgias in the fifteenth and the sixteenth centuries would come to rival the current disgrace.

The timing of this total corruption of the Holy Office seemed especially unfortunate, since the first millennium of Christianity was drawing to a close. Was this not as the Bible had foretold? Had not the Holy Writ prophesied this? Did this complete corruption portend the advent of the Antichrist who was to burst upon the scene at the end of the world? "We see clearer than daylight that in the process of the Last Days, as love waxes cold and iniquity abounds among mankind, perilous times are at hand for men's souls," a French scribe of the time wrote. "By many assertions of the ancient fathers we are warned that, as covetousness stalks abroad, the religious Rules or Orders of the past have caught decay and corruption. Whenever religion hath failed among the pontiffs, when strictness of the Rule hath decayed among the abbots, when the vigor of monastic discipline hath grown cold, what then can we think but that the whole human race, root and branch, is sliding willingly down again into the gulf of primeval chaos."

Also in France, the bishop of Orléans remarked that with the corruption of Rome the churches of Antioch and of Alexandria had been lost, and the churches of Constantinople and of Spain did not respect the word of the pope. "We all are witnesses to the revolt of which the Apostle speaks," proclaimed the bishop, "a revolt not just of people but of Churches. The agents of the Pope who come to Gaul oppress us with all their might. One would say that the Antichrist is ruling us."

Beyond the corruption of the clergy, the other signs, foretold in the Apocalypse of St. John, 13.5, were manifold. There was an abundance of war, where nation rose against nation, kingdom against kingdom. Famine had begun in 970 A.D. and grown worse with each passing year until at its most desperate point, in the year 1000 A.D., cannibalism was rampant. The French historian Glaber, writing when living people still remembered the horrors of the millennial turn, described a mighty famine which raged for five years throughout the Roman world. So severe was the situation that men were "compelled to make their food not only of unclean beasts and creeping things, but even of men's women's and children's flesh, without regard even of kindred. So fierce waxed this hunger that grown up sons devoured their mothers, and mothers, forgetting their maternal love, ate their babes."

Plague was widespread. It took the gruesome form of "St. Anthony's fire," an infection so fierce and deadly—and yet so simple since it came from rotten rye bread—that it could produce its boils in the afternoon and cause death by the following morning. Such a plague seemed aptly named for the impending apocalypse, for in Christian legend the devil had taken the shape of a monk and had offered corrupted bread to St. Anthony as the communion host. In 993 A.D. earthquakes shook Italy before Mount Vesuvius erupted, "belching forth," as Glaber described it, "a multitude of vast stones mingled with sulfurous flames which fell even to a distance of three miles around. By the stench of Vulcan's breath all the surrounding province was made uninhabitable."

In the heavens, too, there were terrible signs. In 998 A.D., two meteorites fell on earth, one near Magdeburg, Germany, the other with a great crash near the river Albia. Then in 1000 A.D., a very bright meteor appeared in the sky that seemed to some to have the head of a snake with deep blue feet. "It appeared in the month of September," Glaber wrote, "not long after nightfall and remained visible for nearly three months. It shone so brightly that its light seemed to fill the greater part of the sky, then it vanished at cock's crow."

If these were the signs of the end-time, who would hold back the onslaught of the Antichrist? Who would be the heroic restrainer of whom the second epistle to the Thessalonians had spoken: "And now ye know what withholdeth that he might be revealed in his time. For the mystery of iniquity doth already work: only he who now letteth will let, until he be taken out of the way. And then shall that Wicked be revealed, whom the Lord shall consume with the spirit of his mouth, and shall destroy with the brightness of his coming."

This role would fall to Gerbert of Aurillac, the first pope from France.

GERBERT WAS AT THE MATURE AGE of fifty-eight when the papal tiara was finally placed upon his head in 999 A.D. In intellect, in breadth of experience and worldliness, in political skill and sheer determination, he was far ahead of his time. A thin, diminutive, balding man, with a sculpted goatee and an aquiline nose, he

was by nature happy, lively, and intense. By 998 A.D., he was somewhat battle-weary. Educator to kings and adversary to popes, he had
acquired a legion of admirers who were awed by his erudition, but
also, in twenty years of fierce ecclesiastical and secular battles, he
had powerful enemies and detractors. Because of his immense intelligence and wide travel, an aura of magic had come to surround him,
and, in the Middle Ages, to be suspected as a sorcerer could be
dangerous.

Born of humble parents in the village of Aurillac in Aquitaine, he
had taken up the religious life early. As a youth he entered the Benedictine monastery of St. Gerauld and bowed to the discipline of a
Latin education. From the start, his superiors had seen his promise.
He was put forward as an example to visitors of the church's bright
future. One such visitor was an important count from Spain, Borrell
II, who came to the Aurillac monastery to be married before returning home to take charge of his lands in the Spanish March, on
the border of the powerful and terrifying Moorish caliphate.

If from past history and prejudice Moorish Andalusia was viewed
with awe in central Europe, it remained the standard of high culture
in the tenth century. In Córdoba and Seville, science and medicine
and poetry flowered in glorious harmony as the learning of the
Arabic, Greek, Hebrew, and Latin worlds fertilized one another in a
celebration of the mind and the spirit. During the reigns of Al
Rahman III, and of his son Al Hakkam II, a spirit of tolerance prevailed toward Christians and Jews. For Muhammad was considered
to be the perfection of all the prophets who had come before him.
Jesus and Moses were not denied as prophets, nor were their teachings dismissed. These prophets were merely absorbed and perfected
in the person of Muhammad.

The knowledge of the caliphate was transported north, across the
barren borderland of La Mancha, to the small Christian kingdoms of
Navarre, Catalonia, Castile, and Aragon. There the learning was embraced and refined and passed further north to central Europe. The
duke of the Spanish March took Gerbert to one of the most important centers for the transmission of this knowledge north. That was
the monastery of Santa Maria de Rispoll, one of the five intellectual
centers in northern Spain (along with Vich, Cuixa, Gerona, and Bar-

celona). Since the ninth century Santa Maria de Rispoll located in a valley next to a river, had been devoted to translating Arabic knowledge into Latin. Its Mozarabic monks labored in the scriptorium over Arabic treatises, and their translations were sent north to the abbeys of Cluny and St. Gall. Gerbert, therefore, had access to the knowledge and the magic of the south without being able to speak or read Arabic.

In this exotic field of cross-fertilization, the French monk took up his studies passionately. Concentrating on mathematics, he became dexterous with the abacus, which was cued to Hindu-Arabic numerals. Later it would be rumored that he also studied astrology, that he practiced divination and was under the spell of the Egyptian magus Neptanebus, and that he wished to become a necromancer. The suspicion of satanic Spanish arts was deep in the rest of Europe.

Like the Renaissance men who were to come later, he was also taught practical knowledge. He learned how to build church organs which were powered by steam. He invented the pendulum clock and learned how to tell time from the stars at night. He also constructed sundials and celestial globes and mastered the science of the astrolabe. To a monk in Fleury, he described the operation of his hemisphere for making astronomical observations, an instrument whose calculations were remarkably accurate and which was, in effect, the precursor of Galileo's telescope. During his three years in Catalonia, he also spent time in Toledo, where he became enamored with the arts of the Orient, especially oriental magic and astrology. He may even have visited Córdoba, the most fabulous city in Europe and to Christians the most forbidding.

This dabbling in the occult would later reverberate harmfully in slanderous gossip. In this age of ignorance, his scientific instruments were seen as the tools of the devil, and his love of books as an occasion for sinister gossip. It would be said that during his sojourn among the Spanish infidels the pope-to-be had learned necromancy and devil worship, that he had divined the language of birds, that he had made a pact with the devil to obtain forbidden knowledge and undeserved honor, and that he dedicated his body to carnal pleasure.

One story had the young monk coming upon a half-naked, gossamer-clad maiden in a forest, sitting on a pile of gold coins. The damsel beckoned with the words "I am Meridiana, of noble birth,

A Mozarabic manuscript with Christian and Muslim influences combined.
(Museum of León)

St. James of Compostela, lopping off the head of a Moor at the Battle of Clavijo.
(Tiepolo, Szepmuveszeti Muzeum, Budapest)

Córdoba portrayed as Gog and Magog.
(*Beatus of Liebana, Pierpont Morgan Library/Art Resource, N.Y.*)

Revelation 20.7–9: And when the thousand years are expired, Satan shall be loosed out of his prison, And shall go out to deceive the nations which are in the four quarters of the earth, Gog and Magog, to gather them together to battle: the number of whom is as the sand of the sea. And they went up on the breadth of the earth, and compassed the camp of the saints about, and the beloved city: and fire came down from God out of heaven, and devoured them.

The Conquest of Hungary by the Magyars.
(*Mihály Munkácsy, Parliament, Budapest*)

The Battle of Lechfeld, presaging the demise of the Hungarian terror.

The crown of King Stephen of Hungary.
(*Hungarian National Museum, Budapest*)

St. Stephen.
(*National Szechenyi Library, Budapest*)

The Abbey at Cluny.
(Reconstruction: according to K. J. Conant)

St. Peter's Basilica, Rome, in medieval times.
(Romische Veduten, *Hermann Egger, National Gallery of Art*)

Gerbert of Aurillac, the Renaissance man of 1000 A.D.
(*Vatican Library*)

Santa Maria de Rispoll, the monastery where Gerbert learned the magic of the Moors.

Empress Theophano, the first diplomat of the first Europe.
(*Parrocchia di S. Ambrogio, Milan*)

The devastating Greek fire, presaging the end of the Viking age.
(Scylitzes Codex, *Biblioteca Nacional, Madrid*)

The Last Judgment, Byzantine-style.
(Par. gr. 74, F, 93 V)

Otto I, known as Otto the Great.
(City of Frankfurt)

Otto II, known as Otto the Red.
(City of Frankfurt)

Otto III, known as *mirabilia mundi*, the wonder of the world.
(Istituto Nazionale per la Grafica, Rome)

The Crowning of Otto III.
(The Bamberg Apocalypse, *presented to Otto III in 1000 A.D.*)

The apocalyptic woman and the beast.
(The Bamberg Apocalypse)
Revelation 12.1–2: And there appeared a great wonder in heaven; a woman clothed with the sun, and the moon under her feet, and upon her head a crown of twelve stars: And she being with child cried, travailing in birth, and pained to be delivered. And there appeared another wonder in heaven; and behold a great red dragon, having seven heads and ten horns, and seven crowns upon his heads.

and desire thee for my lover. I shall take thee to my bed and make thee rich beyond all imagination, because I am madly inflamed by fleshy passion for thee." The future pope purportedly lost himself in the pleasures of the flesh and was easily bought off by the devil's gold. "Thus," the legend concluded, "the wisest of men are brought low by lustful concupiscence and the wiles of the female sex being forever at Satan's service."

Even Gerbert's brilliance at mathematics became the stuff of libel. "Being the first to acquire the abacus from the Saracens he gave it rules which are scarcely understood by the most learned mathematicians," wrote a detractor. "He stayed with an infidel philosopher whose good will he obtained by paying him money. The Saracen had no scruples selling his knowledge. He would talk to Gerbert of matters deep or trivial and lend him books." But there was one book that the Saracen would never lend: the book containing the whole of his diabolical art. "Gerbert was consumed by desire to possess this book by any means, 'for we ever press more eagerly towards what is forbidden.' He implored the Saracen for the love of God and offered many things in exchange for the book, but all in vain. He plied him with wine, and with the help of the Saracen's daughter through carnal intimacy, stole the book from under the infidel's pillow and fled."

If this supposed pact with Satan had been forged in Spain, the devil was to have his due in Rome. In exchange for his false honors and his wicked knowledge, his critics whispered, Gerbert had promised his soul to the devil, and it was to be delivered when Gerbert went to "Jerusalem." To some this accounted for Gerbert's eventual death. The day came when the pope was celebrating the mass in Sante Croce in Gerusalemme near the Lateran Palace in Rome, and suddenly the devil appeared at the holy altar beside him. The terrified Gerbert broke into a cold sweat and died within a few hours, but not before he asked that his body be cut into pieces, so that the devil could not cart it away whole. (So seriously was this legend taken that in 1648 Gerbert's body was exhumed. But the diggers were disappointed to find his bones wholly intact. Still the legend persisted. In succeeding centuries, every time a pope was close to death, Gerbert's bones were said to rattle in his casket, and his tomb was covered with so much cold sweat that it turned the ground around it to mud.)

But we must return to his roots. In 970 A.D. Count Borrell of

Barcelona was bridling under the ecclesiastical jurisdiction of the French archbishop in Narbonne, and he decided to appeal directly to the pope for an independent see in Vich. By this time Gerbert's reputation was in high feather. Thinking the French monk would advance his case for independence at the Vatican, the count took Gerbert on this diplomatic mission.

In Rome Gerbert was quickly noticed. His knowledge of astronomy caught the attention of the pope himself, since the Vatican fathers could not explain the movement of the heavens and still remembered the terrible meteor of fifteen years before, when the big headless dragon had blazed across the sky. Gerbert's skill in music was also of interest, for he was becoming a master on the organ and was experimenting with a new method of finger action. Moreover, he could describe the haunting lute pieces which were making their way from Baghdad across the Mediterranean through the Moorish caliphate north. Inevitably, Gerbert gravitated toward the circle of intellectuals and artists who gathered at Trajan's Market. He was especially attracted to a French philosopher named Gerranus who had come to Rome as the ambassador from the king of the Franks and who was a master of logic.

In due course the pope spoke to Otto the Great about this brilliant new light in their midst. Otto I was then at the height of his power. He was in Rome for the marriage of his son to the Byzantine princess Theophano. After the pope's high praise, the emperor was determined to recruit Gerbert as his court mathematician. An imperial order was proclaimed that on no account was Gerbert to return to Spain. (No doubt the loss of his ward helped Count Borrell obtain his independent see.)

For two years, Gerbert remained in the emperor's court. It was a sojourn which instilled in him forever an abiding sense of gratitude toward the German emperors. Gerbert would later write about this happy circumstance when "I traversed land and sea in the pursuit of knowledge."

In 972 A.D. his thirst for knowledge drew Gerbert on the road once again. Now, with the permission of the pope and the emperor, he followed his tutor in logic back to France. There in the powerful episcopal see of Rheims he accepted a post as the head of the famous Cathedral School. His first responsibility was to shepherd the education of his students: in reading and writing, in grammar and rhetoric, and then in the secondary subjects of the quadrivium— arithmetic, geometry, astronomy, and music. But his own scholarship was equally important to him. With his enormous energy and curiosity, he pursued a wide range of interests, from the natural sciences to philosophy to rhetoric. He became one of the first great collectors of books, building a large library through his travels. "In leisure as in work I teach what I know, and learn what I do not know," he would say later.

In an age of abstraction, he concerned himself with the practical. With his own hands, he built his organs and trained students to play them. Applying his knowledge of Arabic astronomy, he supervised the construction of wooden globes on which the stars were marked. A planetarium was built for him as well, and an armillary sphere for observations. Not one to disparage literature in the face of science, he once traded a globe for a poem. This combination of the scientific and the aesthetic sensibility, this bond of the theoretical with the practical set Gerbert far above his peers and far ahead of his time.

At Rheims, a haven for scholastics, Gerbert emphasized the Greek classics as well. This got him in real trouble. The works of Virgil, Horace, Aristotle, Cicero, Plato, and Ovid were enthusiastically advanced among the students, as if the headmaster wished to restore these ancient authors to their former glory. Without the imagination and eloquence of a poet, Gerbert taught, no man could be an orator. "With my efforts to lead a good life, I have always tried to speak well, as philosophy does not separate these two things," he would write later. "While to live a good life is more important than to be a good speaker, still to those of us in public affairs, both powers are necessary. For it is of the highest advantage to be able to persuade by well-fashioned speech, and by sweet words to restrain angry souls from deeds of violence."

This emphasis on the beauty of words was incendiary. Rheims had come to represent the apex of learning in Christian Europe, and its leading clerics resented the sway of ignorant Roman archbishops over them. They decried the Vatican practice whereby ancient manuscripts were being erased and upon their hallowed pages the lives of minor saints overwritten. No important priest in Rome, the intellectuals of Rheims charged, was conversant with the sciences and the humanities. Without this knowledge, the superior monks of Rheims argued, "a man is incapable of being even a doorkeeper."

Rome reacted in anger. "The representatives of St. Peter and his disciples will have neither Plato, Virgil nor Terence as their masters," wrote an important Roman abbot, "nor the rest of the philosophical cattle, who, like the birds in the air, soar in haughty flight, like the fish of the sea disappear in the deep, and like sheep graze on the earth step by step. You say that those who are not fed with such poetry should never even be invested with the rank of doorkeeper! I tell you that is a lie. Peter knew nothing of these things, and he was appointed doorkeeper of heaven. His representatives and disciples are not adorned with the parade of eloquence, but with the sense and understanding of the Word. From the beginning of the world, God has not chosen philosophers and orators, but the illiterate and unlearned."

By contrast to the erudition of Gerbert and the Rheims intellectuals, Rome put forward the example of Romuald of Ravenna (later a saint), who had established hermitages throughout Italy, who counseled kings and popes, who was wise and holy despite his inability to read the Psalter, and who therefore represented mystical ignorance.

Closer to home, Gerbert's promotion of the humanities put him in direct conflict with the most important cleric in France, the abbot of Cluny. He could scarcely have chosen a worse enemy, for the Cluniac monastic reform movement was the most influential force in the tenth-century church. Centered at the abbey of Cluny to the south in Aquitaine, the Cluniacs had no less ambitious goal than to transform the entire institution of the Catholic church. They had set out to instill discipline in a corrupt congregation by giving it a solid liturgical core and enforcing strict personal rules upon the monks. They were builders, their monasteries dotting Europe from Spain to Hungary. These fortresses provided not only an intellectual but a military bulwark against heathenism and heresy. It was dangerous to cross them.

Among their deepest antipathies was an abhorrence of the Greek classics. Classical works were regarded as so much corrupting garbage, especially those of poetic beauty. Therefore, the very works that Gerbert advertised in Rheims were banned in Cluny. Plato was "vermin." Virgil told "lies." In fact, Virgil gave nightmares to abbots. One early abbot of Cluny had studied Virgil until he dreamed one night of a beautiful, shapely vase, signed by Virgil and filled with snakes. Another abbot fell asleep and dreamed that he was lying on a tangle of snakes. When he awoke in horror, he found a copy of Virgil under his pillow. These tales became gospel in Cluny.

Instead of snakes, Gerbert saw wisdom and beauty in the abbot's vase. His embrace of these classics widened his fame among humanist scholars, as it mobilized his enemies in the church against him. As if associating with Saracens and sorcerers was not bad enough, now he was consorting with philosophers and Hellenists. Twenty years later, when his name was put forward for the papacy, one opponent spat out about Gerbert: "The vicars of Peter and their disciples will not have for their teacher a Plato, a Virgil, or any other of that vile herd of philosophers!" And another prelate delivered the final insult: "You are not a Christian. You are a Ciceronian!"

If Gerbert was a figure of controversy, he was also a figure of envy. By 980 A.D. his reputation for originality had spread far across Europe, and students traveled from great distances to attend his lectures. Over time, he would train kings and emperors, archbishops and important thinkers. But there were also spies. One had been dispatched by the emperor's own teacher at Magdeburg, a professor named Otric, known to his closest friends as the "Saxon Cicero." Otric feared that Gerbert was overshadowing him. Through his spy, he hoped to catch his rival in error. To the Saxon's delight, the intelligence came back that Gerbert was promoting physics as a mere branch of mathematics rather than as a separate discipline. This shocking revelation was gleefully peddled to the emperor himself.

The emperor called for a public contest. In the tenth century these public debates were great sport, with all the spectacle and ceremony of later duels. In November 980 A.D., Gerbert traveled to Italy for the event. A large audience of scholars and students gathered in a Ravenna castle, trembling with anticipation. When the room was quiet, Otto II introduced the contestants lavishly. He extolled the scholars and praised the contests as a way to overcome public sloth. Then, posing the problem of how to divide various categories of natural philosophy, he settled in his chair for the day's entertainment.

Gerbert rose ardently to the challenge. Philosophy, he proclaimed, could be defined broadly as "the science of all things divine and human." As the day wore on and the combatants touched on the cause for the creation of the world and Platonic and Aristotelian definitions were hurled about with abandon, the students cheered the thrusts and recoils of the duelists boisterously. Gerbert began to get the upper hand, through both his natural eloquence and his sheer vigor. At the end, probably as the last man standing, he was proclaimed the winner. The emperor loaded him down with gifts for his return to France.

For Gerbert, this was a genuine turning point. He was perceived now as a useful man of prodigious gifts. By 982 A.D. Emperor Otto II needed all the talent he could gather. In the summer of that year the German emperor had badly overreached himself as a soldier of Christ and suffered a disastrous defeat in southern Italy at the hands of a combined force of Arabs, Greeks, and pirates.

Against this backdrop of defeat and chaos, Otto II summoned Gerbert to Italy and installed him as the abbot of Bobbio. In his nomination diploma, the emperor referred to Gerbert's "greatness of mind," and, dutifully, Gerbert swore allegiance to his "Caesar." To judge from his first letters, Gerbert must have thought this would be a quiet backwater for scholarship. To friends in Rheims, he requested more books: "I urgently ask of you one thing only. It will not expose you to any risk or loss and will tie even more closely the bonds of our friends. You know how many copyists there are everywhere in the countryside of Italy. Without telling a soul, have them copy for me the Astronomy of Manlius, the Rhetoric of Victorinus, Demosthenes treatise on ophthalmia."

To take charge of the monastery of St. Columban was not so much a religious as a political and military calling . . . and a dubious honor at that. Bobbio was one of the more important Italian monasteries, a strategic outpost situated in the Apennines not far from the important episcopal town of Pavia and perched above the river Trebbia. A number of fiefs throughout the length of Italy came under its authority. This gave the abbey an appearance, but not the reality, of great wealth. The abbey was constantly taxed with orders for men and money. Money it did not have, and the fighting ability of its men was questionable. And its monks and landowners resented the appointment of the emperor's Frenchman to its head.

Gerbert's tenure at Bobbio did not go well from the beginning. The new abbot was hounded by the unrelenting solicitations from high and low. He quickly developed a contempt for Italians, a disdain for the avarice of his supplicants, and a distaste for politics in general. The abbey "has troops, but they are Italians, not men," he wrote scornfully on one occasion, and on another, "I dare not rely on the trustworthiness of my knights because they are Italians." "Italy may produce crops," he observed, "but Gaul and Germany breed soldiers."

All around him he found disorder, graft, hostility, and deception. For a product of French monastic discipline, this Italian hubris was hard to take. Once, when he was asked for money, he found "that the whole sanctuary of God has been sold, but its price is not forthcoming. The store houses and granaries are empty, and there is nothing in the monastic purse." In any event, the thought that the church could be sold or bartered offended him.

He tried threat and bluster: "I will not give the sanctuary of God for gold nor for love. Nor will I consent to the alienation, if it has been given away. Restore to this monastery the hay which your people have carried off, if you would not experience what I can effect by the favor of Caesar and by the help of my friends."

Even the imperial Empress Adelaide, the occidental widow of Otto the Great, tried to chivy some lands out of him. His response was full of hurt and self-pity. "How can I take away tomorrow the land which I grant to my dependents yesterday?" he wrote to the empress. "What is my occupation here? If I give away everything, what is left for me to hold?" The empress was not pleased, and Gerbert complained bitterly to the emperor about the hangers-on in the royal court. "Why do the mouths and tails of foxes here flatter my lord? Either let them depart from the palace, or let them present their subordinates who disregard the edicts of Caesar, plot to kill his messengers, even compare him to an ass. The dispossessed have no sense of shame. O the times! O the customs! Where in the world am I living?"

At this early stage in his career as an imperial servant, Gerbert was not cut out to be a politician. He longed for quiet study and reflection, requesting a friend to send him a book on the diseases of the eyes. He was too intellectual or too high-minded or too thin-skinned for the compromises of public men. "The troubles of king-doms are the ruin of the Church," he observed despairingly. "The ambition of the powerful, and the miseries of the times, have turned right into wrong, and no man keeps faith with anybody." He was facing the eternal problem of the moral man in public life.

An unexpected development seemed to relieve Gerbert of his dif-ficulties. In Rome, Otto II, still deep in melancholy over his defeat at Colonna, fell ill, turned to quack medicine, and abruptly died on December 7, 983 A.D.

Gerbert had lost his guardian. The king was dead, and therefore the king's agent must go down as well. Gerbert's sun-baked monks revolted against him, and he fled Bobbio after less than a year as abbot. In flight, he dispatched a pathetic note to Pope John XIV. "Whither shall I turn, Father of the country? If I call upon the Holy See, I am mocked and without opportunity to go to you on account of the enemy. Nor can we freely depart from Italy, even if we wish. To tarry becomes difficult because neither in the monastery nor out-side have I anything left except the pastoral staff and the apostolic benediction." It was a pointless appeal, since John XIV had been driven out of Rome by the Crescenti family, and their mulish anti-pope, Boniface VII, presided at the Vatican. Bitter at his humiliation, Gerbert took refuge in the imperial palace at Pavia, where he joined Empress Adelaide, who seemed to have gotten over her pique about monastic land. They were soon joined by Empress Theophano after her husband's funeral and burial in the crypt of St. Peter's.

The political situation was desperate. For a brief time, Gerbert considered military action to restore his authority at Bobbio. "My knights are prepared to take up arms and to fortify the camp," he proclaimed bravely. "But what hope is there without a ruler of this land. We know so well the kind of fidelity, habits, and minds certain Italians have." But the rebellion of a single monastery was trivial in the larger picture. In Rome the local potentate and his compliant antipope had seized power once again.

To the north, developments were even more distressing. The difficult prince of Bavaria, Henry the Quarrelsome—held in a Utrecht jail for five years on account of his prior treachery—had escaped. Joining forces with Henry of Carinthia and Henry the bishop of Augsburg, he attacked imperial troops and routed them. This would become known as the War of the Three Henrys. Henry the Quarrelsome's clear intention was to seize the throne for himself.

Could the empire be saved? The rightful heir was Otto III, a mere infant three years old. He would not come to majority for thirteen more years, a long time for a holding action, near the end of the first millennium. Who was to rule in the interim? Could the empire survive a regency, where the power rested in the hands of two Byzantine empresses, Adelaide and Theophano? To make matters worse, the child was not in Pavia, but in the care of the bishop of Cologne, well within Henry's sphere of influence, making the boy vulnerable to Henry's designs.

On Christmas Day 983 A.D., the child was taken to Aachen and coronated symbolically as the Holy Roman Emperor. Once the boy was crowned, Henry promptly seized him and took him to Quedlinburg, where the pretender convened an assembly and had himself proclaimed king.

The two empresses turned to Gerbert for help. Only pressure from the outside could save the boy and the empire now. Gerbert, seemingly so ill at ease in the exercise of power before, now went to work. Over the coming months, he appealed for assistance to the prelates and potentates, most significantly to the Carolingian kings Lothair and Louis and to Hugh Capet, the duke of the Franks. The need was to undercut Henry's usurpation and to isolate the usurper. In the service of this goal, Gerbert employed his lethal pen. "Will he [Henry the Quarrelsome], who has attempted to kill two Ottos, be willing that a third should survive," he asked rhetorically. "Remember what Cicero said: 'It is foolish to expect fidelity from those by whom you have been many times deceived.'"

To a wavering, unfaithful duke, he spewed venom: "Swell up, grow stout, wax fat, you who, not following the footsteps of your fathers, have wholly forsaken God your Maker. Remember how often my finger restrained your impudent mouth while you were spreading abroad shameful things."

Slowly, meticulously, Gerbert's coalition came together. When Empress Theophano went to Germany in May, her vassals received her warmly. In the end, the coalition was too much for Henry. At Rohr, on June 29, 984 A.D., a day whose importance was marked in the heavens by the appearance of a brilliant star at midday, the duke of Bavaria handed over the child-emperor to his mother in the presence of Gerbert. Gerbert had "snatched the tender lamb from the jaws of the wolf and had given it back to its mother," it would be said later. And later, Gerbert would remind Otto III of his service to the empire.

"In all the disturbances," Gerbert wrote to Otto fourteen years later, "I stood firm so that I chose death rather than not to see the son of Caesar, then a captive, on the throne."

With the return of Otto III to his mother, Gerbert's reputation as a kingmaker grew. (It would soon get another test.) He wanted his pivotal role in saving the empire recognized and rewarded. "Lorraine is witness that by my exhortations I have aroused as many persons as possible to aid [Otto III]," he wrote in July 984 A.D. He wanted Empress Theophano to entrust him with still greater responsibilities. A passionate, new ambition to be a player on the political stage welled up within this unlikely champion.

"For human feeling, the first sentiment of mankind lies in things of action," he wrote. "The divine sentiment, the second impulse of mankind, lies in things of contemplation."

Would he be returned to the front line of imperial service? he wanted to know. Or

"Shall I remain in France as a reserve soldier for the camp of Caesar?"

IT WAS TO BE THE LATTER . . . except that France would soon enough become Caesar's front line and Gerbert Caesar's point man. After the lamb, Otto III, was safe from the wolf and in the custody of his mother, Gerbert was back in the great metropolitan city of Rheims. Technically, he was still the abbot of Bobbio, a significant fact merely because he remained a vassal of the German Empire. Once again he took up his post as secretary to the archbishop of Rheims, Adalbert, and he returned to his studies.

For insight and knowledge he looked sentimentally to Spain, where the pleasures of the Spanish March remained the source of all inspiration to him. Of friends there he requested the latest books about mathematics and astrology. He was keen to write a treatise on the latest astrolabe.

In 985 A.D. he was even giving thought to returning to Spain for good. The abbot of the Mozarabic monastery at Cuixa had urged him to come south, and Gerbert was tempted. "At times I dream of removing myself near to the Spanish princes," he wrote, but then he thought of Empress Theophano. "I am turned from this desire by the sacred appeals of Lady Theophano, who is ever august and always to be loved." It is well that Gerbert did not follow the pangs of his heart. For on July 6, 985 A.D., Al Mansor captured Barcelona after a five-day siege and put Gerbert's first patron, Count Borrell, to flight. Then, in an example of the Moors' holy war against Christians, the famous Black Rider of Córdoba attacked the monastery of St. Cugat del Valles eight miles from the city and killed its abbot.

If Gerbert's heart was in Spain, his head and his hand were preoccupied with France. Throughout the year 985 A.D. he became more deeply entangled in the intrigues of competing petty royalty. While he was the faithful agent of the German Empire in his native land, he professed allegiance to the French Carolingian king Lothair and his son Louis. "Because the King of Heaven says, 'Render unto Caesar the things that are Caesar's and unto God the things that are God's,' we shall render to our kings, Lothair and Louis an undefiled fidelity," he wrote. "We shall deviate in nothing, and yet we shall make the share owed to the Lord the first consideration." Apparently, his godly duty was to work behind the scenes for the overthrow of Lothair and the elevation of Hugh Capet, the liege of France, to the royal crown.

On April 6, 985 A.D., he wrote a secret and anonymous dispatch proposing an alliance between Hugh Capet and Otto III: "Lothair is the king of France in name only. Hugh, not in name, it is true, but in deed and fact. If with us you had sought his friendship, and had allied his son, Robert, with the son of Caesar, Otto III, you would not just now feel the kings of the French to be enemies."

This was a dangerous double game, and Gerbert, along with his archbishop, Adalbert, soon came under suspicion. To Empress Theophano, Gerbert reported that the prelates had fallen into disfavor, even that their lives might be in jeopardy. "The kings of the French look upon us in an unfavorable light because we do not agree with them about fidelity to you." He considered fleeing to Germany. "What do you wish us to do?" he wrote the empress. "It is no longer a question of Adalbert's expulsion, which would be an endurable evil, but they are threatening his life and blood. The same is true of me, as if I were arousing the archbishop against the policies of the kings."

Inevitably, these tensions and competitions were about land rather than personality. At the core of the dispute was the Lorraine, that vast, rich triangle of land between Flanders and the Rhine and demarcated by the towns of Rheims, Aachen, and Verdun. In mid-985 A.D. the impatient King Lothair marched on Verdun. It was his undoing, for it gave his enemies a pretext for action. Behind the king's back, Gerbert and his cohorts began to plot the demise of the Carolingian dynasty.

On March 2, 986 A.D., the death of Lothair fueled the conspiracy. Cynically, Gerbert wrote an unctuous epitaph to the despised king, full of mock grief and false ceremony. It was an epitaph to the entire dynasty of Charlemagne:

> The dukes met for the funeral of him
> O Lothair, Caesar, sprung from the Caesars—
> whom every good man loved;
> The memorials of grief thou spread before us
> in the second light of terrifying Mars,
> Because thou wert seen clad in purple.

King Lothair's son Louis V succeeded him. History is not quite fair in remembering this last sovereign of the Carolingian dynasty as the Sluggard and King-Do-Nothing. For he energetically prosecuted the see of Rheims as a swamp of treachery and rebellion. Openly now, Gerbert and his archbishop, Adalbert, were charged with treason, and a trial date was set. Not content with the legal process, the increasingly unstable King Louis marched on Rheims. But at the city gates, Gerbert's troops repulsed him, and the king had to content himself with burning a few outlying monasteries.

So, unlikely as it would have seemed ten years before, Gerbert had become a military as well as a religious leader. He found himself at the center of a full-fledged revolt. Great armies were mobilized for him to lead, perhaps against Louis or even to Italy or Saxony in furtherance of the empire's business. Surely this soldier of Christ was the only religious-military leader of the time who was equally concerned with the well-being of his troops and the safety of his organs. "While I endure here the wrath of kings, the disturbances of the people, and the disquiet of discordant kingdoms, I am so wearied that I am almost sorry I undertook the care of the pastoral office," he wrote in January 987 A.D. "Lady Theophano orders me to depart into Saxony with her on March 25, and I have ordered certain of my monks and knights from Italy to assemble there, but I worry about my organs in Italy."

One buck of Louis V's horse averted the final clash between the sacred and the profane forces. While Louis was hunting near Senlis on May 21, 987 A.D., he was thrown against a rock. His doctors struggled to save him, but the prognosis was bad, for his liver had sustained a terrible blow. "Now physicians claim that the liver is the seat of the blood," a contemporaneous reporter wrote. "The king's was ruptured, and the blood flowed freely. Blood even gushed from his nostrils and throat. His chest was afflicted with constant pains. Intolerable fever vexed his entire body . . . and he died."

Within weeks, as Gerbert organized his support within the powerful clergy, Hugh Capet was elected the king of France and crowned on July 3, 987 A.D., near Noyon. With his coronation, Hugh's small demesne, which included Paris, became the royal domain of France.

Thus, through Gerbert's machinations, a new dynasty of French kings began, one that, together with its branches the Valois and the Bourbons, would last for eight hundred years, until the French Revolution.

CHAPTER ELEVEN

Theophano, Almost Purple-Born

AND NOW, the jewels of glorious Byzantium
. . . but first the velvet stage must be set, and
the cunning players must take their places.

After Otto the Great's coronation in 962 A.D., he
gazed covetously at the lands to the south of Rome.
How could he claim to be the modern Roman emperor,
the true successor of Caesar and Caesar Augustus, if he
ruled only half of Italy? Sicily and Calabria, however,
constituted the western flank of the Byzantine Empire,
whose emperors asserted their own claim as the true
heirs of Caesar Augustus. The territory in between—
the provinces of Benvento, Apulia, and Capua—was
disputed and claimed by both empires. For several

centuries these remote lands had been a rich source of slaves for Byzantium, but recently the prince of Benvento, Pandulf Ironhead, had allied himself with the new German emperor and had shut off the trafficking.

To round off his new empire, Otto had two options for his ambition—war and diplomacy. His son Otto II was moving into his adolescence and would soon be of marriageable age. But the first overture to Constantinople was met with oriental vagueness, for the question was premature. From the Byzantine viewpoint, it was still not even clear whether the son would inherit the throne. Otto, however, was impatient. In 966 A.D., he attacked the small and weakly defended town of Bari in Apulia. This was a mistake, for the coastal town put up a stiff defense, and the emperor's troops had to beat a sorry retreat. The consequence of this humiliation was greater than a mere military repulse. The Roman emperor had attacked the lands of the Byzantine emperor. That was enough of an outrage, but for the attack to have failed left the Byzantine emperor with a decided contempt for German capabilities.

After a decent interval of two years, Otto the Great turned back to diplomacy. He commissioned his closest confidant, Bishop Liudprand of Cremona, to travel across the Adriatic to Constantinople. This was a blue-ribbon diplomatic effort, with all the gifts and trappings to demonstrate its true sincerity. Liudprand seemed to be the perfect envoy. He had been pleasantly entertained in Constantinople eight years before and seemed to appreciate the exotic ways of Byzantium. Now he brought with him the full authority of the emperor. Well known for his subtlety and skill as well as for his determination, Liudprand was charged with the mission of bringing home a Byzantine princess for Otto II. Upon all accounts, she must be the issue of the glorious room of porphyry within the Sacred Palace, and the match had to extend Rome's dominance over the boot of Italy. To strengthen the diplomat's hand, Otto the Great had coronated his fourteen-year-old son the previous Christmas as his "co-emperor" and his heir.

Upon his arrival in Constantinople, Bishop Liudprand gazed on the Sacred Palace with awe and wonder. More than a palace, it was a large walled district, a labyrinthine warren of low-slung marble buildings, courtyards, pavilions, churches, audience halls (including the Banquet Hall of the Nineteen Couches, the Hall of Garlands, and the Bronze Hall), bedchambers, terraces, the imperial silk factory with its official purple dyers, baths, gardens, fountains, galleries (such as the Gallery of the Forty Saints), an extensive household of eunuchs, the imperial library, a lighthouse, an armory, a hippodrome, five heavily guarded gates, a large garrison, statues of lions, oxen, and three-headed serpents, an intricate set of arcades and secret passageways, a port, a private racetrack, and a polo field.

The main gate of this spectacular complex was called the Chalke Gate. It faced the vast open square called the Augusteum and was incorporated in a large structure with a bronze dome called the Brazen House. By regulation, the stalls of the royal perfumers clustered around this gate, imparting a sweet fragrance to all who would enter the blessed portal of the Sacred Palace.

To Liudprand, it was the most beautiful and best defended palace he had ever seen. For all its awesome fortress mentality, a sense of free movement dominated the place. The Chalke Gate was thrown open to the public at daybreak and closed again at nine in the morning after the signal "mis" wafted over the hubbub. With considerable excitement, the envoy anticipated his audience with the formidable emperor, Nicephorus II Phocas, in the throne room. The magnificence of the Chrysotriklinos, as it was called, was rumored throughout Europe. It was a golden chamber, octagonally shaped, with splendid mosaics, an incredible gold and enamel tree, complete with singing birds and a golden organ.

Perhaps if he bonded with the emperor, the bishop might hope to see the imperial apartments, perhaps even the blessed purple room itself, the Porphyra, where all imperial children were born. According to rumor, its floor and walls were of purple marble that had been scaled from the crumbling palaces of Rome and brought to Constantinople several centuries earlier. Above the headboard of the royal couch heavy purple drapes were said to sweep dramatically upward to a golden eagle. Against the wall enormous chests housed the lady's vast wardrobe and jewels, and these were managed by the Mistress of the Robes. Off the main chamber were several small rooms, one a tiny chapel, appointed with an epic portrait of the Man-God; the other was a bath and dressing room.

The bishop could only imagine the splendid imperial reception that awaited him on his blessed mission. He expected the emperor to be intimidating, undoubtedly bedecked in his magnificent kaftan of white and purple. Over fifty years of age, Nicephorus was the great general who had reconquered Crete and Mesopotamia for the empire and who had subdued Syria by bringing home the shaved skull of the emir of Aleppo, placing it at the purple-beslippered feet of his predecessor, Romanos II. Nicephorus was also a mystic who had founded monasteries on his spiritual retreat at Mount Athos, where he meditated in a simple cell as an escape from the temptations of the real world. A popular leader known as the "people's king," he wore a hair shirt beneath his armor and slept on stone. The rigors of the campaign trail interested him more than the luxuries and ceremonies of Constantinople. He was also supposed to be desperately in love with his wily and beguiling and utterly corrupt wife, Theophano, a supernatural beauty so extraordinary that she was called a "miracle of nature." She was the widow to the previous emperor and mother to the future emperor, Basil the Bulgar-Slayer.

When the appointed time arrived, Liudprand put aside his weapons, for he knew that within the regulations and ceremonies of the Sacred Palace it was written that ambassadors from the west were to be unarmed in the presence of the emperor, "because they are not barbarian ambassadors." Two eunuch guards marched the bishop to the consistory, down a long passageway decorated with vine tendrils and animals, carved in green marble and black onyx, past the figures of peacocks and eagles, cut from Carian marble, past caged lions and birds which roared and squawked as the prelate passed, and into the gilded Great Chamber. The throne was placed upon a dais of lovely porphyry (whose care was entrusted to the keeper of the emperor's sandals). The throne itself, the bishop noticed, was of immense size, with large golden lions for armrests. The bishop threw himself on his knees in homage. When the bishop lifted his eyes, the throne had risen mysteriously from the floor almost to the ceiling. Had he been able to peer behind the drapes, he would have discovered a rudimentary corkscrew, turned by muscular eunuchs.

To his astonishment, he was greeted not by a figure equal to his surroundings and to his reputation as a fierce man of action, but by thick-necked, big-bellied dwarf, with tiny mole's eyes, short pig-bristled hair, a half-gray beard, and dark, sun-burnt skin, who wore a robe once of fine linen, but now soiled and foul-smelling. This presentiment, this "morning star" to his people, brought to the bishop's mind that line of Juvenal's "You would not like to meet him on a dark night." The bishop took an instant dislike to this smelly eminence. The emperor's slovenly appearance seemed to be an unvarnished insult both to himself and to his emperor.

"It was our desire to give you a courteous and magnificent reception," the emperor Nicephorus said unctuously. "That, however, has been made difficult by the impiety of your master who as an invader has laid claim to Rome. He has robbed King Berengar of his Italian kingdom, has slain some Romans by the sword, some by hanging, while others he has blinded or sent into exile. Furthermore, he has tried to subdue cities belonging to *our* empire! These wicked attempts have proved unsuccessful. And so he has sent you, the promoter of this villainy, under the pretense of peace. But you have come to spy on us."

"My master did not invade the city of Rome," Bishop Liudprand replied stoutly. "On the contrary, he freed her from the tyrant's grasp. Was she not ruled by effeminate debauchers and, worse, by harlots?" This was a reference to the voluptuous Marozia and her dissipated grandson, the boy-pope of the midcentury. "Your power was fast asleep then. The power of your predecessors, who . . . in name only . . . are called the emperors of Rome." This lurid taunt was scarcely diplomatic, and it could only infuriate the volatile Byzantine emperor. "The reality is quite different," the bishop plowed on. "If they were so powerful, if they were the true rulers of Rome, why did they allow the city to be ruled by harlots? Which of your emperors, may I ask, led by the soul of God, troubled himself to punish so heinous a crime? Which of them brought the holy church to its proper state? No, you neglected it. My master did not. As for the Italians, it is a known fact that Berengar was a vassal. He received his kingdom and his golden scepter from my master. At the devil's prompting, Berengar broke his word, and we subdued him. You would do the same to men who swear fealty and then revolt against you."

"There is an Italian here who sees events differently," the emperor said.

"If he denies my version of events," the bishop said hotly, "one of my men, at your command, will prove the truth to him tomorrow in single combat."

"Well, perhaps this is so," the emperor said slyly, as if he wanted to mollify the bishop with a slight concession. "Explain then why your master attacked the borderlands of our empire!" This was a reference to Otto's attack on Apulia several years before, a campaign upon which Bishop Liudprand had accompanied the imperial army. "We were friends," Nicephorus continued, his face displaying his bruised feelings, "and were thinking by marriage to enter into a partnership that would never be broken."

"The land which you say belongs to you is by race and by language a part of the Italian kingdom," Liudprand replied. "For seven years, our ally Pandulf Ironhead, prince of Benvento and Capua, held it under his control. And the friendly partnership which you say you wished to form by marriage, we hold to be a fraud and a snare. Come, come, sire, let us clear away all trickeries and speak the plain truth. My master has sent me to you to see if you will give the daughter of the emperor Romanos and the empress Theophano to my son, my master, the august emperor, Otto II."

A long silence ensued as Nicephorus pondered this bold request following so closely on the bishop's impertinent insults.

"It is past seven o'clock and there is a church procession I must attend," the emperor said finally. "We will give you a reply in due time."

The bishop detested this "monstrosity" of an emperor deeply, passionately, personally. In the succeeding days, the two traded insults. The bishop moved himself to watch the procession of the emperor from the Stephana Palace to the Great Church of the Holy Wisdom, San Sofia, amused at the sight of the pygmy-emperor on horseback, "a very small man on a very large beast." The bishop noted derisively the threadbare costumes of the Byzantine nobles, the garish, oversized jewels on the stump-emperor, and the smarmy cries of adulation from his dirty street-subjects. "Behold the morning star approaches!" they would shout out. "In his eyes the sun's rays are reflected. Long live our prince Nicephorus, the pale death of the Arabs. Adore him ye nations, worship him, bow the neck to his greatness." With his acid pen, as the bishop described this scene later, he wrote that the subjects might have well been chanting, "Come, you miserable burn-out coal, you old woman in your walk, wood-devil in your look, clod hopper, goat-footed, horned, double-limbed, bristly, wild, rough, hairy barbarian." The bishop did not like him.

The envoy was imprisoned in a drafty stone house, without water, and made to sleep on a stone slab with a stone pillow next to cages containing five lions. When he was summoned to dinner, he was seated in a lowly place far down the line from the emperor, beyond the patriarch and the eminent members of the blue and green factions, and without a tablecloth. "Foul and disgusting" goat flesh, swimming in oil and bad fish sauce, reeking of onions and garlic, was put before him. Their wine, the bishop observed, was not wine but brackish water, with overtones of resin and gypsum. Pistachio nuts and lentils were his only recourse. The bishop did not like the food.

Down his line of satraps and sycophants, the emperor bellowed questions about the German army. By his lights, the bishop replied judiciously and soberly.

The emperor would have none of it, for he was keen to bring up the humiliation of German troops by his defenders of Bari two years earlier. "You lie," he thundered. "Your master's soldiers cannot ride, and they do not know how to fight on foot. The size of their shields, the weight of their armor, the length of their swords, the heaviness of their helmets, does not allow them to fight on horseback or on foot." He smiled with pleasure at his wit. "Their gluttony also hinders them. Their God is their belly, their courage but wind, their bravery drunkenness. Fasting for them means panic."

If the bishop's anger got out of control at these taunts, he did not record it. The emperor pressed on. "Nor has your master any force of ships on the sea. I alone have really stout sailors, and I will attack him with my fleets, destroy his maritime cities and reduce his river cities to ashes." The emperor did not mention—but he did not have to—that the Byzantine navy possessed the most terrifying weapon of the Middle Ages, the mysterious Greek fire, which had incinerated the Viking fleet off Constantinople in 941 A.D.

"How can he resist me when I come with forces numerous as corn fields on Gargarus, grapes on Lesbian vine, waves in the ocean, and stars in the sky. . . . You are not Romans but Lombards!"

The emperor leaned back to savor the brilliance of his oration.

"We are Lombards," the bishop spoke up, ". . . and Saxons, and Franks, and Lotharingians, Bavarians and Swabians and Burgundians. You say that we are unwarlike and know nothing of horsemanship. Well, if the sins of the Christians merit that you keep your stiff neck, the next war will prove what manner of men you are, and how warlike we are." At this insult, the bishop was ordered out of the hall. His diplomatic mission did not seem to be going well.

Days passed, and even the emperor's own men began to feel sorry for the bishop. A beardless chamberlain named Basil approached him. "Tell us, brother," he asked disingenuously. "What induced you to come here?" When the bishop answered about the proposed marriage, Basil responded, "It is unheard of that a daughter born in the purple of an emperor born in the purple should contract a foreign marriage. Still, great as your demand, you shall have what you want if you give what is proper: Ravenna . . . and Rome . . . with all the adjoining territories to our possession. If you desire friendship without the marriage, let your master permit Rome to be free, and hand over to their former lord the princes of Capua and Benvento, who were formerly slaves of our holy empire and are now rebels."

And so the price of a purple-born bride was set: Rome and all Italy south of it.

"You must know that my master rules over Slavonian princes who are far more powerful than Peter, king of the Bulgarians, who has married the daughter of the emperor Christopher," Liudprand asserted.

"Ah, but Christopher was not born in the purple," Basil replied.

"Why does your emperor not restore to the apostolic church its rightful lands which lie within his kingdoms?" Liudprand challenged, thinking of southern Italy.

"He will do so," Basil replied, "when Rome and the Roman church shall be so ordered as he wishes."

Liudprand replied with a homily. "A certain man, having suffered much injury from another, reproached God with these words: 'Lord avenge me upon my adversary.' The Lord replied, 'I will do so on the day when I shall render to each man according to his works.' 'How late that day will be!' the man replied."

At this, the chamberlain and his men roared with laughter.

The days became weeks. For long stretches the bishop languished in his stony lion's den and then was abruptly summoned for another oily goat-feast, only to endure more insults. On Assumption Day, things grew even worse for him when a letter from the pope in Rome arrived, which referred to Nicephorus as the "Emperor of the Greeks." This was a catastrophe of bad taste and bad diplomacy, and it sliced to the heart of the Byzantine paranoia.

The central contention between Rome and Constantinople was this: which empire was the true and legitimate heir of the ancient Roman Empire? To the Byzantines they were the true heirs since Constantine the Great had moved the center of the empire east in the fourth century. There had been an unbroken line of "Roman" emperors on the Bosporus ever since. Rome had been deserted to crumble in decay. To Otto the Great and the Germans, they had saved Italy and Rome itself from its corruption and abandonment. Didn't the true Roman Empire have to include Rome?

Liudprand himself had drawn the question in black and white. The competition between Rome and Constantinople was the struggle between the old lion and the whelp. "The ruler of the Greeks wears his hair long, a trailing skirt, wide sleeves, and a woman's cap," Liudprand wrote in his diary. "He is a liar, a cheat, a pitiless and arrogant man as cunning as a fox, full of hypocritical humility, avaricious, covetous, an eater of garlic, onions, and leeks, and a water drinker. The King of the Franks, on the other hand, has his hair cut short, wears clothes utterly different from a woman's, has a hat on his head, is a lover of truth, detests wiles, is compassionate when compassion is proper, but severe when severity is called for, truly humble, never avaricious, drinks wine, does not eat garlic, onions, or leeks like Nicephorus, who wishes to save money that would otherwise be spent on meat, and to hoard what he has gained by selling animals." With the question so framed, how could there be any doubt?

Now Liudprand was immediately summoned.

"The audacity of it!" the eunuch-chamberlain Basil fumed. "To call the universal emperor of the Romans, the great, the august, the one and only Nicephorus, . . . to call him the 'emperor of the Greeks,' and to style a poor barbaric creature 'emperor of the Romans.' O sky! O earth! O sea!" Liudprand was sure that the messengers from Rome would be hanged, as well as himself, but the punishment was more lenient: "They shall be kept in close custody until Nicephorus, the sacred emperor of the Romans, be informed of these insults."

More delay followed since the emperor was in Mesopotamia. As he stewed in his stony, lion-infested prison, Liudprand divined the reason why Nicephorus II Phocas had taken his army to the outer reaches of the Middle East. The emperor was going after profound, apocalyptic scrolls called the Visions of Daniel. They contained apparently contradictory prophecies that would both please and depress the emperor. One prediction stated that this was a fortuitous time to press outward on the eastern front but that after him a less warlike and therefore more wicked Antichrist would overtake his empire and the tables would be turned, allowing the infidels to approach the very gates of Constantinople. In another manuscript, the life span of emperors including himself was foretold, specifically that Nicephorus had only another seven years to live.

Meanwhile, Liudprand had seen another apocalyptic document more to his liking. This had been generated by an obscure third-century bishop of Sicily who had written that "the lion and his whelp shall together exterminate the wild ass." To Liudprand the meaning of this prophecy was clear: at some future time—was it to be sooner or later or perhaps even at the turn of the millennium?—the Romans and the Greeks together would join forces and wipe the infidel Arabs off the face of the earth.

These meditations were finally broken when the emperor's chamberlain came to Liudprand with an explanation of his situation. "The delay in your departure is this: the pope of Rome has sent a letter to our most sacred emperor, unworthy of Nicephorus, calling him emperor of 'the Greeks,' and not 'of the Romans.' Certainly this has been done at your master's instigation. The silly blockhead of a pope does not know that the sacred Constantine transferred to this city the imperial scepter, the senate, and all the Roman knighthood, and left in Rome nothing but vile slaves, fishermen, confectioners, poulterers, bastards, plebeians, and underlings."

This implied the central Byzantine belief: that after Constantine removed the seat of the Roman Empire to Constantinople six centuries before, Rome became the lair of the Antichrist, Babylon itself, and the seven hills of Rome were really the seven heads of the dragon from hell.

"In his noble simplicity," Liudprand replied, "the pope thought that in writing thus he was honoring the emperor, not insulting him."

"Tell us, does your most sacred master wish to confirm friendship with the emperor by a marriage treaty?"

"When I came here, he wished it, but during my long stay he has received no letter from me, and he must think that you have made a faux pas and put me in prison as a captive. He is probably burning with rage, like a lioness robbed of her whelps, and will not rest until he has taken vengeance in just wrath. He hates the idea of a marriage and is only anxious to pour out his anger upon you."

"If he tries to do that," the chamberlain replied, "neither Italy will protect him, nor his native Saxony, that poor country where the people dress in skins. With our money, which gives us power, we will rouse the whole world against him. We will break him in pieces like a potter's vessel, which when broken cannot be put into shape again."

As a final insult, the desexed chamberlain demanded that Liudprand hand over at once any purple garments in his possession, as if he were a petty thief whose real purpose in Constantinople was to steal the secret of silk dyeing from the imperial factory. (The secret of the purple dye was the secretion of a rare mollusk found only in the eastern Mediterranean around Tyre.) "As we surpass all other nations in wealth and wisdom," the eunuch said, "so it is right that we should also surpass them in dress. Those who are unique in the grace of their virtue should also be unique in the beauty of their raiment."

Having no choice, the bishop dutifully handed over five robes . . . but not without real anger. "How insulting!" he wrote later. "To think that effeminate milk-sops, dressed up in long sleeves and female tiaras and mantles—liars, eunuchs, idlers—should go clad in purple, while this is denied to heroes and mighty men of valor. How humiliating!"

Mercifully, this disgraceful piece of anti-diplomacy was at an end. Nicephorus had tired of the game and sent his final rejection of the marriage proposal from the desert of Syria. It was not an official imperial pronouncement written in gold on the emperor's special stationery, but rather was inscribed in silver, with a silver seal, and signed by his brother Leo. Before Bishop Liudprand left on the first leg of his journey home—a forty-nine-day donkey ride to the port of Naupactus—he scrawled his rage and disappointment like a crazy man over the walls of his stone prison:

> Trust not the Greeks; they live but to betray
>
> Nor heed their promises, whate'er they say.
>
> If lies will serve them, any oath they swear,
>
> And when it's time to break it feel no fear.
>
> For lying Greece had promised our son
>
> Her princess as a bride. Ah, would that she
>
> Had not been born nor that land e'er seen me.
>
> All blame I shall decline
>
> The fault, Nicephorus, the fault is thine.

Had his long journey not exhausted him and had he not died soon after his arrival in Italy, Liudprand might have felt some satisfaction at the eventual fate of his nemesis. Nicephorus returned to a Constantinople that had tired of his elaborate campaigns abroad in search of obscure apocalyptic scrolls and of his austerity measures at home. The imperial palace was rife with conspiracy. Chief among the plotters was his own wife, Theophano, and her handsome and athletic Armenian lover John Tzimisces, known as Little Slippers. Once a booster of Nicephorus, one of his best commanders, and a long-legged sportsman who, so it was said, could jump over five horses placed side by side, Little Slippers was now tiptoeing in and out of the imperial palace to the empress's porphyrous bedchamber.

In the late fall of 969 A.D., when this conspiracy was in full flower, the emperor had some inkling that a plot was afoot. On his way to church one day, a shadowy unknown figure thrust a note into his hands. "I am only a worm," it read, "but I know that you will die within a few days." In terror, the emperor retreated to the Bucoleon

Palace by the water, where in his House of Justinian he thought he would be safer. On the fateful night, with high wind and sleet lashing his tower on the Sea of Marmora, he appealed to his brother Leo to reinforce his guard. But Leo was preoccupied with a chess game and laid the note aside.

Meanwhile, the beautiful empress Theophano glided into her husband's bedchamber to calm his anxiety and to lower his guard. As she plied her charms, her chambermaids drew Little Slippers up in a basket from the sea to the empress's porch. With the assassins gathered outside the door, Theophano excused herself "for a moment," apologizing for the need to entertain some Bulgarian visitors a while longer. She cautioned her husband not to bolt the door for she would soon return to satisfy his carnal desires. Alone and fretful, the old commander eschewed the comfort of the imperial bed for a panther skin on the stone floor. There he fell asleep. In his slumber, so the legend goes, he cried out, "Help me, Blessed Virgin!" right before Little Slippers hacked off his head.

TEN YEARS LATER, the new king of France, Hugh Capet, was early in his shaky reign and he was searching every avenue to bolster his weak authority. His kingdom comprised little more than the Ile de France, with the rich county of Paris at its core, and the outlying city of Orléans as its royal seat. The duchies of Burgundy and Aquitaine remained separate principalities, ruled by strong and often hostile lords. Hugh Capet had been elected king of France largely through the power and the skill of Gerbert, the Wizard of Rheims. But for several tense and unstable years, the first monarch of the Capetian line had to contend with the claim of Charles of Lorraine, the last of the Carolingians. Through this tense period Gerbert served as Hugh's scribe and counselor and also the educator of his son Robert, who on December 30, 987 A.D., had been consecrated as the next king of France.

Robert was then seventeen years of age. By nature he was a pious, literary boy, fancying himself as something of a poet. It was said that with his square shoulders and sprouting beard, his straight hair pulled back in a knot, his large aquiline nose and soft mouth, better "to kiss the saint's piece," he looked quite handsome on a royal horse. More than a good steed, he was in need of a good wife. Young Robert did have a general interest in women, especially his first cousin Bertha. This was a problem, for it raised the nasty issue of incest.

Like a good father, King Hugh did his best to eclipse Bertha's hold on his son by securing for Robert the finest wife in all the world. For European royalty, that was an exotic Byzantine princess. This prize was the fantasy of all European royalty at the turn of the millennium, it seemed, and for obvious reasons. The most successful alliance of the tenth century had been the marriage of Otto II and Theophano, for it united, briefly, Rome and Constantinople, the two branches of the ancient Roman Empire.

Thus, in behalf of King Hugh, Gerbert wrote the royal request to the emperor Basil II in Constantinople.

"Not only the nobility of your race but also the glory of your great deeds urges and compels us to love you," Hugh's letter read. "You seem, indeed, to be such a preeminent person that nothing in human affairs can be valued more highly than your friendship. Of great use will be this union with us if it pleases you, and great fruits will it bear. With us in opposition neither a Gaul nor a German will harass the territory of the Roman Empire. To carry out these advantageous plans on a permanent basis we, therefore, seek with especial desire a daughter of the Holy Empire, because we have an only son, himself a king, for whose marriage we can furnish no one equal to him."

Regrettably, Byzantine princesses were in short supply. Not any child of the Greek court would do, moreover, but only those who were born in the Porphyra, the purple marble room which was the bedchamber of the empress. There were four of those, but only one, Anna, was of marriageable age. She was the sister of the Byzantine emperor Basil II, and one year hence, she would marry Vladimir of Russia. Another was Zoe, but she was a mere infant. With this depleted supply, Robert therefore faced considerable competition for only a few jewels from other royal houses in Europe. It was questionable whether they were for sale at all.

Still, because of Theophano, who had set the standard for radiance, power, and wisdom, the urge was strong.

"**S**HE WAS THE FAIR BLOSSOM from the luxuriously poisonous garden of Constantinople."

With that marvelous ambivalence, Gerbert the Wizard described the princess that the Byzantine Empire finally sent to the Holy Roman Empire in 972 A.D. This lovely flower that sprang from poison ground was luxurious and sensuous and exotic, especially in the dry desert of Otto's Rome. When she was sent, she was probably no more than twelve or thirteen years old, but in training and in accomplishment she seemed much older. How the imperial palace of Constantinople finally relented in sending a child of its inner sanctum abroad is an intriguing and typically Byzantine story.

The usurper, John Tzimisces, also known as Little Slippers, was more open to the overtures of the west than had been his victim and predecessor, Nicephorus II Phocas. Having come to power violently, he was compelled to explore every avenue to bolster his shaky and illegitimate rule. Having been driven to distraction and to murder by Empress Theophano, he banished the wicked temptress from the palace promptly, as if the assassination had been all her idea. Then he married the daughter of the much revered Constantine VII, who was the greatest Byzantine emperor of the tenth century. In the Constantinople of the late tenth century, this hypocrisy and cleverness and trickery were simply politics as usual.

On the military front, Little Slippers was tangling with the nettlesome Bulgarians to the north and the Syrians in the east. He dared not lose a battle, and therefore it made no sense for him to continue the needless hostility of his predecessor toward the Ottonians in Rome. Tzimisces anticipated another official proposal from Rome, and he wanted to be prepared. He had no real sway over the children of his now banished lover—they were prizes for later alliances after he was long gone—and so he created a pseudo-princess. Thus his lovely niece was brought into the imperial palace along with her family and began her training as if she were a true product of the purple room.

The emperor's niece was also named Theophano, a common name at the time. In her innocence and in her character, she possessed all the beauty, but none of the sinister qualities of the older Theophano. Her education in court protocol and manners was entrusted to the beardless eunuchs who schooled the child in the refinements of the Greek language and in the subtleties of the Byzantine culture. Their bible was the Book of Ceremonies, compiled at the insistence of Constantine VII in the mid-tenth century. These ceremonies were every bit as elaborate and precise and lengthy as their counterpart, the tea ceremony of Japan.

There was instruction in table settings: who was to sit on the raised dais with the emperor, what the pecking order should be, and who would sit at a separate table; what the color of the silk table covering should be for a given occasion; when the men and women were to be together and when they should part company; what costume was appropriate, especially the wearing of the ceremonial girdle; what comprised alluring and interesting feminine conversation and what subjects were taboo; what the entertainment should be, whether choral singing or theatrical set pieces; when the bawdy cabaret with men in masks and sheepskins and speaking barbarous Gothic jargon was permissible; how dessert should be served and in what different place, especially if the banquet was held in the Hall of Nineteen Couches; how the empress-to-be should relate to the courtiers of high rank like the Mistress of the Robes; how the patriarch's Kiss of Peace was to be received; what the gifts to honored guests should consist of, whether gold or silver or precious stones, and what lesser gifts were appropriate for the guest's entourage; when and how these gifts should be presented.

For a child so young as Theophano, this education was conducted in private. In an age of illiteracy, she learned to read and write in the extensive library of the imperial palace, for Byzantium prided itself in being more cultured and more learned than the barbarians of central Europe. And in an age of piety, she learned to pray and to sing at the hands of important priests who walked briskly across the Augusteum from San Sofia through the Chalke Gate and into the inner sanctum. She was never presented for public view, except in one case, at the victory celebration that Little Slippers staged for himself after his victory over the Bulgarians in 971 A.D.

When Theophano arrived ceremoniously in Italy, it was soon discovered that she was not a true creature of the porphyry palace. Otto the Great's advisers counseled him to send the fraud home, but she was so gracious and lovely, so cultured in her mastery of German and Latin. More important, she came with such a mother lode of dazzling eastern treasure that Otto paused. Perhaps it was better to settle for this princess who was nearly purple-born.

If the Byzantine and the Roman empires seemed like polar opposites, so did the royal couple. Otto II was not much older than his wife, a mere sixteen years of age, but in appearance he was a different species. Next to Theophano's olive skin, her soft loveliness, her raven hair, and dark eyes, Rufus (as Otto was called) was ruddy-haired, homely, and vain. As she was shrewd, strong-willed, willowy, and cultivated, he was crude, short, and impulsive. And yet on April 14, 972 A.D., when they ascended to the altar of St. Peter's in Rome, with Pope John XIII presiding and the bishop of Metz attending, they seemed like a match made in heaven. Their union was sanctified with a magnificent marriage contract, drawn up on an elaborately decorated parchment, resembling Byzantine silk, with animal and tendril designs embedded in the fibers and with gold lettering.

Upon her coronation, Theophano assumed the unique title of co-imperatrix, co-emperor, as if she were equal in authority to her husband. She was imbued with the Byzantine concept of emperorship: to be emperor was to imitate God. In Byzantium, where the women were strong and powerful, there was no concept of the "weaker sex," and Theophano did not mean to adopt German subservience once she was in the west. She established her own independent court, with her personal priest and her ladies-in-waiting who watched over her magnificent jewels and lavish costumes, her linens and rugs, and especially her silk. This fierce independence rubbed certain members of the German court the wrong way. In the corridors, she was referred to as "that Greek woman," who was too talkative and too ambitious.

It was clear from the beginning that she meant to be a player in the affairs of the empire. Imperial documents are rife with references to her interventions in a wide assortment of issues. Her power grew substantially upon the death of Otto the Great on May 9, 973 A.D., even though she maintained a tense relationship with Otto's widow,

Empress Adelaide, who was equally strong-willed. And this power grew exponentially when she finished bearing her children and when the court shifted from Aachen to Rome.

In the first seven years of his reign, Otto II was constantly at war since, even more than his father, he felt the urge to attack the unbelievers on the fringes of his empire. By the end of those seven years, he was known as Otto the Bloody. But he might also have been known as Otto the Spendthrift, for his imperial lifestyle was lavish and extravagant, in part due to the empress's tastes. In 977 A.D., however, she began her childbearing years, giving birth four times between November 977 A.D. and July 980 A.D. Upon the final occasion, she delivered twins, one of whom was her first son. He was named Otto III. As Theophano bore her children, Otto II prosecuted his warfare, campaigning through France on punitive reprisal raids in the Lorraine.

At Christmastime in 981 A.D., Otto and Theophano vacationed at Salerno, south of Naples, and planned the grand campaign of their reign. Both emperor and empress were determined to realize the ambition of their nascent dynasty: at last, to drive the infidel Muhammadans from southern Italy. They sought to undertake this mission, even though it brought Rome into direct conflict with Byzantium. For several decades, Greeks and Arabs had fought over the rugged mountainous terrain of Calabria; successive invasions and plundering between the rivals had left the region without an identity, and therefore it seemed to be ripe for Christian conquest.

In preparation for this final assault, Otto II now took an even grander title, "Emperor of the Romans and the Most Invincible Augustus." Both claims were soon to sound overbold. Reinforced with Bavarians and Swabians, the imperial army marched south, with important bishops at the head of the columns and the zeal of St. Michael in their hearts. The army passed through such ancient places as Rocca Imperiale and Mantera and over roads once traveled by Hannibal's elephants. By March 982 A.D., Otto stood outside the walls of Taranto.

This was a dry, despicable place, the lair of pirates and thieves. Along with Bari, it was the other strategically important Mediterranean seaport in the boot of Italy that remained in Arab hands. But it was scarcely worth staking an empire on. Moreover, it was still part of the Byzantine Empire. Ironically, Theophano egged her husband on toward this confrontation with her own people, for she considered the south of Italy to be part of her legitimate dowry. She was offended that these provinces had not been handed over upon her arrival. (The reason was obvious: her uncle and benefactor, Little Slippers, had himself been assassinated in 976 A.D., poisoned probably by the agents of his spurned lover, the other Theophano. The latter's son Basil II was now the "emperor of the Greeks," and he owed nothing to Empress Theophano in Italy.)

In the ancient reaches of southern Italy, Otto II's impulsiveness finally caught up with him. He threw himself into the fray, without a tactical plan, without a navy or any alliance with local chieftains, and suddenly found himself caught and surrounded on a plain of Cape Colon. The combined Byzantine and Arabic force was strong, and its Islamic elements full of religious zeal. To them, this battle was a dead struggle, a jihad, and they charged into combat with the chant "Victory or dead!" The battle became a complete rout. The German force was obliterated. The bishops of Augsburg and Fulka were killed, as well as two sons of Pandulf Ironhead and the Arabic general Abu al Quasam. Otto II barely escaped with his life when he borrowed a horse from a Jew and swam on it to the boat of a Greek spectator. Before he was allowed to board, the captain demanded to know if he was the emperor. After an initial denial, Otto finally confessed.

"Yes I am," he said. "My sins have brought this disaster upon me. Listen, I have just lost the flower of my realm, and I will never again set foot on these lands. Let's sail to Rossano, where my wife and child await my return. We should pick them up, along with all my money—I have a lot! Look on me, brother. I will be a friend to you as you have been to me in time of need." The suddenly joyous Greek captain savored the royal reward that he would get at Rossano and happily sailed away. But when the town was in view, the emperor leapt unceremoniously overboard and left his Greek rescuer in the lurch, aghast at being stiffed by this imperial skinflint.

Word of the catastrophe at Colon swept through Europe. Nations in the north pounced on Otto's weakness. The Danes of Harald

Bluetooth poured over the Danevirk and attacked an imperial fortress in Schleswig, while the Poles attacked Hamburg and leveled it. There was a massive revolt of Slavic tribes east of the Elbe where Saxon fortresses east of Magdeburg were assaulted and destroyed. And even within Germany itself, from which Otto II had been largely absent for seven years, the criticism of the emperor was fierce.

The brilliant vision of a Holy Roman Empire suddenly seemed to be a dim and fading light. The son of Otto the Great began to look like Otto the Small, even to his own wife, Theophano. She let loose a stream of invective, scorching her husband's pathetic generalship and lambasting the clubfooted performance of the German soldiers. Her own countrymen had performed far better. These impolitic remarks were deeply resented and vividly remembered, as Otto II spiraled downward into depression.

With the empire seeming to crumble, the royal couple made their way north, wintered in Rome, before moving on to the imperial castle in Pavia in the spring. In the summer of 983 A.D. their three-year-old son Otto was sent to Germany, while the emperor and empress struggled to keep control of events. But in November, Otto II, only twenty-nine years of age but run-down and melancholy, fell ill with an intestinal flu. To combat the infection he poured four huge drafts of aloe potion down his throat, which made the illness worse. His diarrhea and swollen hemorrhoids gave him a "superfluity of humors," as it was euphemistically called, and before long the illness was beyond the control of his doctors. On December 7, 983 A.D., he died. He was buried in St. Peter's, the only Holy Roman Emperor of the Ottonian dynasty to be laid to rest there.

Even his contemporaries were harsh in their dirges. Predictably, they placed a lion's share of the blame on Theophano. Bruno of Querfort left a withering analysis of this lesser Otto and his meddling wife:

"Swiftly after his father, did he climb the realm's summit, but he did not know how to reign in the proper spirit and with mature wisdom. While he unwisely thought all men should humbly serve him, he lost the empire and killed the peace which fear of his father had created. Only lost battles opened at last the eyes of the son and shame overcame him for having listened to women's advice. Too late, he rued having taken childish counsel from childish friends instead of from wise elders. He worked for his own honor, not for your victory, Oh Christ!"

After her husband's burial, Theophano traveled north again to Pavia, to mourn with her mother-in-law, Empress Adelaide. What was to happen to them? And to the empire? And to her son, Otto III, who at three years was the rightful heir to the throne? Her husband was scarcely cold in the grave, and her dust had scarcely settled on the road north than the local potentate in Rome and his compliant antipope seized power in the Eternal City once again.

The immediate crisis was the kidnapping of Otto III. As we saw earlier (in "Gerbert the Wizard") the empress turned to Gerbert, then the bishop of Rheims, for help. In his quiet but determined way, over a six-month period, Gerbert built his coalition that finally brought the collapse of Henry the Quarrelsome's pretensions. The boy was returned to his mother on June 29, 984 A.D.

For the next four years, Empress Theophano transformed herself into a subtle and effective diplomat. Still stunningly beautiful in her early twenties, yet resolute, she sought to consolidate the empire and to buy time. Unlike her intemperate husband, she stayed in Germany, moving about from castle to castle within the core of the empire. Through necessity, she pursued a conservative, defensive strategy of accommodation and compromise. Her policy was well-thought-out, consistent in conception and realization, broad-gauged, and far ahead of its time. In modern parlance, it deserved to be called Theophano's European policy. If she was to deliver her empire to her son in a robust condition twelve years hence, she had to avoid confrontation wherever she could. But she did not hesitate to move her legions when her rule and credibility were challenged.

The northern borderlands, ruled by the fierce Scandinavian Vikings, were the most worrisome. Through quiet diplomacy, Theophano reached an understanding first with Harald Bluetooth in Denmark and then with Eric the Victorious in Sweden. In the so called Wildeshauser Proclamations of 988 A.D., it was agreed that an archbishopric should be established in Hamburg-Bremen, as the vanguard for proselytizing Christians in Scandinavia. An alliance with Miescko I of Poland was also concluded, and the Polish king, in gratitude, presented Otto III with a camel when he was six years old. She reached out to Geza, the chieftain of Hungary, to revitalize the friendship that had begun with Otto the Great fourteen years before. And she maintained contact with Vladimir, the Russian prince of Kiev, who would marry a true Byzantine princess of the purple room, Anna, in that same year.

Taken together, these diplomatic initiatives constituted Theophano's "eastern policy." In the west, her stance was the same. Toward the nettlesome problem of Upper and Lower Lorraine, she employed diplomacy and used Gerbert the Wizard as her secretary for western European affairs.

While these alliances were driven by the need to buy peace and to mark time, their effect was to develop the first state system in Europe. Under this remarkable and beautiful woman, the outlines of modern Europe began to take shape. (It has since been called the "First Europe.") By 989 A.D. Theophano could afford to turn her attention south, to Italy and to fickle Rome. This was a strategic campaign but also a sentimental journey, for she wished to revisit the tomb of her husband in St. Peter's just as she wished to tame the local rebels. To meet the grandeur of the moment, she adopted a new title, Imperatrix Augustus. Later she changed it to the masculine form, Imperator Augustus, for she did not want to be perceived as weaker. In the fall of that year she traveled over the Alps, subdued the city of Rome, and brought it back into the imperial fold. She spent an emotional Christmas there and did not return north until the spring of 990 A.D.

"Though she was of the weak sex," a contemporary German chronicler wrote patronizingly, "she possessed moderation, trustworthiness and—a quality not often found in Greece—very good manners. In this way she protected with male vigilance the royal power of her son. She was friendly against all those who were honest, but operated with terrifying superiority against rebels."

This was high praise for a scribe of the Dark Ages. Not all scribes were so fulsome. In Rome hostility remained deep and bitter toward the influence of Byzantium on western Europe. Empress Theophano—this sensuous, elegant, and noble lioness—symbolized the insidious foreign influence. Some from the ascetic monasteries of

Rome resented her extravagant lifestyle, implied that there was something immoral about it, and deplored the presence of Greek churches in their midst. They were quick to spread rumors about Theophano, including one item that the empress, while in Rome, had had an affair, an *obscoeni negotii,* with John Philagathos, the lecherous godfather of Otto III and later the antipope. This was a damning charge, combining forbidden sex with exotic Greek practices and later with heresy. Surely, it was the mark of the devil.

In the spring of 991 A.D., Empress Theophano repaired to her favorite place, the castle of Nijmegen in Holland, which had over the centuries been touched by the Romans, by Charlemagne, and by the Vikings. In her travels, she had returned to this western outpost of the empire eight times. But this would be her last. She died in June of that year.

For her extravagance, later chroniclers of the Roman church were determined that she should pay dearly. In 1050 A.D. a nun testified that the ghost of the empress Theophano had appeared to her and pleaded to the "venerable virgin" to pray for her in her torment. For she was suffering in purgatory.

"I am Theophano. I came into the kingdom of the Franks and was joined in marriage to the emperor Otto," the ghost wheezed.

"How are things with you now?" the nun asked.

"Horribly," the gossamer empress replied. "Because I have been placed into the greatest of torments."

"Why?" the nun asked.

"Because I was the first to introduce many unwarranted, opulent frills of women's attire into the empire which were used by Greece but till then were unknown in the provinces of Europe and France. I adorned myself with them in a manner that was not harmonious with human nature. By dressing in this harmful fashion I caused the sin of vanity in other women who craved for the same. These are my most serious sins for which I deserve to suffer eternal damnation."

For this venial sin of vanity fair, she would be put forward as an object lesson for centuries to come.

CHAPTER TWELVE

Otto the Dreamer

IN 996 A.D., the boy became emperor. At last, Otto III had reached the age of majority, and, frail and effeminate though he was, he was ready to take charge of his destiny. The lure of Rome was strong in him. Caught up in the pomp of his Byzantine ancestry and romantic about the glory of ancient Rome, he longed for a splendid coronation as the emperor of the Holy Roman Empire. Beyond these personal motives, the Eternal City needed attention. Once again the scourge of local dissension that had bedeviled Otto's father and grandfather infested the city. With almost boring predictability, the Roman nobles had seized power and driven out the rightful pope.

This was an old story. For fifty years the struggle between the powerful Roman families who "elected" the popes and the German emperors who imposed them had been unrelenting. In recent years sway over the city had fallen into the hands of the ferocious Crescenti family. This mob shared the blood and the bloodthirstiness of their ancestors Marozia and John XV as they liquidated and installed popes at will. After the death of Otto the Great in 972 A.D., the head of the Crescenti, Crescentius I, had the sitting pope, Benedict VI, strangled in the Castel Sant'Angelo and replaced with his own candidate, Boniface VII. Boniface was no bargain: he himself was implicated in the assassination of Benedict VI. Indeed, he was a thoroughly disgraceful character whom the bishop of Orléans found to be "a horrible monster, surpassing all mortals in wickedness and stained with the blood of his predecessor."

Boniface's installation had drawn Otto III's father, Otto II, back to Italy, and Boniface VII was quickly chased into exile, as the emperor installed his own pope, John XIV, in the chair of St. Peter. But when Otto II left town, the pendulum swung back the other way. The son of Crescentius I, known as John Crescentius, had John XIV killed and brought Boniface VII back from exile.

And so it went in this unending seesaw between the Roman barons and the German emperors. Who was up and who was down depended upon the strength and the proximity of the current emperor. The usurper, Boniface VII, was himself poisoned after a pontificate of just nine months and three days. Being pope had become a dangerous calling. "All Italy seems to be Rome, and at the doings of the Romans the world shudders," wrote Gerbert from Rheims. "Justice is once again put up to auction in Rome." But then Gerbert was not exactly an objective observer, since he was having his own problems with the prevailing regime in the Vatican.

In 996 A.D. John Crescentius remained the tyrant of the Palatine Hill. He tormented the reigning pope, John XV, mercilessly, until the unhappy pontiff was forced to flee Rome and take refuge in Pavia. The very youth of Otto III seemed to embolden Crescentius, and he took full advantage. It was as if he meant to give new life to Solomon's old warning "Woe to thee, O land, when thy king is a child."

Otto III was growing up fast, however. As the beleaguered John

XV appealed for help against Rome's tyrant, the young emperor was already embroiled in a war on the eastern frontier that had lasted for two years. Since 994 A.D. all the Slavs, except the Serbs, were in open revolt against the empire, which had been subjugating them as vassals since the time of Otto the Great. But for Otto III the situation in Rome seemed to take precedence. And so in the winter of 996 A.D. the adolescent emperor made a speedy truce with the Slavs and marched through the Brenner Pass with his army, gleefully contemplating his triumphant arrival in Rome and his coronation.

The emperor celebrated Easter in Pavia, but when his imperial columns moved on to Ravenna, Otto was greeted with the news of the pope's death. The pressures of Rome had simply worn poor John XV out, and he had died of a malignant fever. Falling upon their knees, the nobles and bishops beseeched Otto to name the new pope.

He chose his cousin Bruno, one of his chaplains, a handsome and learned young man of twenty-two years, who took the name Gregory V and became the first German pope. Outside Italy, the emperor's choice was greeted joyfully, for it broke the hold of the Roman nobles over the papacy.

"I have just heard a piece of news at which I rejoice like the sight of gold or topaz," wrote the important Abbo of Fleury. "The dignity of the Apostolic See has been elevated by the election of a member of the imperial family who is full of virtue and wisdom. May the same Holy Spirit who inspired St. Gregory I with such great learning also inspire the present venerable pontiff of the same Holy Roman Church."

This burst of enthusiasm was soon tempered. For Gregory V revealed himself to be impetuous and aggressive, quite open to bribes, and very proud of his Saxon lineage as the great-grandson of Otto the Great. This patriotism was not a good thing.

Together the German duo marched on Rome. With each league that the emperor drew closer to Rome, the Roman tyrant John Crescentius grew milder, and by the time the imperial entourage arrived at the city walls, the Roman potentate was an unctuous greeter. From the Roman viewpoint, the spectacle had all the marks of a foreign conquest. The Germans were oblivious to the resentment all around them. On May 21, 996 A.D., they staged a spectacular Teutonic coronation of the Imperator Romanorum, emperor to the Romans and the Franks, the Saxons and the Swabians, Alsace and the Lorraine, Bavaria and Carinthia and Bohemia. As he ascended the altar of St. Peter's, the young Otto was resplendent in a mantle embroidered with apocalyptic figures, the front displaying a golden zodiac glittering with precious stones, the fringes decorated with 355 tiny gold bells shaped in the form of pomegranates.

After the most solemn moment of the ceremony when the emperor's head, shoulders, and chest were anointed with the holy oil, the bishops proclaimed: "May he defend and exalt your holy church and rule the people committed to him by You with justice." With his sword he was to destroy the heretics and all enemies of Christ, as he was to defend widows and orphans. With his scepter, he must "please the pious and frighten wicked men." Devoutly, Otto III accepted these coronation vows.

Coincidentally, as this grandiose spectacle went forward, Gerbert had come to Italy from France on a personal mission. For five years confusion had reigned over his see of Rheims. In 991 A.D., upon the death of his superior, Adalbert, a council of bishops at St. Basle de Verzy had elected Gerbert archbishop. But a certain faction, seemingly with the initial support of King Hugh Capet of France, regarded this election as improper. The problem became entangled in Gallic politics. Gerbert appreciated what the punishment would be if he were deposed: his ring would be removed; a crosier would be broken over his head; his vestments would be ripped; and he would be made to sit on the ground in humiliation before his peers, as they handed a new crosier to the legitimized rival.

In Rome, where resentment at the arrogance of the Rheims intellectuals remained strong, Gerbert's detractors had found a sympathetic audience for their position. They succeeded in placing Gerbert under a papal excommunication for a time. Determined not to be driven from his see, Gerbert operated extralegally, and those who served and obeyed him did so against papal orders, risking the curse themselves. But in time the situation became intolerable, and Gerbert finally felt compelled to seek out the pope personally to resolve the dispute. And so his trip to Rome.

In the cold and Teutonic Gregory V, however, Gerbert found no friend. In all likelihood, the younger Gregory V saw the older and wiser Gerbert as a rival. The pope preferred to keep the see of Rheims in disarray and in disrepute. And so Gerbert prepared to leave Italy with his episcopal authority still regarded as illegitimate.

On his way home, however, he tarried in Pavia. As luck would have it, Otto III was also still there. The emperor was immediately taken with this Gallic genius of the church and sentimental about his past association with the house of Otto. The young emperor plied Gerbert with endless questions about Arabic astronomy and Egyptian mathematics and especially the Greek classics, and put him to work writing imperial letters. The chemistry between the two men was immediate and magical. Otto had his mentor, and Gerbert his protector.

With the approach of winter, Otto was back in Germany. No sooner was he safely over the Alps than John Crescentius led a revolt of the Roman citizenry against the German pope, drove Gregory V from the city, and installed a Greek antipope in his place. His choice for an antipope was inspired. He was John Philagathos, a slave by birth, who had risen within the ranks of the Catholic hierarchy to be bishop of Piacenza. He was a favorite of Empress Theophano, so favored that he was made the godfather of Otto III and, more pointedly, tasted the favors of the empress's bedroom. Only four years before, this same prelate had undertaken a mission to Constantinople to arrange, unsuccessfully it turned out, for Otto III to have a Byzantine bride. For his godfather to be the antipope could scarcely upset the German emperor too much, except that it would force the emperor to choose between Philagathos and his cousin.

Meanwhile, the cousin, Gregory V, fled to Pavia. From there, he appealed to Otto III to hasten to the defense of papal legitimacy. But Otto was again preoccupied with rebellious Slavs in Brandenburg, and he did not come. Gregory could only wait until Otto III tired of the battlefield and could turn again to the politics and problems of Rome. As the pope waited, a synod was held in Pavia at which both John Crescentius and John the Greek were excommunicated.

Back in Rheims, Gerbert had repaired to his sickbed. While in Italy, he had contracted malaria, and he was feeling his mortality.

"Old age threatens me with my last day," he wrote to Empress Adelaide in February 997. "Pleurisy fills my sides. My ears ring. My eyes fill with water. Continual pains jab my whole body." The real blow, however, had come months before when Hugh Capet, the king he had installed, passed away, and his son Robert, the king Gerbert had educated, took charge of the French throne.

This might have been a passable turn of events, except for one thing: Robert was desperately in love with his first cousin Bertha and had only waited for his father to die so he could marry her. For a king who would later be called "the Pious," this affair was especially seedy. Not only had Robert been the godfather of one of Bertha's children by a former marriage, but the king had conspired in the murder of Bertha's husband. Immediately after his father's death, the new king married this blood relation, and the church reacted by placing Robert under an anathema. Gerbert expressed the dismay of the church directly . . . and also personally, since he had been responsible for Robert's moral education as a child. The consequence was to separate Gerbert from his royal support in Rheims. In the summer of 997 A.D., feeling hurt and abandoned, complaining of the "undeserved persecution of my brothers," he fled to Germany, never to return to his native France. He fretted about the destiny of Rheims, caught as it was between two contenders. "Because Rheims is the head of the French kingdom, if it perishes, the members will follow. And how will it not perish, placed as it is under the names of two men, as if between the hammer and the anvil, while it approves of neither as a leader, as it tosses about midst the waves of the sea without an oars man?"

By contrast, Gerbert found the climate of Germany invigorating. In Aachen, the city of kaisers, Otto III received him joyfully and with great respect. Quickly Gerbert's health and high spirits returned. The time for the two friends was brief, however, since in July the emperor marched off to eastern Germany for his second campaign against the Slavs. Before he left, the friends exchanged gifts. Gerbert presented holy relics which he had brought from Italy, and in turn, the emperor gave Gerbert charge of a monastery in Sasbach, near Strasbourg, south on the Rhine River.

About this gift, confusion soon developed. It was questionable whether the emperor had the right to give it in the first place. Only weeks after Gerbert was ensconced in his splendid new surroundings, imperial forces unceremoniously threw him out, apparently with the connivance of Otto himself. Rightly confused and characteristically hurt and self-pitying, worried that he was destined to be an exile forever, Gerbert wrote with astonishing directness to his benefactor.

"I am at a loss to understand what accusations of mine have injured you. Why has my devotion become so suddenly displeasing? What you gave, you were either able to give or you were not. If you were not able to, why did you pretend to be able to? If you were able to, what unknown emperor without name commands our emperor? In what shadows is that scoundrel lurking? Let him come forth into the light and be crucified so that our Caesar may freely rule."

In his response, Otto was consoling without offering any apology. Instead, he offered something better. Would Gerbert join his court as the imperial teacher? The emperor wanted to cultivate his Byzantine roots as passionately as he wanted to reject the boorishness of his Saxon side. "Show your aversion to Saxon ignorance," the emperor wrote to Gerbert, "and, with God's help, cause in me the lively genius of the Greeks to shine forth. Explain to me the book of arithmetic, so that I may learn of the attainments of the ancients." Poignantly, the emperor closed his invitation with a verse, as if he needed to show that he would be a worthy pupil.

> Verses have I never made
> Nor in such study ever stayed.
> When to its practice myself I apply
> And can write successfully,
> As many men as has Lorraine,
> To you, then, songs I'll send the same.

In accepting, Gerbert beseeched the emperor to live as long as the last number of the abacus, 999,999, into infinity. "If we are aglow with the slightest spark of knowledge, it redounds to your glory through the excellence of your father who nourished it and the magnificence of your grandfather who matched it," Gerbert wrote in October 997 A.D.

"I do not know what more evidence of the divine there can be than that a man, Greek by birth, Roman by empire, as if by hereditary right seeks to recapture for himself the treasures of Greek and Roman wisdom."

The seeds of a glorious vision had been planted. But before the emperor could think of that, he had to turn his mind to some dirty business.

LATE IN 997 A.D., the youthful German Caesar finally came south to "cleanse the Roman sink." As the imperial legions approached the city, John Crescentius, at last humbled and cornered, locked himself into Castel Sant'Angelo while the terrified antipope, John the Greek, fled into the countryside.

With the Teutonic brigades in their midst, the Romans abruptly switched their allegiance, expressed their outrage at the usurpation, and joined the emperor's forces. Their lord and his antipope, the Romans suddenly declared, were evil people and must be hunted down. A combined force of Germans and Italians rose passionately to the challenge. They first went after the Greek and found him cowering in a castle tower in the Campagna. Setting upon him like ravens, they plucked out his eyes, cut out his tongue, and mutilated his nose and ears. Piously, the soldiers held the Bible high and said they were only following the prescription set out in Ezekiel 23.24–25: "They will come against you with chariots, with a host drawn from the nations, armed with shield, buckler, and helmet. They will beset you on every side. I will give them authority to judge, and they will use that authority to judge you. I will turn my jealous wrath loose on you, and they will make you feel their fury. They will cut off your nose and your ears, and in the end they will kill you with the sword."

In time the wretch was dragged before Otto and Gregory. The horrified Otto shrank from the gruesome sight of his mauled godfather, his mother's lover, as if he had not understood the consequences of revenge. His guilt intensified when the aged, ethereal figure of Nilus of Rossano, the most famous holy man of Italy, came to plead for mercy. Like John Philagathos, Nilus was a Greek born in

Calabria, and he was now close to ninety years of age. For many years the Muslims of southern Italy had harassed and pursued him, and he had been forced to live in a cave. He gave up eating meat, wore a goatskin, and now was mentor to an ascetic community of Basilian monks in Serperi. Rarely did this decrepit, otherworldly, pious old man stray from his rocky retreat, but now he came to Rome to plead for his fellow Calabrian. The young Otto listened with respect to the holy man, but the emperor seemed incapable of action. In frustration at the emperor's paralysis, Nilus finally raised a crooked finger in warning:

"If you have no pity on him, sire, so the Lord will have no pity on you when you stand before his Throne." Otto shuddered at the threat from this ghostly holy man.

Gregory V, however, was unmoved. For Philagathos's ambition and usurpation had been directed at him personally and at his legitimate seat upon the papal throne. Seized with the desire for revenge, the pope demanded further public degradation. As the emperor remained stricken and silent, the papal vestments were torn and turned inside out and placed on the culprit. Philagathos was deposited backwards on a donkey, commanded to hold the ass's tail, and paraded through the city before the prurient citizens of Rome, with a herald walking before him announcing that this was the John who dared "to play the pope." The Romans jeered at the pathetic figure.

"Thus let the man suffer who has endeavored to drive the pope from his see," they shouted.

Such was the justice of the age. Official and diplomatic Rome wallowed in the pornographic extravaganza. Even the Greek ambassador, who might have been thought to be sympathetic toward his blood brother, reveled in the madness. "This Philagathos, who fortunately has no equal, whose mouth is ever full of curses, blasphemies, and calumnies, this man to whom no one can be compared, and who is not to be likened to anyone, this Pope with hands imbued in blood, this Pope so arrogant and haughty, has stumbled and fallen," he wrote to his brother. After the ambassador described the mutilation in graphic detail, he concluded the letter:

"I would counsel all to refrain from doing what he has dared to do. For justice never sleeps."

When the humiliation of the antipope was complete, he was

handed over to the monks of St. Nilus and taken away to a remote monastery.

Meanwhile, John Crescentius was still holed up in the supposedly impregnable Castel Sant'Angelo. Knowing that his situation was hopeless, Crescentius disguised himself in a hooded monk's cowl, slipped into the emperor's palace on the Aventine, and pleaded for his life. At the appearance of this hoary figure, Otto was furious. The emperor demanded to know who admitted this dark "Prince of the Romans" into his presence, and ordered the villain to be returned to Castel Sant'Angelo.

"Take him back to the throne of his highness," said the emperor, "until we have prepared a reception worthy of his dignity."

The reception was chilly. When the culprit was back at Sant'Angelo, the imperial soldiers leapt from their movable towers over the fortress walls, seized the baron, and dragged him to the highest tower. There, as the throng of Romans below cried out for blood, Crescentius was beheaded and his body thrown into the moat. Then the corpse was retrieved, dragged on the skin of a cow across the Neronian Field to the Vatican Hill (known alternately as the Hill of Joy or the Hill of Evil), and hung upside down by its heels. The execution "inspired all present with unspeakable fear," a chronicler would write later.

Revulsion might have been a better word. If the Vatican was a swamp of corruption, the foreign emperor was just as bad in his gratuitous violence. In private, the sensitive Otto retreated into despair and mourned his new calloused reputation. Racked with guilt, he was haunted by the image of the headless Crescentius and the maimed Philagathos. The warning of the Greek hermit Nilus tormented him; it was as if the violence which had been done to the antipope had been done to God himself.

Rather than terror at his execution, the Romans wallowed in Crescentius's fate and turned their late patrician into a martyr. On the streets it was said that Crescentius had agreed to surrender only when the emperor promised him safety. Only the perfidy of the emperor had done the Roman noble in. The patrician of Rome became memorialized as Crescentius of the Marble Horse, a valiant figure battling for his life and liberty against the foreign oppressor and then tortured mercilessly before death. On his grave the following epitaph was inscribed:

> He to whom Rome her glad allegiance gave,
>
> Lies now unhonored in this obscure grave,
>
> The mighty Duke Crescentius, to whose share
>
> Fell noble ancestry and beauty rare.
>
> Strong stood the land of Tiber in his day,
>
> Then turned submissive to her Pontiff's sway.
>
> For round the fickle wheel of Fortune spun,
>
> And horror closed what glory had begun.
>
> Oh thou, whoe'er thou art, who passest by,
>
> Under like chance 'tis thine to live and die;
>
> Then spare thy fellow man at least a sigh.

The antipathy toward the German emperor increased, but Otto III did not notice it. He had receded into a mystical trance. To Gaeta he traveled humbly in search of St. Nilus. Before the hermit, the emperor dropped to his knees and asked for forgiveness. Beseeching Nilus to return with him to Rome, he placed his gold crown in the hands of the holy man. But Nilus was not moved. He merely prayed for the emperor's salvation.

On February 18, 999 A.D., Gregory V died (and the rumor promptly spread that he had been poisoned). The alien and despised German pope had expired, and the way was clear for Otto to placate the resentment of the Romans by restoring their primacy in electing popes.

Instead, Otto turned at last to Gerbert of Aurillac. Rome was appalled. To elect the first French pope after the first German pope was more salt in the Roman wounds. Otto was adamant. Political compromise was beneath him. The great teacher was the obvious choice. He was the towering intellect of the age and the profound conscience of the Catholic church. He was the man for the millennium.

Gerbert took the title Sylvester II. It was a name carefully chosen. For the first Sylvester had ruled Rome in the fourth century, as the companion to the Roman emperor Constantine. Together, Constantine and Sylvester I had forged a powerful Christian theocracy that was an inspiration to the ages. Now Otto III and Sylvester II set out to restore a kingdom of God on earth, to bring the glory of ancient Rome and the wisdom of ancient Greece to their contemporary enterprise. Their universal dominion would be worthy of Constantine the Great, of the greatest Byzantine emperor, Justinian, of Charlemagne.

"Ours is the Roman Empire," Gerbert had written to his Caesar. "Italy is fertile in fruits, Lorraine and Germany are fertile in men, and even the strong kingdoms of the Slavs are available to us. Our august emperor of the Romans art thou, Caesar, who, sprung from the noblest blood of the Greeks, surpass the Greeks in empire and govern the Romans by hereditary right. You surpass both in genius and eloquence."

Thus did Gerbert flatter his romantic, idealistic pupil at this historic moment, and in many moments in the years to come. Without the power of the emperor, the pope knew that he would get nowhere in reenergizing the Catholic church. Without Gerbert, the emperor knew that his romantic notions would have no shape or substance or moral authority. Flattery would become commonplace in their communication. For his part, Otto addressed his messages to his teacher, "To the most wise Gerbert, crowned in the three classes of philosophy." It was a genuine example of mutual admiration.

They would soon find out, however, that genius and beautiful words and fertile imagination were not enough.

T HE ROME OF 999 A.D. was a pale shadow of its luminous former self. Ancient Rome, at the time of Christ, had been a bustling, vibrant metropolis of about a million people, full of colossal buildings and sweeping marble spaces, parade grounds and magnificent vistas. But in the centuries that followed, the invasions of Goths and Saracens and Norsemen as well as plague and general neglect had left the city in ruins. At the turn of the millennium, its population had shrunk to a paltry fifty thousand citizens. St. Peter's Cathedral remained the heart of Christendom, but its dome and grand parade ground would come later during the Renaissance. In 999 A.D. Gerbert's papal basilica looked much like another church in Rome called St. Paul's: rectangular, simple, faced with crumbling, ocher brick, and vaguely Byzantine. The pope himself reigned at the Lateran Palace while the emperor had his residence at the old Savelli fortress on the Aventine Hill.

But the other glorious sites of the Holy Roman Empire had fallen into disrepair. Trajan's Market still bustled, but in a semirural setting with sheep grazing on its terraces. The Forum of Augustus had become a quarry for foreign and native scavengers and pastureland for cattle. The Colosseum had been turned into an apartment house, with clothes hanging out to dry and squatters squawking at one another. The Field of Mars was strewn with broken marble relics and covered with vines and vineyards. And the imperial mansions on the Palatine were colossal ruins. Fishmongers and butchers sold their products from the prostrate marble slabs in the Theater of Marcellus. The carved sarcophagi were troughs for pigs.

If Otto III and Sylvester II wished to make Rome once again worthy of being an imperial capital, much work lay ahead of them. The emperor turned his mind first to the colossal ruins of the Palatine. From his palace on the Aventine, he looked across the pasture of the Circus Maximus to the monumental arches where Caesar Augustus and Livia had once walked, to the squalid shacks that covered the sacred ground where Romulus and Remus had been nourished by their lupine mother, where the Temple of Apollo had once drawn the faithful. Almost stripped naked over the centuries, its palaces were filled still with crumbling statues, torn draperies of golden cloth, marble halls, and overgrown gardens. The restoration of Rome's glory had to begin at the Palatine.

In the first few months of their partnership, the emperor and the pope nurtured their plans for a universal Christian empire. Europe was to have no borders. Between the Atlantic Ocean and the Black Sea there was to be a perfect union of church and state, where no distinctions came between lands and peoples, but only between Christians and infidels. Rome was to become again the capital of the world. The motto of the new empire was enshrined as *Renovatio Imperii Romanorum,* and this was inscribed on the imperial seal surrounding a veiled woman, bearing a shield and a lance.

At the outset, Otto concerned himself with the ceremonies of the new court. He began to sign his edicts with the moniker Emperor of the Romans, or Consul of the Senate, or, simply, Augustus, Romanus, or Saxonicus. Drawing upon his Greek roots, he conferred the magnificent titles of the Byzantine court on his lieutenants. There was the Count of the Sacred Palace and the Prefect of the Fleet (even though there was no navy). Greek titles were suddenly fashionable. His chamberlain became the Protovestarius whose subordinates were the Protospatharius and the Hyparch. These Greek names were presented imposingly in the Greek alphabet, and speaking the Greek language in court was encouraged. This created an element of low comedy: to see German bluebloods stammering superciliously in halting Greek was a sight to behold.

When the emperor dined, he was served on gold plates, seated at a semicircular marble table, with his chair raised above the others. On any given day, he might wear one of ten crowns whose derivation he had found in the formularies of the Byzantine court: ivy, olive leaves, poplar branches, oak and laurel, peacock feathers, the mitra of Janus, the Trojan frigium of Paris, the iron crown of Pompey, or the golden crown of Persia with the inscription *Roma caput mundi regit orbis frena rotundi* (Rome, the head of the world, rules and restrains).

For all his obsession with ceremony during the last year of the first millennium, Otto's mood swung, without notice, toward the opposite extreme of penitence, renunciation, and mysticism. In the summer of 999 A.D., the emperor spent fourteen days in a hermit's cell in the basilica of San Clemente in Rome. In August he proceeded east to Subiaco where he mortified the flesh at the monastery of St. Benedict. Was he a Caesar or an Anchorite? It depended on the day.

In the meantime, Sylvester II adopted the title universal pope. In the months leading up to the millennium, he acted boldly and universally, as befit his vision and this historical moment. By day, stern directives flowed from his hand, especially in his determination to punish simony and lapses of priestly chastity, while by night he watched the stars from his Lateran observatory. His reach extended as far north as Norway, east to the Volga, west to Santiago de Compostela. On October 23, 999 A.D., he commanded King Olaf Trygvesson of Norway to revoke the use of the pagan runic letters in his country. Such stick writing was vulgar and needed to be replaced with the civilized Latin alphabet. This was a condition of Norway being recognized as a Christian nation. He welcomed Vajk's envoy from Hungary and gave his blessing to the first Christian king of Hungary as Stephen I. Thus he officially welcomed Hungary into the community of Christian nations. Poland was welcomed likewise when the ambassadors from Boleslav the Brave came as eager supplicants. To them he promised a visit from the emperor in the following year, at the congress of Gniezno . . . and someday a holy crown. With Vladimir, the prince of Kiev, he kept up a warm and spirited correspondence, nurturing his embryonic Christian state.

The intensity of events was picking up considerably, as if the church had entered a period of preparation.

The affairs of France required Gerbert's special attention, since King Robert still lived wickedly and incestuously with his queen Bertha and under an anathema of the church. The pope was aware of the interpretation that certain learned French clerics put on this and other evil events in his native land. Several years before, the bishop of Orléans had proclaimed France to be in the grip of the Antichrist.

This imagery was echoed by the Abbo of Fleury, a respected and learned teacher as well as a worthy opponent of Gerbert's in the struggle at Rheims. In 998 A.D., the Abbo had raised the possibility of the apocalypse. In a work called *Apologeticus,* dedicated, with a certain irony, to King Robert of France, the Abbo spoke of anxiety about the end-time sweeping through the Lorraine. He recalled the predictions of the end-time from his adolescence, when in Paris a priest had predicted that the day of wrath would come when Annunciation Day, March 25, the day when the Church announces the incarnation of Christ, coincided with Good Friday. In other words, the alpha and the omega, the beginning and the end, the holy conception and the last breath of Christ: the combination could be deadly. Twice in the first millennium of Christianity this terrifying conjunction had happened: in the first century after Christ and again in 992 A.D. But the actual day of wrath remained a mystery and beyond human prediction or understanding.

"Of that day and hour knoweth no man," the Abbo said, and he quoted that terrible passage in Paul's first epistle to the Thessalonians: "The day of the Lord cometh as a thief in the night."

The emphasis on the timing of the apocalypse was upsetting. Would it be in a matter of weeks or months or even years? Would it not make more logical sense for it to fall a thousand years after the death of Christ? If so, the world had another thirty-three years to live. Or perhaps it could fall somewhere in between, signaled perhaps by some strange apparition like a comet in the heavens or rain turning to blood. (In 1010 A.D. the Turks captured Jerusalem, and this set off a panic about the imminence of the end-time.)

Within the context of his apocalypse, the Abbo of Fleury warned King Robert of France that certain things needed to be corrected in his kingdom, and he was making an item-by-item list. The menacing suggestion of a looming apocalypse was a powerful incentive toward self-examination.

If Gerbert thought of himself as the last Vicar of Christ, he showed no sign of it. In the final months of 999 A.D., bold and stern directives about lines of authority and disputes over property flowed prodigiously from his hand. Immediate problems pressed in on him. In the north of Italy a bishop had been assassinated in a plot orchestrated by a local count. While the count of Vercelli had not handled the murder weapon, he had guided the assassins to their victim and had entertained them after the deed. The pope convened a synod in the basilica of St. Peter's, and the kingpin of the conspiracy was tried on the dais before the altar. Upon a guilty verdict, the ecclesiastical court handed down its punishment. The count of Vercelli was never again to bear arms, never again to eat meat, never again to kiss a man or a woman, nor ever to wear linen vestments. He was never to stay more than two nights under any roof (except in the case of illness) and was never to receive the holy host in church until he lay on his deathbed. This condemnation to perpetual motion, this curse of the pariah was harsh, but the culprit's life had been spared. The crime was capital, but Gerbert abhorred capital punishment.

Nor, in this charged atmosphere, did Otto III act as if he were the last emperor. Instead, both at the Lateran and Aventine Palaces, optimism and hope and excitement about the future prevailed. Renewal, restoration, vitality, rededication, redemption were in the air. While the pope thought globally, the emperor pored over his plans to restore the palaces of ancient Rome and to establish a church dedicated to St. Bartholomew on the island in the Tiber.

They seemed to be conscious, perhaps too conscious, of their own nobility. It was as if they anticipated martyrdom, as if, somehow, tragically, their grand quest was about to be cut short. Busy as he was with massive correspondence and endless decisions, the pope still had time in this period to write his most touching poem. It was, significantly, a eulogy to Boethius, the sixth-century Greek philosopher and statesman who had combined piety with wisdom, to whose work on music and mathematics Gerbert was indebted, and who was executed by barbarians. Why would Gerbert identify so closely with this figure of the past?

Powerful Rome, while it declared laws by itself to the world

You, Boethius, father and light of the world

You arranged the guidance of the state as Consul

You shine light on knowledge

You need not yield to the Greeks

Your divine mind keeps order in the world

By the wild sword of the Goths, Rome lost its freedoms

You Consul and exile, you leave behind in your famous death
   remarkable honors

Otto III, now the pride of the Empire, understands the highest arts

He judges you worthy for his palace

And forever sets up monuments to your labors.

He well adorns your worth with distinguished rewards.

Whoever drinks deeply in the mead of your book

To raise the curtains of wisdom's obscure realms

You direct their excited steps through the grass.

Whither the instruments of the learned adorn wisdom's fortress;

Take the throne gleaming with praise,

And wisdom will make utterances such as these to you:

Dear friend, hasten always to my halls

There we may rule the kingdoms together without end:

We will distribute honor with accompanying pride,

You will bear a name joined to mine in the stars.

More and more you will see the multitude

Like a rower glides over the oceans of language

Following our new path and direction.

S 999 A.D. drew to a close, the emperor felt compelled to travel north to Germany. He did so reluctantly, for he had become Roman in a grand, historical sense and had ceased to think of himself as German. In his own mind, he was Emperor of the World now, the ruler of the Kingdom of God on earth. Not everyone saw him as such, however. His absence in Germany had hurt his standing and had given quarter to his rivals. On December 16, 999 A.D., the last of his feminine minders, his grandmother, Empress Adelaide, had died. This followed the death of his aunt Mathilda, the abbess of Quedlinberg, ten months earlier. Otto stood absolutely alone.

Together with the martyrdom of Adalbert his teacher and the poisoning of his pope, Gregory V, this spate of important deaths close to the emperor stood beside other distressing signs in his realm. In July 998 A.D., a terrifying earthquake rocked all Saxony, and then, as if to put an exclamation on the point, a ball of flaming rock fell from the sky and slammed directly into the imperial cathedral in Magdeburg. What did these disasters in the fatherland portend?

Other events pulled him north from his beloved Rome. The Polish leader, Boleslav, had consolidated his large gains among the Slavic tribes between the Oder and Elbe Rivers and was now a powerful leader and potential rival in central Europe. Technically, Poland was still a vassal state of the empire, but this was in name only. As a practical matter, it was fast becoming a competing empire on the empire's eastern flank. But Boleslav had been vigorous in propagating Christianity, and this earned him high marks with Otto and Sylvester. Boleslav's motives were geopolitical rather than religious, of course, since by converting the Slavs to Christianity, he had removed their hate of mother Poland. The emperor and the pope well understood such pragmatic motives.

The chief missionary for the Slavic conversions had been Adalbert, Otto's former teacher, who had been nearly as influential as Gerbert in the emperor's upbringing. But in 997 A.D., when he was on a mission to Prussia, pagans had captured and beheaded Adalbert. From this tragedy, both Otto and Boleslav profited. Otto promoted his old teacher as a saint and commissioned a saintly biography about him to be written. And Boleslav, after purchasing the saint's bones from his murderers, brought the relics back to Gniezno, where they were deposited in the basilica. Boleslav then petitioned for a new, independent episcopal see to be established at Gniezno. Rome smiled on the notion. At a synod in 999 A.D., presided over by Sylvester II, a new archbishop for Poland was approved.

As the second millennium was ushered in, Otto III left Rome, his magnificent columns festooned with holy men and nobility. Once over the Alps, the procession passed through Ratisbon, Zeitz, Meissen, and Bautzen before it arrived at the Polish border. There, Boleslav met the emperor's legions and conducted them to Gniezno. With the rooftops of the city in view, Otto dismounted and walked barefoot the rest of the way as a humble pilgrim.

The days that followed were filled with pomp and feasting and, on Otto III's part, an excess of charity. The state visit began with a solemn consecration of the saint, as Adalbert's bones were laid upon the altar of the basilica. Over these holy relics a papal bull was read, establishing the dioceses of the country, including one at Cracow.

Thereafter, the banquets began. The Polish nobles, like gentry of the nouveaux riches, turned out in brocaded caps and garish robes, gold jewelry jangling from their necks and wrists. "Gold was commonly used instead of silver," wrote an observer, "for silver was thought to be something ordinary like straw." Boleslav flattered the impressionable emperor with gushing praise and lavished him with gifts.

Otto responded magnanimously. Instead of gifts, he gave Boleslav more important things. Upon the Polish leader he bestowed the prerogative of creating and investing new bishops, a power hitherto reserved to the Ottonian emperors. And the emperor conferred on Boleslav official jurisdiction over the conquered Slavic lands, sanctioning and blessing a Polish state that could be an awesome enemy later. Then, in a surfeit of enthusiasm, Otto lifted his own crown from his head and placed it upon Boleslav's head.

"It is not fitting that such a great man should be called a mere duke or count," the emperor proclaimed. "Rather he should be elevated to the royal throne and crowned with the ornament of kingship." This impromptu coronation lacked only the ampulla and the oil of catechumens. Rome later frowned on the emperor's spontaneity.

With one imperial visit, Boleslav had achieved the liberation of his state and the dignity of kingly power. Poland came officially into existence, alongside the "apostolic state" of Hungary. The eastern tier of modern Europe began to take shape.

From Poland Otto marched west across his homeland for a brief stay at the holy city of kaisers. The haze of death hung over Aachen, as the emperor paid his final respects to his aunt Mathilda and his grandmother Adelaide. The city must have seemed strange to him, for he had been in Germany for only several months since 996 A.D. As a result, his own countrymen scarcely knew him. The German bishops especially viewed him with suspicion. Discontent with the emperor's Italian fixation was only barely below the surface, and it would not be long before the plots were hatched.

Otto was oblivious. Swept along by the competing emotions of nobility and martyrdom, as if every day in the year 1000 A.D. was a day of purification and preparation, he proceeded to put his affairs in order. The opinions of mere mortals did not concern him. The gods in heaven and the gods on earth approved of what he was doing, he was sure. Was he, after all, the Emperor of the Last Days?

Inevitably, his behavior became bizarre. In Aachen, Charlemagne remained the greatest of all historical figures, the true champion of Christ who had defended Christianity against the infidels and who had established the Kingdom of Christ in Europe. To Otto III, he was the supreme model for kingship. It was said that between Charlemagne's shoulder blades he bore the impression of the cross, the sign of his divine election. The Emperor of the Last Days, it was said, would also bear this sign. To this hero of Christ and to man, it was only fitting that the emperor of the millennium should pay homage. No doubt, Otto III believed the popular notion that Charlemagne lived. He had never died, but was only sleeping.

Ordering Charlemagne's monumental tomb to be opened, Otto, along with a companion, the count of Lomello, approached the sarcophagus with fear and reverence. "We entered in unto Charles," the count was to relate later. "He was not laying down, as in the manner with the bodies of other dead men, but sat on a certain chair as though he lived. Crowned with a golden crown, he held a scepter in his hands which were covered with gloves, through which the nails had grown. Above him was a magnificent tabernacle of marble and brass. There was a vehement savor in the tomb. We bent to our knees and did worship forthwith to him. Straightaway Otto the Emperor clad him with white raiment and pared his nails and made good all that was lacking about him. None of his members had corrupted and fallen away, except a little piece of the end of his nose. This Otto caused at once to be restored with gold. And the emperor took from Charles's mouth one tooth . . . and departed."

After this encounter with Charlemagne's uncorrupted body, Otto began to have premonitions of an early death. Inevitably, these premonitions became bound up with nightmares about the death of the world.

In June 1000 A.D., the emperor set out on the journey south to Rome. Traveling along the Rhine River, he tarried in the cloister of Reichenau, where the monks presented him with a magnificent work of art. Three years in production, it was a series of forty illuminations depicting scenes from the last book of the Bible. It was called the *Bamberg Apocalypse*. In the pictures where a stoic figure bearded the seven-headed dragon or overthrew the false prophet or where the Savior was crowned, the face looked remarkably like that of Otto III. The last savior, the last dragon-slayer, the last emperor had melded into one.

In Rome, Gerbert received his friend with great affection and a sense of relief, for the pope worried when the emperor was away. Without the emperor, of course, the pope was powerless. This time, the Romans turned out to welcome the emperor back warmly. Through the summer the mood of Rome was a strange mixture of joy, piety, and nervousness, as if the city and the empire stood at a great moment in its history, a turning point of some unspecified and unpredictable nature. Talk of renewal mixed with fear of judgment.

On August 15, the festival of Mary's Assumption, reflected this surreal atmosphere. The emperor and the pope joined a nocturnal procession from the Lateran Palace to the basilica of San Lorenzo, as the devout worshipers held high a sacred picture of Mary. When the celebrants gathered in the basilica, a hymn was sung, in which the Rome of the past was portrayed alternately as the fourth beast of Daniel and as the Great Whore of the Apocalypse who was unafraid of the Lord. In the eyes of the optimistic worshipers, the Rome of the present had repented of her old lusts and hoped for the redemption of the Lord.

"Rejoice, Pope. Rejoice, Emperor. Let the Church rejoice. Let there be great joy in Rome. Under the power of the Emperor the Pope purifies the centuries." That was the joyful side. And in the next breath, the line rang out:

"Now you are renewed at the price of martyrdom."

And then: "The face of the Lord is here, before whom the whole world lies prostrate. The face of the Lord is here with the sign of Judgment."

In this transitional year to the second millennium of Christ . . . if there was to be a second millennium . . . Otto III himself seemed transformed. More than ever before, he gave himself over to his mystical side. Instead of the grandiose imperial titles, he presented himself increasingly as Servant of Jesus Christ, and Servant of the Apostles. He encouraged his courtiers to speak not of his victories in war, but of his gentleness in peace, to talk not of his relations with noblemen and popes, but of his good works for the poor. "Strong in war, great in peace, he is always gentle," ran one acclamation. "In war or in peace he was always kind to the poor. Therefore he is called the father of all the poor."

But the emperor could find no peace. In the summer the pope

complained to the emperor about the desecration of a holy mass in the Sabina region when competing nobles drew swords on one another during the liturgy. In October of 1000 A.D., the entire city of Tivoli revolted against imperial control. This ancient retreat of Augustus, Horace, and Hadrian prized its tradition of independence, and its citizens killed Otto's ambassador as an act of contempt. However much military activity was abhorrent to the emperor in his current state of mind, Otto III promptly marched on the city and laid siege. Soon enough, Tivoli's defenses cracked, but not before Pope Sylvester II and St. Romuald were entangled in the negotiations and concessions. The defeated nobles were paraded before the emperor in humiliation, clad only in loincloth as a humiliation. But that was the extent of their punishment. Otto softened and pardoned the city. This leniency bought Otto even worse trouble, for the Romans were outraged at his weakness. Rome and Tivoli had long been rival encampments. Between the two cities animosities ran deep. Rome wanted blood.

In February 1001 A.D., using the Tivoli event as pretext, the Romans revolted against their German emperor. They barred the gates of the city and attacked the imperial palace on the Aventine. Otto was cut off from his troops outside the city walls, but he rallied his palace guard—two cohorts of 555 men each—into a spirited defense and prepared to lead them out against the rebels. He clutched the sacred lance, carried by his grandfather Otto the Great in the epic triumph over the Hungarian pagans at Lechfeld, the lance in which a nail from the cross at Calvary was embedded. On a high place, he presented himself to the rebels below, at one moment striking a defiant, at another moment a tragic pose.

"Are you my Romans?" he bellowed. "For whom I have left my country and my relatives. For love of you I have shed the blood of my Saxons and of all Germans, even my own blood. I have led you to the farthest corners of our Empire, to places where even your fathers when they ruled the world never set foot. Romans, I have borne your name and fame to the very ends of the earth! You were my favorite children. For you I incurred the ill will and the jealousy of nations.

"Now, in response, you desert your father. You have slaughtered my trusted friends. You have shut me out. But this you cannot do.

For I cannot banish from my heart those whom I have loved with a father's love."

These noble words melted the fury of the Romans. For a brief moment, it seemed as if the crisis were defused. But Otto's problems were not over. The conspirators against his rule remained strong. Hints of plots were rife in the palace. Pressure on the emperor to leave mounted. Discouraged that his subjects were so caught up in petty concerns and were unable to appreciate the grand destiny that he had charted for them, Otto fell into melancholy.

In his rich imagination, he was the incarnation of the Holy Roman Empire, its alpha and its omega. If he failed, the empire would fail. He knew the prophecy of Ephraem the Syrian, the fourth-century prophet: the end of the Roman Empire would bring the end of the world. "When the Roman Empire begins to be consumed by the sword, the coming of the Evil One is at hand," Ephraem had proclaimed. "It is necessary that the world come to an end at the competition of the Roman Empire. And so the Adversary will be loosed. In those days many will rise up against Rome." The petty citizens of Rome were their own executioners.

On February 16, 1001, the emperor fled his beloved city. With Sylvester II in tow, Otto tarried outside the city walls for some days, hoping that the citizens of Rome would see the error of their ways, beseech him to return, and sweep him triumphantly back to his throne on the Aventine. But no citizens came for him.

In the succeeding months he raced around Italy frantically, at one time the warrior and at another time the monk. He ordered reinforcements from Germany to recapture Rome and crush his enemies; he besieged cities in the north and south; he mobilized his troops for the glorious recapture of his imperial capital. And he also made a clandestine visit to Venice, a city Otto admired not only for its marriage to the sea, but for its marriage of the west and Byzantium.

Venice was suddenly bursting with renewed vitality under its young, vigorous doge, Peter Orseolo II. After years of drift, the city had recovered its pride and its power. After years of harassment, the pirates of the Dalmatian coast had finally been subdued, and Venice was free to pursue its true calling. That mission was trade. But the commercial success of Venice depended upon good relations with both Rome and Constantinople. For several years the doge had been cultivating the emperor in Constantinople. Now the opportunity presented itself to turn his attention to Rome. That Otto III was traveling outside the borders of his empire was a tribute to Venice, even if the doge was mystified by Otto's insistence that the visit be clandestine. For Venice to forgo the great spectacle of a state visit was a high disappointment. The basilica of St. Mark's, which had been destroyed in the great fire of 976 A.D., was now half-rebuilt, and the new doge was eager to show off his prized reconstruction.

Otto's purpose was straightforward. He was coming to solicit the help of the Venetian doge in recapturing Rome. Mystified though he was at Otto's bizarre, secretive behavior, the doge treated the emperor graciously. Presents were exchanged: the emperor received an ivory throne and footstool, while the doge was released from the old burden of paying an annual tribute of 50 pounds of silver to the empire, an obligation imposed upon the city by Otto the Great years before. Otto III was sent on a predawn sightseeing trip to the church of St. Zaccaria, but in the light of day, after all the ceremony was over and the evasions exhausted, the doge refused the emperor's request for ships. Venice's business was commerce, not war. If its warships were going anywhere, it would be against the islands of Curzola and Lagosta, the pirate lairs from which pesky attacks were continually launched on Venetian galleys.

Amidst his disappointment in Venice, Otto tarried in the company of the illiterate saint, St. Romuald, and closeted himself in the monastery of Classe. There, clothed in a tattered cowl, he considered becoming a priest. But his penitence competed with his anger. When he heard that troops were trickling in from the north, he shed his cowl for his armor. His moods swung wildly between euphoria and melancholy. One minute elated at the massing of troops, he would suddenly become depressed at the vision of all Italy in revolt against him. Italy . . . that wicked place of "a thousand languors and a thousand deaths" . . . he loved it. His admirers gathered around to support him but the emperor saw only enemies and rebels. He complained bitterly that all the bishops and counts of Italy opposed him. The reports from Germany did not lighten his mood. With the long absence of the emperor, there were threats to depose him and crown another.

In a life lived so intensely, there was little time for serenity or patience . . . unless the rumor of his love affair with the widow of his victim the Roman patrician John Crescentius was true. Women were certainly on his mind. Once again, he requested a princess from Byzantium. It seemed like a hopeless pipe dream, since only once before, in the marriage of Vladimir of Russia and Anna of Constantinople, had the Byzantine court ever given away the genuine issue of the sacred Porphyry Room. Now Otto sent the wealthiest and most cosmopolitan archbishop in Italy, Arnulf of Milan, to Constantinople.

The archbishop arrived at the court of Basil II on a magnificent horse which was draped with richly embroidered regalia and shod with golden horseshoes attached with silver nails. Basil II received Otto's ambassador warmly and entertained him lavishly. This time, the court of the purple marble throne room smiled on the union of east and west. If the prince of Rome and the princess of Constantinople were to have a son, their issue would rule the greatest empire since the Byzantine emperor Justinian united the continent in the sixth century.

In January 1002 A.D., Princess Zoe, the attractive twenty-three-year-old daughter of Constantine VIII, prepared to come to Italy. As he waited for her, Otto boasted to St. Romuald that he would soon leave Ravenna for his final assault on Rome.

"If thou goest to Rome," Romuald responded quietly and ominously, "thou shalt never see Ravenna again." But the "adulterous beauty" of Rome pulled on the emperor too strongly. Besides, he longed for a monumental imperial wedding, fitting for the joining in marriage of the two great empires of Europe.

With his fresh troops he marched south to Rome. But the Romans would not open the gates, and the emperor was loath to wreak havoc on his favorite city. For days he tarried in the countryside outside the city in the fortress of Paterno. Then, wavering and frazzled, he grew ill. Within a few days, a few days short of his twenty-second birthday, Otto III died. The shock was widespread. Given his youth and apparent health, it was whispered that his mistress, the beautiful widow of John Crescentius, had poisoned him, eager as she still was to avenge the death of her husband or desperate as she may have been to prevent the marriage of her lover. The royal barge of Princess Zoe arrived at Bari after Otto was dead, turned around, and was on its way back to Constantinople within a day. The dream of uniting east and west into a Justinian empire was over.

In Rome, the grief was genuine, if belated. It was as if the Romans finally realized what a great heart and generous spirit had been in their midst and how lofty had been his master plan for a universal empire. In Germany too, sadness was widespread. "Thou who are the Alpha and the Omega, confer much upon the Humble and upon the mortal, grant Eternity now and forever," the mourners prayed. In death his stature grew. Suddenly he became the wonder youth, a marvel to the world, and a martyr to an ideal.

Upon his tomb in the cathedral of Charlemagne in Aachen were inscribed the following lines:

> Let the world lament, let Rome weep
>
> Let the Church mourn,
>
> Let there be no song in Rome
>
> Let the palace wail.
>
> Under the absence of the Emperor
>
> The ages are distressed.

Before the year was out, Sylvester II, the emperor's mentor and friend, but most of all his partner in the fleeting dream of universal empire, was also dead. Their dream seemed dead as well . . . except that the Holy Roman Empire of the German Nation survived until 1806 A.D.

EPILOGUE

December 31, 999 A.D.

IN THE LAST FEW MONTHS of writing this
book, when I was not sawing and polishing the
walnut of my Viking bed, several moments stick in my
mind. One afternoon in November, high on the Janicu-
lum Hill in Rome, I stood at a window, telephone in
hand, looking down on a scene of mayhem. Below me
lay the Porta San Pancrazio, one of the ancient gates to
the city, around which several narrow roadways have
been cut through the Roman walls. The cars race wildly
at this lovely impediment from five separate directions.
Hell-bent Italian drivers slow, try to merge, honk, ma-
neuver for inches and any advantage that will allow
them to navigate around the hell-mouth and into the

narrow funnel on the other side a few seconds faster. Where that road on the other side leads, I have no idea, but someday I will explore it.

As I listened to the endless, annoying rings of the Vatican telephone, it occurred to me that here was my metaphor for the millennium: a beautiful yet imposing landmark with ancient significance and modern difficulty. It was like an opening in a great wall, separating the past and the future, through which we all must pass warily into the funnel on the other side, before we fan out again into exciting, unknown pathways beyond.

At last someone at the Vatican picked up. He was an Irish priest, a plenipotentiary to the eminence who runs the important Vatican office for the "Great Jubilee" of the year 2000 A.D. The priest was harried and impatient and somewhat self-important in a pious sort of way. Did I not know that his office was trying to plan for thirty million pilgrims? he said in a patronizing tone. What was my book about anyway? I tried to explain. Well, his office had nothing to do with the last millennium, he said. Was I not up on the history of jubilees? The church had not celebrated them until the year 1300 A.D. I should read my church history. Boniface VIII was the important, millennial pope, not Gerbert of Aurillac (of whom he seemed unaware). Had I read the pope's pronouncement on the millennium? Well, I would find everything I needed to know in there. The Book of Revelation? What did the year 2000 A.D. have to do with that?

"You'll get no discussion of apocalypse in this office," he said tersely. "Certainly not from me. You need a theologian!" I thanked him and hung up. It was as if the plumber had suggested an electrician. I decided not to pursue the matter.

A month earlier I had been in Princeton for a football game. On Sunday morning, eager to get home, I waited fretfully in the car for my wife and child to come down from our hotel room. Finally, in boredom, I switched on the radio. Through the morning gloom the voice of the preacher was energetic and shrill, redolent with Protestant certainty and moral rectitude. His tone had none of the Vatican self-satisfaction, but it was urgent. This was no raw evangelical from the snake-handling hollows of West Virginia or the mineral-rich moonscape of Phoenix. Nor was it a voice from the Middle Ages. We were in Princeton, New Jersey, after all, a place of high cultivation, and the year approached 1999 A.D.

His theme was the time of tribulation which will precede the Second Coming when the forces of evil deploy themselves and when we could expect ten thousand saints to appear, in white robes, and banish the Antichrist. White robes, he said importantly, white robes in a field of blood. "When the thousand years are expired," he quoted Revelation 20, "Satan shall be loosed out of his prison." We must purify ourselves and be ready. We must wash our linens . . . I looked over to a bin of hotel linens being wheeled by.

My gaze wandered to the sterile streets and storefronts of the suburban America where we had stayed the night. No one but me, it seemed, was listening. The streets were empty, the stores closed, the world asleep and comfortable. Alarm was not in the air, although the Princeton football team had been upset by Brown the day before, and the Tigers had fallen to 1–2. Could it have been like this a thousand years ago?

Between avoidance and terror, there must be another way to approach this passage of time and this subject of apocalypse.

In considering the millennium, at least if we are to judge from the experience of the last time the calendar turned three digits, people are looking for the apocalypse in the wrong place. It cannot be found in the thunderous arrival of ten thousand angels on a field of blood, in some final epic clash between the forces of good and evil. In 1000 A.D. when, by rights, the great battle should have happened, it did not happen. Nor can it be found in an atmosphere of terror. No frightened mobs raced through the streets on New Year's Eve 999 A.D. There is simply no evidence of it.

In their disappointment, a few modern historians have tried to invent the evidence. They imagine Gerbert on the altar of the old basilica of St. Peter's, dressed in white robes, the legend of his interchange with the devil still hovering in the smoke of incense. Was he the successor of St. Peter or the emissary of the Antichrist? The throng is terrified. The devout weep uncontrollably at their impending death and the certain death of the world itself. Only the monotonous voice of Gerbert soothes their terror. And afterward, with such a collective sigh of relief as the world had never heard before, the legions spread out over the continent and build Christian churches in such number that defy counting.

Regrettably, there is nothing to support either the terrifying mass at St. Peter's or the wholesale building of churches afterward, not a letter, no poem or prayer, no remembered story, no chronicle.

Perhaps it is the attention in modern times to an exact day or year or hour that is misleading. In an illiterate age, there can be no awareness of the calendar. But even if ignorance were not a factor, what would have been the date to fear? By what measure do we identify this Doomsday, the Julian calendar or the Gregorian that followed it? Must we date it from Christ's birth or death? If the latter, we get a reprieve of another thirty-three years. Since the ancients had no concept of zero, how does that change things? The gift of another year's grace?

In recent years, there have been astonishing discoveries in astronomy. Suddenly we see clusters of galaxies and protoplanets. We actually see the birth and the death of stars. We perceive infinite possibilities for other intelligent life. We appreciate that stellar life is measured in millions of light-years. By this measure the earth's perspective on time seems puny and simple-minded. But in a thousand years, it seems, we have never tired of imposing a human, earthbound perception on our concept of deity and of time.

In managing His universe, does God really count the way we do? By a twenty-four-hour day, from sunrise to sunrise on earth? That would be like managing the ocean by the rules of a sand pebble. When the cosmos is His dominion, isn't it possible that He counts by some quite different measure, where the days and the years are somewhat longer? Our view of a deity as the alpha and omega must alter. The "fullness of time" is also the vastness of time.

If counting time might be different, could the very nature of apocalypse, as we generally understand it, be different as well? We understand apocalypse to be sudden, but what, to a deity, is suddenness? We understand it to be total and all-encompassing, but who says it can't be limited? It must be dramatic, but in the modern attention span, a four-hour drama is boring by its nature. We also understand an apocalypse to be violent, something like the revenge of Santiago de Compostela on a global scale. The human imagination is a wonderful thing, but it has a nasty side. Lastly, we understand an apocalypse to be miraculous. It must result in a total transformation of the world, one where the state of things is considerably better. To the believer, it is an act of God.

In 999 A.D., the apocalypse lay in the forces of history. It can be found in the collective clash of personalities . . . and the outcome of these clashes, taken together: in the determined cruelty of Olaf Trygvesson, in the wisdom of Thorgeir and the jealousy of Sigrid, in the brave curiosity of Leif Eriksson, in the weakness of Ethelred and the strength of Canute the Mighty, in the overreaching brutality of Al Mansor and the silliness of his sons, in the saintliness of Vajk and the diplomacy of Theophano, in the dreams of Otto III and the brilliance of Gerbert. The violence of the human battlefield plays a part: the pivotal battles of Poitiers and Calatañazor, of Lechfeld and Roncesvalles, the devastation of the Viking fleet by Greek fire on the Black Sea. In Spain the constant grinding humiliation on the battlefield during Al Mansor's jihad created a backlash that led to the Christian reconquest of the peninsula. The apocalypse lies in the concatenation of these dramatic personalities and battles and social forces. In this machine of history, was there a God at work?

Over a period of forty years there had been many battles between pagans and Christians, but the Christians won the war. The Vikings had been defeated and converted and absorbed. The Magyars had been tamed and had joined the apostolic community of Gerbert. The Moorish caliphate had collapsed, and the seeds of the Spanish reconquest had been planted. More important were the conversions: Olaf Trygvesson in 991 A.D., Boleslav the Brave of Poland in 996 A.D., Vladimir I of Russia in 988 A.D., Thorgeir of Iceland in 1000 A.D., Harald Bluetooth of Denmark in 974 A.D., Leif Eriksson of North America in 1000 A.D., Svein Forkbeard and Canute the Mighty in 1014 A.D., the rise of Sancho the Great in Spain in 1000 A.D., and, finally, the glorious coronation of Vajk as King Stephen of Hungary in 1000 A.D. With those conversions came a concerted campaign to expunge the vestiges of pagan religion, especially in Iceland, Hungary, and Norway. Was this just random action, like the cars that just happened to arrive at the Porta San Pancrazio when I was looking out of the window?

Christian Europe had become a reality. It became a community of nations, with a continental view, rooted in the Rome of Gerbert and Otto. The dream of civilization had been recaptured. The last apocalypse was a process rather than a cataclysm. It had the suddenness of forty years. Limited to Europe, its drama lay in the deliverance from terror rather than terror itself. The victory culminated in peace and tranquility. As the new millennium began, the absence of terror was the important thing. Hope and excitement about the future was the mood.

However this quiet, even ironic apocalypse happened, through random convergence or deliberate orchestration, the hinge of the last millennium signified a miraculous transformation.

Acknowledgments

DURING THE FIRST EIGHT MONTHS of work on this book, as I read broadly without putting pen to paper, I struggled with a nagging question. Could I tell the story of 999 A.D. through a series of interlocking portraits? The goal seemed difficult, especially with a tale of a "dark" and largely illiterate age. Moreover, the form of textured biography, with shadings of character, is a modern invention and not easily achieved from meager sources. Quickly it became apparent that I would have to dig very deep for personal details that might bring these distant characters alive.

At least in those early days, I had the most splendid circumstances to ponder my problem. For the first seven months I was a fellow at the Woodrow Wilson Center for International Scholars, and when I got dejected, I could look out mullioned, Gothic windows of the Smithsonian Castle to the inspiring sights of downtown Washington. Under the circumstances, it was hard to feel sorry for myself when everything seemed right at my fingertips and with two eager interns, Ernesto Sancho and later Dennis Paul, ready to meet my every request. At the Wilson Center, I was encouraged, comforted, and downright coddled by the director of that institution, Charles Blitzer, and by the director of Historical, Cultural, and Literary Studies, James Morris. During the hard conceptual stage, when the resources of the Wilson Center were so important, their good cheer was invaluable, as was the company of my colleagues. Several Wilson Center fellows, especially Warren Treadgold and Robert Lerner, were to advise me in Byzantine studies and the literature of Apocalypse. Carol Armbruster was my point person at the Library of Congress, ever cheerful and always ready to help. Far fewer bullets will come her way now that this book is completed.

Once I had taken the library research as far as I could, I began to travel. Scandinavia was my first stop, since the Viking lore seemed to be the easiest entry point for the year 999 A.D. In planning for that first literary journey, in the spring of 1995, I'm indebted to a covey of cultural attachés in the embassies across Washington who were eager to make my arrangements in their respective countries: Petur Thorsteinsson of Iceland, Jorgen Grunnet of Denmark, Ingomar Bjorksten of Sweden, and Eivind Homme of Norway.

With their help, I was blessed from the beginning with the most knowledgeable and liveliest of guides. In the wild and lovely landscape of Iceland I arrived with a suitcase of questions about the Norse sagas: how they were written, where the saga writers found their inspiration, what was their reliability. At the University of Iceland, a number of scholars dealt patiently with my inquiries: the historians Helgi Thorlaksson, Jon Hnefill Adalsteinsson, and Gisli Gunnarson; the religionist Hjalti Hugason; and the literary expert Asdís Egilsdóttir. Both Asdís Egilsdóttir and Petur Thorsteinsson helped with Icelandic translation. For my several visits to the Thingvellir, I had the privilege of being shown around by the almost otherworldly priestess–park superintendent of that sacred place,

Hanna Maria Petursdóttir. I would return three more times to Iceland after that first visit—so much did the country appeal to me—and for those subsequent visits I must thank Sigurd Helgasson and Debbie Scott of Icelandair for their generosity. I only regret that in this enterprise I never got to play midnight golf or ski cross-country during midwinter across the colossal glaciers.

Elsewhere in Scandinavia I encountered a superb collection of Viking scholars. In Denmark Lars Jorgensen and Niels-Knud Liebgott at the Danish National Museum in Copenhagen were most accommodating, as was Dr. Morten Warmind, a great mind and a huge man, who educated and entertained me over a liter of beer and an immense potato-and-beef stew in the Tivoli Gardens (I felt as if I were dining with Thorstein the Cod-Biter). In Sweden, Björn Ambrosiani of the Birka excavations, Carin Orrling at the Museum of National Antiquities, and Johan Engström of the Military Museum in Stockholm were gracious, as was the wonderful saga aficionado Dr. Lars Lönnroth of the University of Göteberg. In Norway, Dr. Signe Fuglesang of the Center for Viking and Nordic Medieval Studies, at the University of Oslo, was accommodating, as was Professor Arne Emil Christensen at the Vikingship Museum.

These experts were all helpful in sharpening my focus. On a subsequent trip I was to travel to York in England, where Dr. Sid Bradley of York University put me onto the Blickling Homilies and imparted his trenchant and quite patriotic analysis of the *Battle of Maldon*. (He was quite appalled at the recent trend in "sanitizing" these grubby Nordic invaders of his homeland.) Simon Keynes at Cambridge University was equally helpful in discussing, over lunch of Stilton and green pudding at Trinity College, the shortcomings of Ethelred the Unready, before he sent me on my way to Ely Cathedral to search for the tomb of Byrhtnoth.

Once the Viking chapters were in hand, I turned to the exotic history of Hungary. In Budapest, my agenda was arranged by Peter Becskehazy of the United States Information Service (USIS), who seemed to be able to deliver Magyar authorities in a matter of hours. With his help, I had useful exchanges with the historians Andras Gero, Gabor Klaniczay, Nemeskürty István, András Róna-Tas, and Pal Engel; with Tamás Hofer of the Ethnographic Museum; and with the art historian Eva Kovacs. Once I was back in Washington, fortified with a packet of indecipherable documents from Budapest, I received extensive Hungarian translation help from a very generous Catholic priest in Rockville, Maryland, Father Josef Zolatay, and from Kenneth Nyirady at the Library of Congress. (Father Zolatay was also to help me with Latin translations.)

For my two trips to Spain, I again tapped the resources of Washington. The cultural attaché at the Spanish embassy, Mr. Alvaro de Erice, sought to outdo his Nordic rivals. Through his good offices, and with the additional help of Jeanne Miserindino of the Spanish Tourist Office in New York, during May 1996 and again in January 1997 I consorted with Arabists and medievalists across Spain. These included Dr. Manuela Marin, Dr. Cristinia de la Puente, Dr. Eduardo Manzano Moreno, and Dr. Ana Rodríguez López at Consejo Superior de Investigaciones Cientificas (CSIC) in Madrid; Dr. Maria Jesus Viguera Molins at the University of Madrid; and archaeologist Dr. Juan Zozaya, a director of the National Archeological Museum. In Córdoba I was guided on my tour of Al Zahrâ by the director of the site, Dr. Antonio Vallejo Triano; in Barcelona, Julio Samsó Moya imparted his knowledge of medieval Islamic science; and in Santiago de Compostela, I discussed the myth of Santiago with Ermelindo Portela. Back home, my sister-in-law Vicki Kiechel helped with Spanish translation whenever she could tear herself away from my infant nephew and namesake, James. On Spanish matters, I also conducted a lively correspondence with the novelist Homero Aridjis, author of *The Lord of the Last Days: Visions of the Year 1000*.

When the manuscript was nearly completed, I spent three weeks at the American Academy in Rome. This was more familiar turf for me. As I expected, under the steady guidance of the estimable prefect of the library, Father Leonard Boyle, and with the assistance of Barbara Jatta, I found materials at the Vatican Library about Otto III and Sylvester II that were unavailable in America. At the Farnesina collection, Dr. Rita Parma Baudille searched for visual materials from the year 999 A.D. and then showed me where to buy the best bread in Rome.

Finally, I must thank my agent, Joe Regal, and the Doubleday-Anchor editor, Roger Scholl, who together conceived this idea in an inspired lunch late in 1994 . . . and my editor, Bill Thomas, who guided me so ably toward its execution.

Selected Bibliography

MEDIEVAL SOURCES

Adam of Bremen. *History of the Arch-Bishops of Hamburg-Bremen*. Trans. Tschan, Francis J. New York: Columbia University Press, 1959.

Adler, Elkan Nathan, ed. *Jewish Travelers in the Middle Ages: Nineteen First-hand Accounts*. New York: Dover, 1987.

Anglo-Saxon Chronicle. Trans. Garmonsway, G. N. New York: Dutton, 1953.

Anglo-Saxon Poetry. Selected and trans. Gordon, R. K. New York: Dutton, 1926.

Book of the Icelanders. Hermannsson, H., ed. and trans. Ithaca, NY: Cornell University Library, 1930.

The Correspondence of Leo, Metropolitan of Synada and Syncellus. Trans. Vinson, Martha Polland. Washington: Dumbarton Oaks, 1985.

Coulton, G. G. *A Medieval Garner*. London: Constable & Co., 1910.

Damian, St. Peter. *Letters*. Washington: Catholic University Press, 1992.

The Earliest English Poems. Trans. Alexander, Michael. Berkeley: University of California Press, 1966.

Egil's Saga. Trans. Eddison, E. R. New York: Greenwood, 1968.

The Elder Edda: A Selection. Trans. Auden, W. H., and Taylor, Paul B. New York: Vintage, 1970.

Encomium Emmae Reginae. Ed. Campbell, Alistair. London: Offices of the Royal Historical Society, 1949.

English and Norse Documents Relating to the Reign of Ethelred the Unready. Ed. Ashdown, Margaret. New York: Russell & Russell, 1972.

Eyrbyggja Saga. Trans. Palsson, Hermann, and Edwards, Paul. Toronto: University of Toronto Press, 1973.

Florence of Worcester. *Florentii Wigorniensis monachi Chronicon ex chronicis.* 2 vols. London, 1848–49.

Gerbert of Aurillac. *The Letters of Gerbert.* New York: Columbia University Press, 1961.

Glaber, Rodulfus. *Historiarum libri quinque.* Oxford: Clarendon Press, 1989.

Hallfred's Saga. Trans. Boucher, Alan. Reykjavik: Iceland Review Saga Series, 1981.

The Homilies of Photius, Patriarch of Constantinople. Ed. and trans. Mango, Cyril. Cambridge: Harvard University Press, 1958.

Hroswitha of Gandersheim: Her Life, Times, and Works. Ed. Haight, Anne. New York: Hroswitha Club, 1965.

Ibn Hazm. *The Ring of the Dove.* London: Luzac & Co., 1953.

Laxdaela Saga. Trans. Magnusson, Magnus, and Palsson, Hermann. New York: Penguin, 1969.

Liudprand. *The Works of Liudprand of Cremona.* London: Routledge & Sons, 1930.

Njal's Saga. Trans. Magnusson, Magnus, and Palsson, Hermann. Penguin Classics, 1959.

Orkneyinga Saga: The History of the Earls of Orkney. Trans. Palsson, Hermann, and Edwards, Paul. London: Hogarth Press, 1978.

Russian Primary Chronicle: Laurentian Text. Trans. Cross, Samuel, and Sherbowitz-Wetzor, Olgerd. Cambridge: Medieval Academy of America.

Scriptores Rerum Hungaricarum, vol. 2. Ed. Szentpétery, Emericus. Budapest: Academia Litter. Hungarica, 1938.

Saga of Gunnlaugur Snake's Tongue. Trans. Durrendberger, Paul and Dorothy. Rutherford, N.J.: Fairleigh Dickinson University Press.

The Saga of the Jomsvikings. Trans. Hollander, Lee M. Freeport, N.Y.: Books for Libraries Press, 1971.

Seven Viking Romances. Trans. Palsson, Hermann, and Edwards, Paul. London: Penguin, 1985.

A Spanish Apocalypse: The Morgan Beatus Manuscript. New York: Brazilier, 1991.

Sturlason, Snorre. *Heimskringla.* Trans. Laing, Samuel. New York: Dutton, 1915.

————. *The Prose Edda: Tales from Norse Mythology*. Selected and ed. Jean I. Young. Berkeley: University of California Press, 1954.

Thietmar of Merseburg. *Chronik*. Darmstadt: Wissenshaftliche Buchgesellschaft, 1970.

Vikings in Russia: Yngvar's Saga and Eymund's Saga. Trans. Palsson, Hermann, and Edwards, Paul. Edinburgh: Edinburgh University Press, 1989.

Vinland Sagas. Trans. Magnusson, Magnus, and Palsson, Hermann. Baltimore: Penguin, 1965.

Widukind of Corvey. *Rerum gestarum Saxonicarum*. Ed. and trans. Claude J. Dolan, 1957.

MODERN WORKS

Adalsteinsson, Jon Hnefill. *Under the Cloak*. Uppsala: Amquist & Wiksell, 1978.

Alexander, Paul J. *Byzantine Apocalyptic Tradition*. Berkeley: University of California Press, 1985.

Aridjis, Homero. *The Lord of the Last Days: Visions of the Year 1000*. New York: Morrow, 1994.

Beladiez, Emilio. *Almanzor*. Madrid: Coleccion Textos Universitarios, 1995.

Bloch, Marc. *Feudal Society*. 2 vols. Chicago: University of Chicago Press, 1961.

The Cambridge Medieval History, Vols. 3–4. Cambridge: Cambridge University Press, 1966–.

Carlyle, Thomas. *The Early Kings of Norway*. London: Chapman & Hall, 1878.

Chadwick, H. Munro. *The Heroic Age*. Cambridge: Cambridge University Press, 1912.

Charles, B. G. *Old Norse Relations with Wales*. Cardiff: University of Wales Press, 1934.

Cohn, Norman. *The Pursuit of the Millennium*. New York: Oxford University Press, 1970.

Conde, Jose Antonio. *History of the Dominion of the Arabs in Spain*. London: Henry G. Bohn, 1854.

Coppee, Henry. *History of the Conquest of Spain by the Arab-Moors*. (Boston, 1881.)

Davids, Adelbert, ed. *The Empress Theophano*. Cambridge: Cambridge University Press, 1995.

Dozy, Reinhart. *Spanish Islam*. Karachi: Karimsons, 1976.

Du Chaillu, Paul. *The Viking Age*. 2 vols. New York, 1889.

Eckstein-Diener, Bertha. *Imperial Byzantium*. Boston: Little, Brown, 1938.

Eichengrun, Fritz. *Gerbert (Silvester II) Als Personlichkeit*. Berlin: B. G. Teubner, 1928.

Emmerson, Richard K., and Herzman, Ronald B. *The Apocalyptic Imagination in Medieval Literature.* Philadelphia: University of Pennsylvania Press, 1992.

Emmerson, Richard K., and McGinn, Bernard. *The Apocalypse in the Middle Ages.* Ithaca: Cornell University Press, 1992.

Erdoes, Richard. *A.D. 1000: Living on the Brink of Apocalypse.* New York: Harper & Row, 1988.

Ethelred the Unready: Papers from the Millenary Conference. Ed. Hill, David. Oxford: BAR British Series 59, 1978.

Evans, Joan. *Monastic Life at Cluny, 910–1157.* Oxford: Oxford University Press, 1931.

Focillon, Henri. *The Year 1000.* New York: Frederick Ungar, 1969.

Gerberto: scienza, storia e mito. Symposium, Bobbio, Italy, 1983.

Godkin, Edwin Lawrence. *The History of Hungary and the Magyars.* New York: Alexander Montgomery, 1853.

Gregorovius, Frederick. *History of Rome in the Middle Ages.* Books 6–7. London: George Bell & Sons, 1896.

Greenfield, Jeannette. *The Return of Cultural Treasures.* Cambridge: Cambridge University Press, 1989.

Gyorffy, Gyorgy. *King Saint Stephen of Hungary.* New York: Columbia University Press, 1994.

Harnischfeger, Ernst. *Die Bamberger Apokalypse.* Stuttgart: Urachhaus, 1981.

Helgaldus, Benedictine Monk of Fleury. *Vie de Robert le Pieux.* Paris: Éditiones du Centre National de la Recherche Scientifique, 1965.

Jackson, Margaret, and Hodder, Elisabeth. *The Seven Sovereign Hills of Rome.* London: Longmans, Green, 1936.

Jenkins, Romilly. *Byzantium: The Imperial Centuries, A.D. 610–1071.* New York: Random House, 1967.

Jones, Gwyn. *A History of the Vikings.* Oxford: Oxford University Press, 1973.

———. *The Legendary History of Olaf Tryggvason.* Glasgow: Jackson & Co., 1968.

———. *Scandinavian Legends and Folk-Tales.* New York: Henry Z. Walck, 1956.

———. *Four Icelandic Sagas.* Princeton: Princeton University Press, 1935.

Kendrick, Thomas Downing. *A History of the Vikings.* New York: Scribner's, 1930.

Komjathy, Anthony Tihamer. *A Thousand Years of the Hungarian Art of War.* Toronto: Rakoczi Foundation, 1982.

Kosary, Dominic G. *The History of the Hungarian Nation.* Astor Park, Fla.: Danubian Press, 1969.

La Fay, Howard. *The Vikings.* Washington: National Geographic Society, 1972.

Lane-Poole, Stanley. *The Story of the Moors in Spain*. Baltimore: Black Classic Press, 1990.

Lebe, Reinhard. *Als Markus Nach Venedig Kam*. Frankfurt: Wolfgang Krüger Verlag, 1978.

Leyser, K. J. *Rule and Conflict in an Early Medieval Society*. Bloomington: Indiana University Press, 1979.

Lukinich, Imre. *A History of Hungary in Biographical Sketches*. London: Simpkin Marshall, 1937.

Lund, Niels. *Lid Leding og Landevaern*. Roskilde: Vikingeskibshallen, 1996.

Mann, Horace. *The Lives of the Popes in the Early Middle Ages*. Vol. 5. London: Kegan Paul, Trench, Trubner, 1925.

MacCabe, Joseph. *Splendour of Moorish Spain*. London: Watts & Co., 1935.

McCall, Andrew. *The Medieval Underworld*. London: Hamish Hamilton, 1979.

McGinn, Bernard. *Visions of the End: Apocalyptic Traditions in the Middle Ages*. New York: Columbia University Press, 1979.

Melville, Charles, and Ubaydli, Ahmad. *Christians and Moors in Spain*. Warminster, Eng.: Aris and Phillips, 1992.

Muñoz Molina, Antonio. *Córdoba de los Omeyas*. Barcelona: Ciudades en la Historia, 1991.

Norwich, John Julius. *Byzantium: The Apogee*. New York: Knopf, 1996.

———. *A History of Venice*. New York: Knopf, 1982.

Oman, Sir Charles. *England before the Norman Conquest*. London: Methuen & Co., 1949.

Painter, Sidney. *A History of the Middle Ages, 284–1500*. New York: Knopf, 1953.

Picavet, Par F. *Gerbert: Un Pape philosophe*. Paris: Ernest Leroux, 1897.

Riché, Pierre. *Gerbert d'Aurillac, le pape de l'an mil*. Paris: Fayard, 1987.

Rosenwein, Barbara H. *Rhinoceros Bound: Cluny in the Tenth Century*. Philadelphia: University of Pennsylvania Press, 1982.

Sawyer, Birgit (and Sawyer, Peter, and Wood, Ian, eds.). *The Christianization of Scandinavia*. Alingsas, Sweden: Viktoria Bokfarlag, 1987.

Sawyer, P. H. *The Age of the Vikings*. London: Edward Arnold, 1971.

Scales, Peter C. *The Fall of the Caliphate of Córdoba*. New York: E. J. Brill, 1994.

Steblin-Kamenskij, M. I. *The Saga Mind*. Odense: Odense University Press, 1973.

Stone, James S. *The Cult of Santiago*. London: Longmans, Green, 1927.

Stromback, Dag. *Conversion of Iceland: A Survey*. London: Viking Society, 1975.

Sutherland, Jon N. *Liudprand of Cremona: Bishop, Diplomat, Historian*. Spoleto: Centro Italiano di Studi sull'Alto Medioevo, 1988.

Thorpe, Benjamin. *Northern Mythology*. London: Edward Lumley, 1851.

Togan, Ahmed Zeki Velidi. *Ibn Fadlan's Reisebericht.* Nendeln, Lichtenstein: Klaus Reprint, 1966.

Toynbee, Arnold. *Constantine Porphyrogenitus and His World.* London: Oxford University Press, 1973.

Turville-Petre, G. *The Heroic Age of Scandinavia.* Westport, Conn.: Greenwood, 1976.

————. *Myth and Religion of the North: The Religion of Ancient Scandinavia.* Westport, Conn.: Greenwood, 1975.

Vajay, Szabolcs de. *Der Eintritt des Ungarishen Stammebundes in die Europeaeishe Geschichte (862–933).* Mainz: Hase & Koehler, 1968.

Vambéry, Arminius. *The Story of Hungary.* New York: Putnam's, 1886.

Velázquez Bosco, D. Ricardo. *Medina Azzahray Alamiriya.* Madrid, 1912.

Winks, Robin W., ed. *The Historian as Detective: Essays on Evidence.* New York: Harper & Row, 1968.

Wolf, Gunther. *Kaiserin Theophanu.* Cologne: Bohlau Verlag, 1991.

Wolf, Kenneth Baxter. *Christian Martyrs in Muslim Spain.* Cambridge: Cambridge University Press, 1988.

Index